GRAMMATICIZATION, SYNCHRONIC VARIATION, AND LANGUAGE CONTACT

STUDIES IN LANGUAGE COMPANION SERIES (SLCS)

The SLCS series has been established as a companion series to STUDIES
IN LANGUAGE, International Journal,
sponsored by the Foundation "Foundations of language".

Series Editors

Werner Abraham
University of Groningen
The Netherlands

Michael Noonan
University of Wisconsin-Milwaukee
USA

Editorial Board

Joan Bybee (University of New Mexico)
Ulrike Claudi (University of Cologne)
Bernard Comrie (Max Planck Institute, Leipzig)
William Croft (University of Manchester)
Östen Dahl (University of Stockholm)
Gerrit Dimmendaal (University of Leiden)
Martin Haspelmath (Max Planck Institute, Leipzig)
Ekkehard König (Free University of Berlin)
Christian Lehmann (University of Erfurt)
Robert Longacre (University of Texas, Arlington)
Brian MacWhinney (Carnegie-Mellon University)
Marianne Mithun (University of California, Santa Barbara)
Edith Moravcsik (University of Wisconsin, Milwaukee)
Masayoshi Shibatani (Kobe University)
Russell Tomlin (University of Oregon)
John Verhaar (The Hague)

Volume 52

Rena Torres Cacoullos

Grammaticization, Synchronic Variation, and Language Contact
A study of Spanish progressive -ndo constructions

GRAMMATICIZATION, SYNCHRONIC VARIATION, AND LANGUAGE CONTACT

A study of Spanish progressive -ndo constructions

RENA TORRES CACOULLOS
University of New Mexico

JOHN BENJAMINS PUBLISHING COMPANY
AMSTERDAM/PHILADELPHIA

The paper used in this publication meets the minimum requirements of American National Standard for Information Sciences — Permanence of Paper for Printed Library Materials, ANSI Z39.48–1984.

Library of Congress Cataloging-in-Publication Data

Torres Cacoullos, Rena.
 Grammaticization, synchronic variation, and language contact : a study of Spanish progressive -ndo constructions / Rena Torres Cacoullos.
    p.   cm. -- (Studies in language companion series, ISSN 0165-7763 ; v. 52)
 Includes bibliographical references and index.
 1. Spanish language--Gerund. 2. Spanish language--Adverbials. I. Title. II. Series.
PC4312.T67   2000
465--dc21   00-028922
ISBN 90 272 3055 2 (Eur.) / 1 55619 938 4 (US) (alk. paper)   CIP

© 2000 – John Benjamins B.V.
No part of this book may be reproduced in any form, by print, photoprint, microfilm, or any other means, without written permission from the publisher.

John Benjamins Publishing Co. • P.O.Box 75577 • 1070 AN Amsterdam • The Netherlands
John Benjamins North America • P.O.Box 27519 • Philadelphia PA 19118-0519 • USA

To the memory of
Alejandro Torres
1966–1998

Table of Contents

List of Figures — xi
List of Tables — xiii
Acknowledgments — xv

Chapter 1
Introduction — 1
1.1 Grammaticization — 1
    1.1.1 Diachronic evolution and synchronic variation — 1
    1.1.2 Retention — 4
1.2 The set of *-ndo* constructions — 6
    1.2.1 Classifications of *-ndo* constructions — 7
    1.2.2 Auxiliary status — 8
1.3 Mechanisms of change — 12
    1.3.1 Semantic and formal reduction — 12
    1.3.2 Frequency effects — 12
    1.3.3 Subjectivity — 14
1.4 Spanish — English language contact — 15
    1.4.1 *-nd*o constructions as a locus of convergence — 15
    1.4.2 Register considerations in language contact — 17
1.5 The data — 20
    1.5.1 Old Spanish (OldSp) — 21
    1.5.2 Present-day Mexican Spanish — 22
        1.5.2.1 Mexico City popular (MexPop) — 22
        1.5.2.2 Essays — 22
        1.5.2.3 Chihuahua (Chih'97) — 23
    1.5.3 New Mexican Spanish — 23
        1.5.3.1 New Mexico near monolingual (NMmon) — 24
        1.5.3.2 New Mexico bilingual (NMbil) — 26

	1.5.3.3 New Mexico transitional bilingual (NMtb)	26
1.6	Summary	26

Chapter 2
Formal reduction in grammaticization:
Diachronic changes in the form of *-ndo* constructions — 31

2.1	From positional variation to positional fixing	33
2.2	The decline of multiple gerund constructions	35
2.3	Reduction of intervening material	38
	2.3.1 Diachronic changes	38
	2.3.2 English interference?	43
2.4	Clitic climbing as an index of formal reduction	45
	2.4.1 Clitic position in Old Spanish	46
	2.4.2 Factors in clitic climbing	51
2.5	Construction frequency	55
2.6	Register differences in construction frequency	60
2.7	Clitic climbing in the New Mexico corpus	65
2.8	Summary	69

Chapter 3
Evidence for semantic reduction:
Changing patterns of cooccurring locative and temporal expressions — 71

3.1	Semantic retention and reduction in the distribution of locatives	73
	3.1.1 Counting cooccurring locatives	73
	3.1.2 *Estar* + *-ndo* locatives	76
	3.1.3 *Ir* + *-ndo* locatives	78
	3.1.4 *Andar* + *-ndo* locatives	80
	3.1.5 Loss of locative features	82
3.2	Analogy in the extension of *estar* + *-ndo* to mental verbs	84
3.3	*Estar* + *-ndo* temporal expressions: Expansion to present habitual uses	88
3.4	*Ir* + *-ndo* temporals: Inceptive-continuative and gradual development	93
	3.4.1 Inceptive and continuative	93
	3.4.2 Gradual development	99
3.5	*Andar* + *-ndo* temporals: "Going around" in space and time	102
3.6	Locatives and temporals in New Mexico Spanish	104

3.7	Usage effects in the conventionalization of aspectual meaning	109
3.8	Summary	111

Chapter 4
Frequency effects and layering in the domain of progressive aspect:
The shifting semantic territory of *-ndo* constructions — 115
4.1	The changing distribution of *-ndo* auxiliaries	115
4.2	Token and type frequency in semantic generalization: *Estar* + "talking"	120
	4.2.1 Diachronic ordering of main verbs	120
	4.2.2 Early postural meaning: "watching" perception verbs	124
	4.2.3 Entrenched locative meaning: "waiting" verbs	127
	4.2.4 Subject involvement: talking and "bodily activity" verbs	129
4.3	Experiential meaning (= subject and speaker involvement): "*Ver*" *estar* + *-ndo*	132
	4.3.1 Experiential uses	132
	4.3.2 Evidentiality: "see" *estar* + *-ndo*	134
	4.3.3 Subjectivity: pragmatic strengthening?	140
4.4	Harmony and generalization: Gradual development *ir* + *-ndo*	142
	4.4.1 Motion verb harmony	142
	4.4.2 Process verbs, telicity	145
	4.4.3 "Manner" expressions	147
	4.4.4 Routinization of *ir creciendo*	150
4.5	Frequency constraints on generalization	152
4.6	Layering and sociolinguistic variation: *Andar buscando*	157
	4.6.1 Plural objects and parallel gerunds in frequentative meaning	158
	4.6.2 General activity main verbs	160
	4.6.3 A newer construction — negative nuances	165
	4.6.4 Routines and sociolinguistic factors in variation	168
4.7	Specialization in New Mexican Spanish	170
4.8	Summary	175

Chapter 5
From progressive to experiential habitual — 177
5.1	Change in progress in the grammatical status of *estar* + *-ndo*	178
	5.1.1 Definitions of *estar* + *-ndo*	178
	5.1.2 Obligatoriness	180

	5.1.3 Restriction of the simple present to stative and habitual	182
	5.1.4 Token frequency increases	184
5.2	Experiential habitual uses	188
	5.2.1 From progressive to experiential habitual	188
	5.2.2 Indices of habituality: frequentative adverbials and general activity main verbs	193
5.3	Subjectivity and deixis in *estar* + *-ndo*	195
	5.3.1 Subject animacy	195
	5.3.2 Grammatical person	198
	5.3.2 Deictic time and place adverbials	200
5.4	Generalization to motion verbs	204
	5.4.1 *Estar yendo*	204
	5.4.2 General motion and experiential habitual	208
	5.4.3 Frequencies of *estar*-plus-motion verb	212
5.5	Generalization to statives	213
	5.5.1 Frequencies of *estar*-plus-stative	213
	5.5.2 Experiential uses with statives	216
5.6	Subjective vs. transitory: Back to locative origins	219
5.7	Summary	224

Conclusion 227

References 231

Appendices
Appendix I. Corpora, word counts, and *-ndo* construction totals 243
Appendix II: Old Spanish corpus: Editions, concordances, translations 244
Appendix IIIA: Essays corpus 245
Appendix IIIB: *-ndo* construction frequencies in Essays texts 246

Index 247

List of Figures

1.	Predictions of convergence and acceleration hypotheses with respect to *estar + -ndo*	17
2.	Emergence of *estar + -ndo* unit	55
3.	*Estar* + mental verb: Schematic associations based on *en*	87
4.	Layering (variation) in the domain of progressive and continuous aspect	119
5.	Order of appearance of *estar + -ndo* main verbs	124
6.	Original elements of meaning in *estar + -ndo* progressives	131
7.	Generalization of *estar + -ndo* contexts	131
8.	Locative bounding and speaker participation (Locative origins, part I)	140
9.	Emergence of gradual development *ir + -ndo* construction	151
10.	Slots in *ir + -ndo* construction (*ir + -ndo* contexts)	151
11.	Steps in bleaching of *estar + -ndo*	189
12.	Synchronic variation in the uses of *estar + -ndo*	189
13.	Locative — temporal bounding and speaker — subject participation (Locative origins, part II)	222

List of Tables

1.	Distribution of gerunds in *Estoria de España* (partial list)	5
2.	Frequency of *estar* + *-ndo* (Clegg and Rodríguez 1993)	19
3.	Proportion of gerunds cooccurring with an auxiliary (Clegg and Rodríguez 1993)	20
4.	Frequency of *-ndo* constructions in Essays and in oral popular Mexico City corpus	23
5.	Positional variation: *-ndo* forms preceding *estar*, *ir*	34
6.	Multiple gerund constructions in Old Spanish	36
7.	Multiple gerund constructions in present-day corpora	37
8.	Intervening material in *estar* + *-ndo*	40
9.	Intervening material in *ir* + *-ndo*	41
10.	Clitic climbing (CC) in *estar* + *-ndo* in Old Spanish	48
11.	Clitic climbing (CC) in *ir* + *-ndo* in Old Spanish	49
12.	Diachronic increase in token frequencies of *-ndo* constructions (tokens per 10,000 words)	56
13.	Diachronic increase in proportion of gerunds in construction with an auxiliary	58
14.	Distribution of *-ndo* constructions in the *Corbacho*	61
15.	Token frequencies of *-ndo* constructions in present-day corpora (per 10,000 words)	62
16.	Clitic climbing (CC) in present-day corpora	63
17.	Proportion of gerunds in construction with an auxiliary in present-day corpora	64
18.	Cooccurring locatives in *-ndo* constructions	75
19.	*Estar* + *-ndo* locatives in Old Spanish texts	76
20.	*Estar* + *-ndo* locatives by semantic class of main verb in Old Spanish texts	87

21.	*Estar* + *-ndo*: Cooccurring temporal adverbials	89
22.	*Ir* + *-ndo*: Cooccurring temporal adverbials	93
23.	*Andar* + *-ndo*: Cooccurring temporal adverbials	104
24.	*Estar* + *-ndo* locatives in Mexico and New Mexico corpora	105
25.	*Estar* + *-ndo* temporal adverbials in Mexico and New Mexico corpora	106
26.	Relative frequencies of *-ndo* auxiliaries in Old Spanish texts	116
27.	Relative frequencies of *-ndo* auxiliaries in present-day corpora	116
28.	*Estar* + *-ndo*: Most frequently occurring main verbs (gerunds)	122
29.	*Estar* + *-ndo*: Semantic classes of main verbs in Old Spanish	123
30.	*Estar* + *-ndo*: Distribution by clause type in Old Spanish	135
31.	*Ir* + *-ndo*: Semantic classes of main verbs in Old Spanish	143
32.	*Ir* + *-ndo*: Most frequently occurring main verbs (gerunds)	145
33.	*Ir* + *-ndo*: Distribution by clause type in Old Spanish	149
34.	*Estar, ir* + *-ndo*: Tenses	153
35.	*Estar, ir* + *-ndo*: Animacy of subject	155
36.	Token frequency of *-ndo* constructions (per 10,000 words)	156
37.	Plural objects in *andar* + *-ndo*	159
38.	*Andar* + *-ndo* multiple gerund constructions	160
39.	*Andar* + *-ndo*: Distribution by clause type in Old Spanish	164
40.	*Andar* + *-ndo*: Animacy of subject	166
41.	*Andar* + *-ndo*: Tenses	168
42.	Relative frequencies of *estar* and *andar* by speaker level of education	170
43.	Uses of simple Present (Moreno de Alba 1978:18–41)	182
44.	Token frequencies of *estar* + *-ndo* (per 10,000 words)	185
45.	Uses of *estar* + *-ndo* Present (Moreno de Alba 1978:39)	188
46.	Frequentative adverbials in Present-tense *estar* + *-ndo*	193
47.	Animacy of subject in *estar* + *-ndo* (Chihuahua and New Mexico)	196
48.	Person and number in *estar* + *-ndo* (Chihuahua and New Mexico)	199
49.	First person object pronouns with third person subjects in *estar* + *-ndo*	200
50.	Deictic temporal adverbials cooccurring with Present-tense *estar* + *-ndo*	201
51.	Deictic locative adverbials cooccurring with Present-tense *estar* + *-ndo*	203
52.	Distribution of motion verb gerunds (main verbs) by auxiliary	212

Acknowledgments

This study owes the most to grammaticization and usage-based functionalism, particularly as developed in the work of Joan Bybee. In variationism and language contact I have been influenced, in different ways, by Carmen Silva-Corvalán and Shana Poplack. At the University of New Mexico I enjoyed fruitful discussions with Alan Hudson on register variation, Garland Bills and Eduardo Hernández-Chávez on New Mexico Spanish, Joanne Scheibman on subjectivity, and Melissa Axelrod on semantics. I owe a special debt of gratitude to my dissertation director John Lipski, for guidance and support throughout my doctoral studies. This research would not have been possible without a Fellowship (1997–1999) and Field Research Grant (Fall 1997) from the Latin American Institute of the University of New Mexico; the UNM Office of Graduate Studies also supported this work with a Research, Project, and Travel Grant (Spring 1997). *Gracias a los chihuahuenses y a los nuevomexicanos que me aguantaron con mi grabadora. A Alex y a Anna Iris, que me aguantaron con todo.*

Chapter 1

Introduction

1.1 Grammaticization

1.1.1 *Diachronic evolution and synchronic variation*

Grammaticization or grammaticalization — the development of grammatical morphemes out of lexical morphemes — may be viewed from both a diachronic and a synchronic perspective.[1] Since the resurgence of grammaticization studies in the 1970s most work has been on a diachronic axis, as scholars have investigated paths of semantic and formal evolution followed by grammaticizing items. But grammaticization also affords insights on synchronic variation, on two fronts. One is variation in form, or the competition among different forms that express the same grammatical meaning. The second is variation in meaning, or the existence of multiple uses of the same form. The present study is about diachronic evolution and synchronic variation in Spanish auxiliary-plus-gerund periphrases.

In grammaticization, new layers emerge without necessarily replacing older layers in the same domain, so that the same grammatical function may be carried out by different forms. This is known as layering (Hopper 1991: 22). An example from English is the variation between the three futures, *will*, *shall*, and *be going to* (Bybee, Perkins, and Pagliuca 1994: 21) or the Past Tense, where vowel alternations (*I broke*) coexist with the alveolar *t/d* suffix (*I walked*) (Hopper and Traugott 1993: 124). In layering we have variation in forms that serve the same or similar functions. In this sense grammaticization as an approach to language study is in conflict with structuralist views of grammatical morphemes as based on maximal contrasts or the presence versus absence of features (cf. Bybee et al. 1994: 22, 148). Instead, there are affinities with sociolinguistic variationism, which has demonstrated that meaning distinctions among different forms can be neutralized in discourse (Sankoff

1988: 153). The layering hypothesis provides diachronic insights on the existence of variables above and beyond phonology as demonstrated by synchronic variationist studies.

A second implication of grammaticization for present-day variation is the existence of multiple uses for a single form. Synchronic variation in meaning or use corresponds to successive stages on the diachronic path of evolution of a grammaticizing item (Bybee et al. 1994: 17, 300). The existence of multiple uses stands in conflict with attempts to define a single, invariant, abstract meaning for grammatical morphemes. In analyses of Spanish verbal morphology this approach has a long tradition in the distinction between invariant systemic meaning and secondary non-systemic meanings.[2] Although the objective of succinct definitions of systemic meaning has appeal, when faced with variation in real data the problem quickly becomes one of "stalking the wild invariant" (Timberlake 1982: 305, cf. Hopper 1982).

Let us now come to Spanish auxiliary-plus-gerund periphrases. Variation in form occurs as layering in the functional domain of progressive aspect. Layering is illustrated in the set of examples in (1), where periphrastic constructions with three different auxiliaries, *estar* 'be (located)', *ir* 'go', and *andar* 'go around', are available to express present progressive or continuous meaning. In all three cases the actions take place simultaneously with the moment of speech.

(1) Variation in form (layering) in progressive territory

    a. *estar* 'be (located)' + *-ndo*

        Talking about a computer print job:
        *Por eso **está diciendo** ahí que faltó papel.* (Chih'97#12B)
        'That's why it **is saying** there that it is out of paper.'

    b. *andar* 'go around' + *-ndo*

        R: *A ver qué están haciendo.*
        P: *Yo creo que **andan jugando** ai.* (Chih'97#2B)
        'R: Let's see what (the children) are doing.
        P: I think they **are playing** around there.'

    c. *ir* 'go' + *-ndo*

        Talking about the price of farm machinery:
        *Sí pues va, **va subiendo** no más con la sencilla razón de que de*

que- Por ejemplo ahorita, por decir así es que le cuesta el dólar siete, siete ochenta, siete noventa. Pero ya pa mañana le cuesta a ocho pesos y tiene que comprarlo.(Chih'97#21A)
'Yes well it **is going up** for the simple reason that- For example right now, let's say the dollar costs you seven, seven-eighty, seven-ninety. But already by tomorrow it costs you eight pesos and you have to buy it'[3]

We will see that overlapping uses as in (1) are the result of parallel evolutionary paths involving semantic bleaching in all three constructions. As specific features of spatial — locative and motion — meaning are lost, the constructions generalize to more contexts of use, with primarily temporal — aspectual — meaning.

Variation in meaning, or the existence of multiple uses of a single auxiliary-plus-gerund construction, is illustrated for *estar + -ndo* in the next set of examples. In example (1a) above, repeated below as (2b), the meaning is progressive. But the same periphrasis may have locative meaning. In (2a) *estar + -ndo* answers a question about the subject's location.[4] Or, it may have habitual meaning. In (2c) the situation is one that is customarily repeated, as indicated by cooccurring frequentative adverbial *a la semana* 'a week'.

(2) Variation in meaning in *estar + -ndo*

　　a.　locative

　　　　R:　*¿Aquí está?*
　　　　V:　*Sí **está cuidando televisión**.*
　　　　R:　*Oh.*
　　　　V:　*Ai en en en el cuarto allá del otro lado. Está durmido en la silla.* (NMbil/Vig)
　　　　'R:　Is he here?
　　　　V:　Yes **he is watching television**.
　　　　R:　Oh.
　　　　V:　There in in in the room over there on the other side. He's asleep in the chair'

　　b.　progressive

　　　　*Por eso **está diciendo** ahí que faltó papél.* (Chih'97#12B)
　　　　'That's why **it is saying** there that it is out of paper.'

c. habitual

*Que ahorita nos **están pagando** 580 a la hemana.* (Chih'97#VIA)
'Now **they are paying** us 580 a week.'

We will see that these three sets of present-day uses correspond to stages in the diachronic evolution of *estar* + *-ndo*.

1.1.2 Retention

Grammaticizing constructions retain features or nuances of meaning from the source construction. This is known as the retention (Bybee and Pagliuca 1987) or persistence (Hopper 1991) hypothesis. Retention is reflected in differences in the gerund or main verb types with which the different auxiliaries are used.

The skewed distribution of gerunds in the 12th c. chronicle *Estoria de España* provides a nice introduction to the discussion of retention that I will develop in the following chapters. *Fablando* 'talking' cooccurs with *estar*. This is an activity usually circumscribed in one location, which is consistent with the 'be located' meaning of *estar*. *Llegando* 'arriving', *entrando* 'entering', *yendo* 'going' are most compatible with the directional motion or allative meaning of *ir* (indeed, *yendo* is the gerund form of *ir*!). These gerund types cooccur with *ir*. Even more closely associated with *ir* is the process predicate *creciendo* 'growing', in a gradual development use we will discuss in following chapters. All tokens of *creciendo* are in construction with *ir*, in other words, whenever *creciendo* appears it is preceded by a form of *ir*. On the other hand, *buscando* 'looking for', *predicando* 'preaching', *preguntando* 'asking about' are activities consistent with the non-directional motion "going around" meaning of *andar*. These gerunds tend to cooccur with *andar*. Table 1 gives some figures.

Auxiliary-plus-gerund collocational patterns emerging from Old Spanish texts are vigorous in present-day data as well. Returning to the set of examples in (1), we see that *diciendo* 'saying' combines with *estar*, *jugando* 'playing' with *andar*, and *subiendo* 'rising' with *ir*. In the data from which these examples are taken, 90% (29/32) of *diciendo* tokens pair up with *estar*, 80% (8/10) of *jugando* tokens pair up with *andar*, and 75% (3/4) of *subiendo* tokens pair up with *ir*.

The same gerund type may combine with a different auxiliary depending on the kind of activity referred to, in support of the retention hypothesis. In the next set of examples, *limpiando* 'cleaning' combines with *estar* in (a) and with

Table 1. Distribution of gerunds in "Estoria de España" (partial list)

Gerund (main verb)	Tokens total	Tokens with an auxiliary	Tokens with particular auxiliary	% with that auxiliary
			ESTAR	*ESTAR*
catando 'watching'	16	7	4	57%
fablando 'talking'	11	4	4	100%
			IR	*IR*
creciendo 'growing'	8	8	8	100%
entrando 'entering'	9	4	4	100%
fuyendo 'fleeing'	25	10	7	70%
llegando 'arriving'	10	4	4	100%
subiendo 'rising'	4	3	3	100%
viniendo 'coming'	16	3	3	100%
yendo 'going'	30	6	6	100%
			ANDAR	*ANDAR*
buscando 'looking for'	11	8	7	88%
conquiriendo 'conquering'	11	5	4	80%
destruyendo 'destroying'	16	9	7	78%
predicando 'preaching'	2	2	2	100%
preguntando 'asking for'	2	2	2	100%

andar in (b), but in the first case the activity is washing dishes while in the second it is clearing up land to build houses. One stands in one place — *estar* — (usually indoors) to do the former but moves about — *andar* — (outdoors) to do the latter.

(3) a. *una hermana de mi mamá **estaba lavan- limpiando** los trastes [ ] Y ella oía bulla. Pero no se daba cuenta ella que [] que los niños andaban jugando* (NMmon/Mar)
'one of my mother's sisters **was (*estar*) wash- cleaning** the dishes. And she heard noise. But she didn't realize that the children were playing'

b. *Tenía como- como ocho hombres conmigo cuando **andábanoj limpiando** el- 'onde iban a hajer laj casas y todo* (NMmon/NMCSS#311)[5]
'I had about- about eight men with me when **we were (*andar*) cleaning** the- where they were going to build the houses and all that'

Thus, although there is layering or variation between auxiliaries in expressions of progressive aspect, not all auxiliaries are as likely to combine with a particular gerund. In some cases the distribution of gerund types clearly reflects retention, as in the pair above. In other cases the choice of auxiliary reflects the routinization of a frequent collocation, being simply the residue of earlier meaningful differences. Sociolinguistic factors, especially dialect and register, also play a role. I come back to factors contributing to the choice of auxiliary in Chapter 4.

1.2 The set of *-ndo* constructions

The term "*-ndo* construction" in what follows is applied to periphrastic expressions composed of an auxiliary plus a main verb in the gerund (or present participle) *-ndo* form. "Auxiliary" is a convenient cover term for *estar*, *ir*, and *andar*, and is meant to be neutral as to the extent of lexical meaning (or conversely, the degree of grammaticization) of these verbs in *-ndo* constructions. I use the term construction in the general sense of a conventionalized form-meaning pair (cf. Goldberg 1995; Kay and Fillmore 1999), although here "function" is not so much a single meaning as a set of diachronically related uses.

There is no standard name for what I am calling *-ndo* constructions. In works by European or Latin American Hispanists, they are commonly referred to as *perífrasis de gerundio* 'gerundial periphrases' (e.g. Gili Gaya 1964; Luna 1980; Roca Pons 1958). Grammars and studies of Spanish written in English tend to use "progressive", either for all *-ndo* constructions (e.g. Solé and Solé 1977; Spaulding 1926) or, more commonly, for *estar* + *-ndo* alone (e.g. Comrie 1976; Green 1988; Klein 1980; Whitley 1986). Another name for *estar* + *-ndo* is "continuous" (e.g. Butt and Benjamin 1994) or *durativo* 'durative' (e.g. Lenz 1925: 399, §256). Some scholars simply opt for labels such as *estar* + gerund or *estoy cantando* 'I am singing' (e.g. De Bruyne 1995; Fernández 1960; Kattán-Ibarra and Pountain 1997). In the absence of a standard label, "*-ndo* constructions" seems preferable to "progressive" or "continuous", which might be misleading as to the range of uses.

A rich array of locative and motion verbs participate in *-ndo* constructions. *Estar* 'be located' is included in all mentions of the phenomenon. Most studies also include *ir* 'go', *andar* 'go around', *venir* 'come'. Other auxiliaries often cited are *seguir* 'follow' or 'continue' and *quedarse* 'remain, stand still'. Appearing on some lists are *continuar* 'continue', *hallarse* 'be, find oneself', *llevar* (plus a time expression) 'have spent time, have been', *pasar* (plus time expression) 'spend time', *permanecer* 'remain', *soltarse* 'begin, start', *salir* 'leave' or 'start'. Results from four different quantitative studies indicate that the five most frequent auxiliaries are *estar, ir, seguir, andar,* and *venir* (Arjona 1991; Clegg and Rodríguez 1993; Keniston 1937b; Luna 1980). In popular Mexican conversational data the three most frequent are *estar, ir,* and *andar* (Arjona 1991). These three are the focus of the present study.

1.2.1 Classifications of -ndo constructions

Different classifications for *-ndo* constructions are quite congruent, with discrepancies primarily with respect to *andar*.[6] Hamplová (1968: 216–22) proposes a three-way classification for the group of what she calls *perífrasis durativas*:

(4) Perífrasis durativas (Hamplová 1968)
    a. *estar* + *-ndo*   simple duración
    b. *ir, venir, llevar, andar* + *-ndo*   progresivas
    c. *seguir, continuar, quedar(se)* + *-ndo*   continuativas

Luna (1980: 200–11) follows essentially the same classification, with the difference that she considers *andar* + *-ndo* together with *estar* + *-ndo* as a *durativa neutra* 'neutral durative'. For Coseriu (1977b: 250–1), Spanish *-ndo* constructions belong to a Romance aspectual category of *visión* 'vision', in particular to a *visión parcializadora* (cf. Keniston's 1936: 170 partial view of a situation). Dietrich (1983: 211) slightly modifies this classification.

(5) Visión parcializadora (Coseriu 1977b; Dietrich 1983)
    a. *estar* + *-ndo*   angular
    b. *andar* + *-ndo*   comitativa
    c. *ir* + *-ndo*   prospectiva
    d. *venir* + *-ndo*   retrospectiva
    e. *seguir, continuar, permancer* + *-ndo*   continuativa
    f. *quedar(se)* + *-ndo*   extensiva

In a comprehensive description of Spanish periphrases, Olbertz (1998) arrives at essentially the same characterization under Functional Grammar (Dik 1987,

1989) labels. All *-ndo* constructions belong to the class of Inner Aspect: *estar, continuar-seguir, venir*, and *quedarse* as expressions of Inner Phasal Aspect, *ir* as an expression of Qualificational Aspect (Olbertz 1998: 324–45). An exception is apparently elusive *andar + -ndo*, which is said to express Quantificational Aspect, within the domain of Outer Aspect (Olbertz 1998: 370–2).

(6) Periphrastic expressions of Aspect (Olbertz 1998: 338, 437–8)

Form	Label	Description
a. *estar + -ndo*	Progressive	be SoA-ing
b. *andar + -ndo*	Distributive	SoA occurs here and there
c. *ir + -ndo*	Gradual	SoA gradually
d. *venir + -ndo*	Anterior-Persistive	have been SoA-ing so far
e. *continuar, seguir + -ndo*	Continuative	continue SoA-ing
f. *quedar(se) + -ndo*	Posterior-Persistive	keep SoA-ing

SoA = State of Affairs (event)

The characterization of *ir + -ndo* as "prospective" in the sense of expressing movement from the present toward a goal, of *venir + -ndo* as "retrospective" in expressing movement toward the present, and of *andar + -ndo* as expressing movement without a fixed direction is found in most grammars and analyses (e.g. Gili Gaya 1964: 114–5, §98; Keniston 1936: 172–3; Lenz 1925: 417, §270; RAE 1973: 448, §3.12.5; Roca Pons 1958: 66; R.Seco 1966: 172; Solé 1990: 63). The diachronic data we will be looking at show that these specific meaning components follow from the lexical uses of *ir, venir,* and *andar*.

1.2.2 Auxiliary status

Spanish has more periphrastic forms than any other standard Romance language (Green 1988: 101), at over 60 (De Kock 1975; Olbertz 1998: 31; cf. Dietrich 1983: 427, note 79). But verbs participating in periphrastic expressions may be more or less auxiliarized, to borrow a term from Benveniste (1968). Numerous attempts have been made to delimit auxiliaries in Spanish.[7] Many involve a semantic criterion of debilitated lexical meaning or, in Heine's (1993) terms, desemanticization. Examples are early treatments by Spaulding (1926), Gili Gaya (1964), and Roca Pons (1958). Others propose criteria related to syntactic restrictions and autonomy, or Heine's decategorialization. Examples are the absence of arguments (Coseriu 1977a: 73), clitic climbing (Lenz 1925, §247; cf. Myhill 1988a, 1988b; Harre 1991: 22–3), and more generally, the applicability of syntactic manipulations (Fontanella de Weinberg 1970; Gómez Torrego 1988: 15–17; Fernández de Castro 1990: 39–40; Olbertz 1998: 38–44).

Implicit in most treatments is an assumption that auxiliary status is a "yes or no" matter, based on traditional views of linguistic categorization as discrete (see Lakoff 1987 and Taylor 1995 for different approaches to categorization). Yet as Green (1987: 259) observes, "if an auxiliary is defined as a grammatical marker of tense and aspect devoid of any lexical meaning, then Spanish has no true auxiliaries." The "yes or no" view is consistent with a view of grammatical change as fairly abrupt, as with parametric change in generative approaches (e.g. Lightfoot 1991).

The alternative is a scalar view of auxiliaries based on gradual diachronic evolution (cf. Heine 1993; Ramat 1987). In support of this view, the data we will describe in the following pages show that there is synchronic variation in the uses of periphrastic expressions, corresponding to successive diachronic steps in the evolution of lexical toward grammatical meaning. It is important that synchronic variation may include cases of ambiguity or merger between more lexical and more grammatical uses (Coates 1983: 15–7; 1995: 61; Heine 1993: 52). In example (2a), *está cuidando televisión*, *estar* means both 'he is here, in front of the television' (locative — lexical) and 'he is in the midst of an activity at reference time, i.e. watching television' (progressive — auxiliary). In this sense, bleaching **can** be observed synchronically (pace Squartini 1998: 21–2). The range of uses in the set of examples in (2), from locative to progressive to habitual, is a synchronic manifestation of bleaching in *estar + -ndo*.

The approach here differs from other treatments in that I make no attempt to assign different *-ndo* constructions to fixed classes based on degree of grammaticization. Olbertz (1998), for example, delimits three classes to which gerundial constructions are assigned, lexical, semi-auxiliary, and periphrastic. But even in this classification allowances have to be made. Thus, although *seguir/continuar* 'go on' are assigned to the semi-auxiliary class, they are (partially) periphrastic "when their restrictions as semi-auxiliaries are violated" (Olbertz 1998: 270). And not only must some constructions have a double assignment, low frequency *acabar/terminar* 'finish' end up in the same class as *ir* and other much more frequent auxiliaries (Olbertz 1988: 271ff.). An alternative might be to try to quantify degree of grammaticization. So, for example, Quesada (1995) assigns numerical values to factors based on Lehman's (1995: 121ff.) parameters of weight, cohesion, and variability. Thus, *estar* + *-ndo* scores a number of points and achieves 73%, while *acabar* 'finish, end' only garners 6.66% (Quesada 1995: 17–23). But in this classification motion verb-plus-gerund constructions (*venir, andar, ir*) are said to belong to an Aktionsart category of direction (retrospective, neutral, prospective), together with motion verb-plus-past participle constructions, rather than to the category of aspectual markers to which *estar*-plus-gerund belongs (Quesada 1995: 23–4).

I treat *-ndo* constructions as a set based on both form and meaning and based also, crucially, on diachronic patterns. First, these constructions share the same auxiliary-plus-gerund form. Second, they show semantic overlap. Semantic overlap is supported by diachronic and synchronic evidence. Diachronically, all these constructions evolve from lexical spatial expressions to grammatical aspectual morphemes. Synchronically, they compete as expressions of progressive aspect. Meaning overlap points to semantic bleaching along similar paths. At the same time, *-ndo* constructions retain different specific meaning components that follow from their original lexical meaning, such as that described as prospective or gradual for *ir* + *-ndo*.

Rather than complete or partial grammaticization there is variation. The following is a nice example of variation between more lexical and more grammatical uses of the same construction, on the one hand, and between competing constructions as progressive morphemes, on the other.

(7) *Y nos **fuimos acercando** a la troca que estaba completamente destrozada del frente en el poste.[ ] Y entonces **nos estábamos acercando** y yo me detuve. [ ] Es que atropellaron a una pareja que **venía caminando** por la banqueta. **Iba** la pareja **caminando**, venían a gran velocidad y no sé se trataron de esquivar a otra troca que tambien venía se voltearon con el poste.* (Chih'97/#11A)

'And **we gradually approached** [lit: went approaching] the pickup which was completely destroyed in the front at the post. [ ] And **we were approaching** and I stopped. [ ] What happened is that they ran over a couple who **was walking** [lit: came walking] on the sidewalk. The couple **was walking** [lit: went walking], they were coming very fast and I don't know they tried to avoid another pickup that was also coming and they hit the post.'

The speaker is describing an accident. She first uses *nos fuimos acercando* 'we went approaching' with auxiliary *ir*, to indicate gradual progress in physical space toward the scene of the accident, thus combining spatial (motion) and aspectual (gradual) meaning. Then she uses *nos estábamos acercando* 'we were approaching' with *estar* to indicate that the approaching was in progress when it was interrupted by her stopping, *yo me detuve*. Further down in the same example she uses *iba caminando* and *venía caminando*, both translatable as 'was walking'. What is lost perhaps in the English translation is lexical meaning: the directionality of the walking which is viewed as either toward, *venía*, or away, *iba*, from the vehicle. All three Imperfect periphrases, *nos estábamos acercando*, *venía caminando*, and *iba caminando* express past progressive in that the situations were in progress at reference time, when the speaker stopped, when the couple was run over, when the pickup hit the post. *Venía caminando* may further specify "retrospective" that is, that the walking began before the moment of reference or that the couple 'had been walking'. On the other hand, *iba caminando* does not seem to carry "prospective" connotations of future-projecting movement toward a goal in this case. Examples like this one illustrate the richness of variation between and within forms.

Another reason to treat *-ndo* constructions as a group is the changing pattern of the relative frequencies of the auxiliaries, which will turn out to be crucial in evaluating changes in bilingual varieties of Spanish. In the earliest Old Spanish text, the *Poema de mio Cid* (c.1207), *ir* is most frequent relative to other auxiliaries, with about 70% of all *-ndo* constructions. About three centuries later, in the *Celestina* (1499), *ir* is down to about 27%, and first place belongs to *estar*. In present-day oral varieties the relative frequency of *estar* is 52% in popular Mexico City Spanish and 76% in educated Madrid Spanish. In the corpus of New Mexico bilingual Spanish we will be studying, it is 82%. In short, we have a reversal in the ordering of *ir* and *estar* with respect to relative frequency. The results suggest the initiation of a process of specialization (Hopper 1991: 26) in the group of *-ndo* constructions. I return to this point in Chapter 4.

1.3 Mechanisms of change

1.3.1 *Semantic and formal reduction*

An ongoing debate in grammaticization studies is whether the development of expressions of tense and aspect from lexical sources is a metaphorical change from the spatial to the temporal domain. This study provides textual evidence that the development of progressive morphemes does not involve metaphorical extension but rather semantic reduction. From patterns of cooccurrence with locative and time adverbials, we will see that Old Spanish *-ndo* constructions have had a temporal dimension from their earliest uses. What happens is that spatial — locative and motion — meaning is lost (cf. Bybee et al. 1994: 292–3). I will refer to the loss of features of meaning as semantic reduction to emphasize parallels with phonetic or formal reduction (Bybee et al. 1994: 19). Other familiar terms are bleaching (Givón 1975), semantic generalization (Bybee and Pagliuca 1985), and desemanticization (Lehmann 1995: 127ff.). This is the topic of Chapter 3.

Formal reduction results in the emergence of auxiliary-plus-gerund sequences as fused units. Auxiliaries and gerunds lose their independence as erstwhile lexical items and increasingly cooccur as a single unit. Evidence of formal reduction is the fixing of the position of the gerund with respect to the auxiliary, the reduction of open class material intervening between these two elements, and the more frequent positioning of object clitic pronouns preposed to the entire sequence. We will see that concurrent with this series of formal changes is a shift in the proportion of gerunds in construction with an auxiliary. That is, there has been an increase in the frequency of gerunds cooccurring with an auxiliary relative to those gerunds that are manner adverbials or non-restrictive relatives. I will call this construction frequency. We return to these questions in Chapter 2.

1.3.2 *Frequency effects*

Just how locative gives rise to progressive — continuous and then habitual meaning, as in the set of examples in (2), is a major question. Much work has been done to describe cognitive processes, such as metaphor (e.g. Heine, Claudi and Hünnemeyer 1991) or pragmatic inference (e.g. Traugott and König 1991) underlying grammaticization. For Spanish periphrases in particular, there is a growing number of studies based on present-day corpora, among others Olbertz (1998), Quesada (1995), and Squartini (1998). Admirable studies of Old Spanish are provided by Spaulding (1926) and Yllera (1980). Yet we still do not have much quantitative data. The main contribution of this study lies in the detailed description of cooccurrence patterns. My goal is to draw attention to the vagaries of use and how they may propel linguistic change.

In usage-based functionalism, lexical and grammatical structures emerge from patterns of language use (Bybee 1998; Hopper 1987). Linguists are now paying more attention to the role played by frequency in propelling the changes that occur in grammaticization. Bybee (1995) and Bybee and Thompson (1997) have shown that frequency of use operates in language change, in support of the view put forward by Haiman (1994) that grammatical constructions emerge as conventionalized patterns of language use through mechanisms effective more generally in ritualization.

We will see that token and type frequency play an important role in the development of aspectual expressions. Spatial meaning in *-ndo* constructions is reduced as *estar, ir,* and *andar* are used frequently with particular gerund types (or main verbs) not typically associated with location or physical movement. It turns out that *estar hablando* 'be (located) talking' and *ir creciendo* 'be (go) growing' are high token frequency combinations. That is, these particular auxiliary-plus-gerund combinations account for a large number of tokens. For example, *estar hablando* makes up more than 10% of all *estar* + *-ndo* tokens in our Old Spanish corpus, and *ir creciendo* 5% of all *ir* + *-ndo* tokens. The strong association of *estar* with *hablando* 'talking' and *ir* with *creciendo* 'growing' in experienced linguistic usage, neither of which are situations linked to location or motion, detracts from the spatial meaning component of the emerging auxiliaries.

In addition, frequent main verbs belong to semantic classes with a large number of types participating in the *-ndo* construction. For example, the class to which *hablando* belongs has 16 different verbs of speech combining with *estar* in the Old Spanish corpus. This verbs-of-speech class makes up more than 25% of all *estar* + *-ndo* tokens. The cooccurrence of *estar* with a large number of different types leads to the development of a more generalized *estar*-plus-verb-of-speech schema, where temporal meaning is more important than locative. We will look at main verb cooccurrence patterns in Chapter 4. In Chapter 5, we will see that extension to habitual contexts as in example (2c) is also linked to high frequency collocations, but now with general activity main verbs. *Estar trabajando* 'be working' makes up close to 10% of all *estar* + *-ndo* tokens in three different corpora of present-day Spanish. *Trabajar* 'work' is a general activity not circumscribed to a particular location or a particular physical manifestation.

1.3.3 Subjectivity

Much if not most linguistic analysis has assumed the primordiality of the referential or propositional function of language (Silverstein 1976). As linguists turn to real data, more attention is also being paid to subjectivity or expressivity (cf. Lyons 1982, 1994). Finegan (1995: 1) gives the following definition: "Subjectivity concerns the involvement of a locutionary agent in a discourse and the effect of that involvement on the formal shape of discourse". In grammaticization, Traugott (1989: 31) has proposed that paths of semantic change go from propositional (to textual) to expressive. Subjectification is the process whereby concrete, objective meanings later become based in speaker attitude (Traugott 1995).

In this study we will see that subjectivity plays a role throughout the development of *estar* + *-ndo*, not just in later stages. From early uses subject and speaker involvement are part of the meaning of the construction. Evidence of subject involvement in the activity is cooccurrence with verbs of speech and verbs referring to uniquely human bodily activities. Evidence of speaker involvement in the description is the occurrence of *estar* + *-ndo* in clauses subordinated to *ver* 'see', which points to an evidential meaning component. Furthermore, we will see that subjective meanings of subject and speaker involvement follow from the locative origins of the construction. I return to these points in Chapter 4 (Section 4.3). In Chapter 5, I will show that newer habitual and stative uses are experiential (cf. Lyons 1982; Wright 1995), rather than just temporally transitory (cf. Langacker 1991), in that they express the speaker's viewpoint on the situation as noteworthy and/or personally experienced.

1.4 Spanish — English language contact

1.4.1 -ndo constructions as a locus of convergence

Convergence as defined by Silva-Corvalán (1994: 5, cf. Gumperz and Wilson 1971) is "the achievement of greater structural similarity in a given aspect of the grammar of two or more languages, assumed to be different at the onset of contact." In an influential study, Klein (1980) compared the relative frequencies of Present tense *estar* + *-ndo* and simple Present forms in bilingual and monolingual speakers of Puerto Rican Spanish in New York City. She found that bilinguals presented a significantly higher frequency of *estar* + *-ndo* in contexts where English admits only the Progressive *be* + *-ing* form (Klein 1980: 70):

(8) a. Look, the sun **is coming** out
 b. *Look, the sun **comes** out

 a'. *Mira, **está saliendo** el sol*
 b'. *Mira, **sale** el sol*

The difference, it is claimed, is that Spanish allows either the simple (*sale*) or periphrastic form (*está saliendo*) where English admits only the periphrastic (*is coming out*). Klein (1980) concluded that bilinguals are losing the Spanish option to express present progressive meaning with the simple Present. Convergence of the bilinguals' system of present reference with English is favored by parallelism of form in combination with meaning overlap, as illustrated in (8) (Klein 1980: 71). It is important that convergence is facilitated because it does not give rise to ungrammatical utterances, but appears as a change in frequency of a native form (Klein 1985: 539).

Klein's conclusions were refuted by Pousada and Poplack (1982), who compared verb form frequencies in bilingual and monolingual varieties with English data and found no overall increase in *estar* + *-ndo* among bilinguals. Klein (1985) subsequently took Pousada and Poplack (1982) to task for not distinguishing cases where the two languages coincide, which are habitual uses of the simple Present, as in 'every morning the sun comes out over the Sandia mountains', from those where they purportedly do not, that is, progressive moment-of-speech uses of the simple Present, as in (8b). I will refer to the hypothesis that bilinguals' usage of *estar* + *-ndo* is becoming similar to the usage of English *be* + *-ing* as the convergence hypothesis.

Studies of Spanish varieties spoken in the Southwest region of the United States also cite increased frequency for *estar* + *-ndo*, especially use of Present and Imperfect periphrastic forms to the detriment of corresponding simple forms. A series of studies of Spanish in Texas in the 1970s all suggested deviations from monolingual norms (see Floyd 1978 and Chaston 1991 for reviews — but see Mrak 1998 for contrary findings). Lavandera (1981) analyzed the distribution of past tense verb forms in a bilingual narrative and found that Imperfect is often realized in an *-ndo* auxiliary. She suggested that contact with English, which has more periphrastic verb forms than Spanish, accelerates an internal linguistic change; the change is internal since other varieties manifest the same phenomenon (Lavandera 1981: 69).

In her extensive study of Spanish in Los Angeles, Silva-Corvalán (1994: 135) found that "the permeability of a grammar to foreign influence [depends]…on the existence of superficially parallel structures…". This finding is in agreement with the constraint on contact-induced grammatical change proposed by scholars such as Meillet (1914: 84–7), Jakobson (1938), and Weinreich (1953: 25), that is, structural similarity between the languages in contact (but see Thomason and Kaufman 1988; Harris and Campbell 1994). Silva-Corvalán (1994: 135) showed that permeability is manifested in (1) the extension of discourse-pragmatic functions in accordance with the corresponding structure in English; (2) increased frequency to the detriment of variants without a counterpart in English (cf. Klein 1980); and (3) loss of semantic-pragmatic constraints not operative in the English counterpart. This scholar (1994: 5, 214) concluded that the effect of language contact is to accelerate nascent processes already present in the language. In Weinreich's (1953: 25) formulation, language contact has a "trigger effect". I will refer to the hypothesis that internal changes are more advanced in bilinguals as the acceleration hypothesis.

Most scholars of language contact recognize multiple causation, that is, that an external cause of change does not exclude an internal one. However, there is not complete agreement on the identifying criteria. In the case of *-ndo* constructions, both a convergence and an acceleration hypothesis make roughly the same predictions, as shown in Figure 1.

Introduction 17

Predictions about bilingual varieties	Convergence hypothesis	Acceleration hypothesis
estar + *-ndo* will...	since...	since...
• have a higher token frequency	...*be* + *-ing* is more frequent in English	...the diachronic tendency in Spanish is toward increased frequency
• have a higher frequency relative to motion verb constructions	...these variants have no English counterpart	...the diachronic tendency is for use of *estar* to the detriment of *ir, andar*
• *estar* + *-ndo* will be used for situations not actually in progress at the moment of reference	...English *be* + *-ing* is not a true progressive but a continuous, as in 'I'm writing a book on X (but right now I'm actually talking to you on the phone)'	...the diachronic tendency is toward semantic generalization

Figure 1. Predictions of convergence and acceleration hypotheses with respect to ESTAR + -NDO

We could continue the list in this fashion, with more specific predictions with respect to structural variables such as tense form distribution, grammatical person, and main verbs. An important difference, though, is that a convergence hypothesis, but not an acceleration hypothesis, would predict futurate uses in bilingual varieties. That is,

• Present tense *estar* + *-ndo* will be used to refer to future situations

since English *be* + *-ing* is used for expected future situations, as in 'I'm leaving tomorrow'.[8]

1.4.2 Register considerations in language contact

Poplack's (1997) study of French subjunctive usage along the Quebec-Ontario border in Canada reveals a set of factors largely ignored in studies intending to show contact-induced simplification and loss in bilingual varieties. Poplack showed that differences among French bilinguals in subjunctive use were due to differences in the distribution of matrix verbs. None of the factors related to degree of contact showed a consistent effect. Instead, once the lexical effect of matrix verb was factored out, social class emerged as the one factor contributing consistently to the choice of the subjunctive, which turns out to be a prestige form. Thus, the effects of extralinguistic factors such as those related to degree of language contact may be epiphenomenal when a linguistic factor is distributed differently across speakers (Poplack 1997: 304). This scholar (1997: 306) concluded, "We submit that claims regarding loss or simplification of the French subjunctive derive from notions of the 'standard' and/or of an earlier stage of the language that are highly idealized." Reliance on idealized notions of the language is related to the absence of comparative base studies of monolingual varieties, without which conclusions about bilingual situations are premature (cf. Lipski 1996).

The frequency of a form can be interpreted in two very distinct ways, according to Lavandera (1984: 41). It may convey social and stylistic information, as in the original Labovian studies of phonological variables. Or, it may simply reflect the frequency of occurrence of appropriate contexts. Lavandera's example is the alternation between the adjectives *exhausto* 'exhausted' and *reventado* 'beat' as meaning *muy cansado* 'very tired'. Differences in frequency for *reventado* between informal and formal contexts derive from the fact that an informal variant is more appropriate in informal contexts. Similarly, Givón (1990: 963) points out that the distribution of verbal tense, aspect, and mood categories is genre-dependent. As an example, he shows that in academic writing imperfective uses are overwhelmingly habitual and stative. This would lead us to expect fewer *estar* + *-ndo* tokens in academic writing.

Differences between oral and written varieties in the frequency of *-ndo* constructions may originate in functional differences between genres as observed by Givón. But distribution differences can also acquire social meaning. The English passive is a good example of the interplay between functional and register factors. Passives may be functionally motivated by factors such as the status of the subject as new or given information, but at the same time, the circumstances in which they are used are more formal than those in which the active is used. They may thus acquire an association of formality.[9] Similarly in Spanish, the kinds of things talked about in formal, written language may require fewer *-ndo* constructions and a proportionally higher number of gerunds as adverbials and relatives. Then, in its own right, *-ndo* construction frequency may come to convey a social-stylistic meaning of level of formality.

Dorian (1981: 154) suggested that the lack of prescriptive monitoring may be an important factor on the rate of grammatical change in communities undergoing language shift. Although Spanish in New Mexico is not in the same situation as the Scottish Gaelic dialect studied by Dorian, exposure to formal, written varieties is minimal. The present-day southwest region of the United States was excluded from the standardization of Mexican Spanish in the 19th century, first because of isolation from the political center and later because of occupation by the United States (Hidalgo 1987: 170–1). Spanish foreign language instruction in U.S. schools is based on norms from non-local varieties and so-called bilingual education programs are transitional to English-only instruction (Hernández-Chávez 1992). In general, varieties of Spanish in the Southwest are characterized by popular oral features (Sánchez 1982: 14).

The possibility that higher *estar + -ndo* token frequency might be a feature of informal, oral varieties rather than a manifestation of convergence with English has not been considered in studies of bilingual Spanish. However, a comparison between spoken and written corpora suggests that *estar + -ndo* token frequency is highly stratified by register. Initial results from Clegg and Rodríguez (1993) indicate that the construction is at least twice as likely to occur in popular oral varieties than in literary language. As shown in Table 2, the average occurrence of *estar + -ndo* per 10,000 words of text is 10 in a corpus of 15 novels, but 25 and 21 in Lope Blanch's (1990) oral Southwest Spanish corpus and popular Mexico City corpus (UNAM 1976), respectively.

Table 2. Frequency of ESTAR + -NDO (Clegg and Rodríguez 1993)

Corpus	Word count	*Estar + -ndo* tokens	Average per 10,000 words
Southwest (oral)	83,835	209	25
MexPop (oral)	172,699	366	21
Novels	1,300,000	1318	10

Southwest = Lope Blanch (1990), MexPop = UNAM (1976)

Table 3, also based on Clegg and Rodriguez's study, indicates that the proportion of gerunds cooccurring with an auxiliary relative to the proportion of gerunds appearing "unaccompanied" as manner adverbials or relatives is at least three times greater in oral than literary varieties. The proportion of gerunds occurring in an *-ndo* construction is 22% in the novels corpus, but 70% and 76% in the two oral corpora.[10] I return to register differences in construction frequency in Sections 2.6 and 5.1.4, and to dialect and register differences in the relative frequency of the different auxiliaries in Sections 4.6.4 and 4.7.

Table 3. Proportion of gerunds cooccurring with an auxiliary (Clegg and Rodríguez 1993)

Corpus	Gerund tokens N	Gerund adverbials, relatives N	%	Gerunds with an auxiliary N	%
Southwest (oral)	443	131	30%	312	70%
MexPop (oral)	925	226	24%	699	76%
Novels	13,242	10,340	78%	2,902	22%

The higher token frequencies of *estar* + *-ndo* in oral varieties compared to literary language may also reflect a change in progress. Traditionally it has been held that in Spanish *estar* + *-ndo* is not an obligatory expression of progressive meaning, in contrast to English Progressive *be* + *-ing* (e.g. Comrie 1976: 33). The claim is that, in Spanish, one can use the simple Present for a situation in progress at the moment of speech, as in Klein's (1980) example (example 8), *Mira, sale el sol* = *the sun is coming out*. But in what contexts and with what frequency do speakers actually use the simple Present with progressive meaning? Klein's (1980) conclusion that bilinguals are losing the option of using the simple form to express progressive meaning can only be evaluated in light of actual use and not according to prescriptive or idealized notions of the standard. I come back to the changing status of *estar* + *-ndo* toward becoming an obligatory progressive in Chapter 5 (Section 5.1).

Returning to the predictions about the effects of language contact outlined above (Section 1.4.1, Figure 1), it turns out that we do not find expected future uses in our bilingual data, against the convergence hypothesis. More generally, our results indicate that mechanisms of change with *-ndo* constructions are the same as in monolingual varieties, as outlined in Section 1.3, rather than a cognitive process of convergence (Klein 1980) or simplification (Silva-Corvalán 1994: 6). With respect to comparable oral varieties, the most important change in our bilingual data is the decline of the frequency of *ir* relative to *estar*, and here our results are more consonant with the acceleration of an internal process of specialization than with contact-induced convergence with English (Section 4.7).

1.5 The data

I draw on three sets of data to enable diachronic and synchronic comparisons: Old Spanish, Mexican, and New Mexican Spanish. Appendix I presents in summary fashion the corpora, words counts, and number of *-ndo* constructions.

1.5.1 *Old Spanish* (OldSp)

Data were collected from Old Spanish texts spanning three centuries, beginning with the *Poema de mio Cid* (1140/1207) and ending with the *Celestina* (1499). Rather than sampling a large number of units of small size, as in Keniston (1937a; 1937b), preference was given to a small number of well-studied texts with printed or electronic concordances. I read through all the texts (with the exception of the very long *Estoria de España*) to become familiar with contexts of use. The corpus is a little over half a million running words of text. Although this is not very large, the results agree with those reported in Spaulding (1926) and Yllera (1980). Our purpose here is to describe broad changes between Old and present-day Spanish, rather than to track developments by century. While a sample distributed over more texts may yield a precise chronology, it is unlikely that major new patterns would be revealed by a larger database.

The texts were selected to include works that are conserved in a manuscript fairly close to the date of composition (for example, not included is *Libro de Alixandre*, a composite of fragments from different sources). Excluded are works based on translation (in the case of *Apolonio,* which is based on a Latin work, an oral version was in circulation prior to the written text; the *Estoria de España* was composed originally in Spanish although some passages are adaptations from other-language texts). Since the earliest Old Spanish texts are in verse, both prose and verse are included. All texts have narrative and quoted speech. Works ostensibly incorporating language from popular speech are included, as in parts of the *Corbacho* and *Celestina*, as well as those written in more formal or stylized language.

For ease of future reference, a list of abbreviations is given below; the basic information about each text is from Deyermond (1971). Editions and concordances are listed in Appendix II. In the citation of examples, the original text as listed in the appendix is reproduced exactly and omitted parts are shown by three dots [...]. Numbers in parentheses following examples refer to verse number for the PMC, Apol, and LBA; Cátedra edition page number for Luc and Corb, and folio location for EE1 and C01.

(9) OldSp = Old Spanish corpus
PMC = *Poema* (or *Cantar*) *de Mio Cid*, 1140/1207, verse, epic
Apol = *Libro de Apolonio*, c.1250, *cuaderna vía* verse, epic
EE1 = *Estoria de España*, Alfonso X, 1270–89, prose, chronicle
LBA = *Libro de buen amor*, Juan Ruiz, Arcipreste de Hita, 1330/1343, verse, sermon — autobiography — exempla
Luc = *Libro de los enxiemplos del Conde Lucanor e de Patronio*, Don Juan Manuel, 1335, prose, didactic exempla
Corb = *Arcipreste de Talavera o Corbacho*, Alfonso Martínez de Toledo, 1438, prose, sermon — exempla
C01 = *(Tragi)comedia de Calisto y Melibea* or *Celestina*, Fernando de Rojas, 1499, prose, novel in dialogue

1.5.2 Present-day Mexican Spanish

The Mexico data set is composed of three corpora.

1.5.2.1 Mexico City popular (MexPop)

MexPop contains the transcriptions of interviews conducted as part of the popular Mexico City companion to the educated Mexico City data collected for the *Norma Culta* project (UNAM 1976; cf. Lope Blanch 1986). It is approximately 450 pages long, with 170,000 words of running text, from 17 hours of recordings (Arjona 1991: 8). I will draw on previous studies of this data (Arjona 1991; Clegg and Rodríguez 1993; Torres Cacoullos 1999a) for comparisons with the Old Spanish corpus in Chapters 2, 3, and 4. There are a total of 648 *-ndo* constructions in MexPop, conveniently close to the number of tokens in OldSp, at 616. Examples from MexPop will be cited by UNAM (1976) page number.

1.5.2.2 Essays

This is a corpus of essays, formal speeches, and scholarly writings by well-known Mexican writers. It represents a formal as opposed to colloquial style (cf. Biber's 1986 abstract vs. situated content), with works by Rosario Castellanos, Néstor García Canclini, Juan M. Lope Blanch, Carlos Monsiváis, Carlos Montemayor, Octavio Paz, and Alfonso Reyes. The texts are listed in Appendix IIIA. The corpus covers approximately 1,350 pages of text. Appendix IIIB gives the frequency of *-ndo* constructions per 100 pages, by text. Even though the number of pages is three times greater than the number of pages for MexPop, the number of *-ndo* constructions is less than half. In particular, *estar + -ndo* is 15(!) times more likely to appear in MexPop than in Essays. Table 4 shows differences in token frequency, which confirm the importance of register considerations.

Table 4. *Frequency of -ndo constructions in Essays and in oral popular Mexico City corpus*

| | ESTAR | | IR | | SEGUIR | | TOTAL* | |
	N	Aver	N	Aver	N	Aver	N	Aver**
Essays (1344 pp.)	67	5	101	8	81	6	278	21
MexPop (450 pp.)	340	76	146	32	39	9	637	142

* Total includes cases of *continuar + -ndo, venir + -ndo, andar + -ndo*.
** Average number of occurrences per 100 printed pages

1.5.2.3 Chihuahua (Chih'97)

This is oral data I recorded in the city of Chihuahua and the village of Ascención, in the northern Mexican state of Chihuahua just across the border from New Mexico. The data used here come from 15 hours of recordings with 37 speakers made in June and December 1997. The variety is mostly popular.[11] About half the recordings are interviews or two-way conversations and half are interactions involving at least three speakers. I draw on Chih'97 in addition to the published MexPop materials for comparisons with the New Mexico corpora to ensure that the conditions under which the data were obtained were as similar as possible, since I was present at most of the Chihuahua and bilingual New Mexico recordings. A second reason is the historical bond between the two border states, which is reinforced by present-day immigration. Traditional New Mexico Spanish is more related to northern Mexican Spanish than to any other dialect group, at least with respect to lexical items, although New Mexico has many unique terms (Bernal Enríquez 1996; Vigil and Bills 1998). Examples from Chih'97 will be cited by tape number.

1.5.3 New Mexican Spanish

In situations of language contact, time-depth, extent, and type of bilingualism have been shown to have linguistic effects (cf. Poplack 1993; Thomason and Kaufman 1988; Weinreich 1953). In particular, bilingual communities may be transitional, as in cases of language shift (Mougeon and Beniak 1991) and obsolescence (Dorian 1981), or they may be stable (Poplack 1989). Spanish in the United States can be said to cover the range of possibilities, depending on the sample chosen by the investigator. In non-immigrant varieties in the Southwest region of the United States, census data analyzed by Hudson, Hernández-Chávez, and Bills (1995) suggest an unrelenting shift to English. As Dorian (1981: 94) observes, societal bilingualism of the transitional type may take the form of two groups each monolingual in a different language. It is not clear whether Spanish-English bilingual contact in the Southwest has always been primarily of this form; Hernández-Chávez (1993: 59), for example, suggests that earlier periods were characterized by stable bilingualism.

As Poplack (1997) has argued, it is important to distinguish between the concomitants of regular interaction in both languages, or stable bilingualism, and the manifestations of language acquisition or attrition, or transitional bilingualism. While grammatical transfer from English may be possible in either case, the first is relevant to questions about possible (relatively lasting) changes in Spanish, while the second is most relevant to questions about the acquisition and especially loss of Spanish. Transitional bilinguals or semi-speakers (Lipski 1993a) are unlikely to transmit "changes" to future generations.[12]

A difficult question in studies of bilingual speech communities is how to appropriately operationalize factors related to parameters of bilingualism. Poplack (1997), for example, includes neighborhood of residence and English proficiency in her study of French subjunctive use along the Quebec-Ontario border in Canada. Silva-Corvalán (1994) uses generational distance from immigrant monolingualism in her study of Spanish in Los Angeles. Generational groupings would not be appropriate for New Mexican Spanish, which has been spoken in the region for over three hundred years in relative isolation, although there is increasing contact with immigrant varieties. Instead, for the present study I group the speakers by Spanish and English proficiency as rated by the interviewer. In nearly all cases proficiency rating coincides with age grouping (cf. Bernal-Enríquez 1999; Hudson-Edwards and Bills 1982). The three groups are near monolingual (NMmon), bilingual (NMbil), and transitional bilingual (NMtb).

1.5.3.1 *New Mexico near monolingual* (NMmon)
The near monolingual group is "near" because just about all speakers of

Spanish in New Mexico at least manage to get by in English. A nice formulation for the state of affairs in this group is the following, from one of the interviews:

(10) – *¿Y según usted, habla el inglés bastante bien, usted?*
– *Pos, eh, **ahi le-** [] **jamacheo**.* {Risa}(NMCSS#217)
'– And according to you, you speak English pretty well, do you?
– Well, uh, I get by'[13]

The NMmon data are from the New Mexico-Colorado Spanish Survey (NMCSS) corpus, housed at the University of New Mexico (Vigil and Bills 1993). All 15 speakers in this group received an interviewer rating of 5 for Spanish and 3 or less for English, on a scale of 1 to 5. They were all born before 1920. All are from towns to the north of the largest city in the state, Albuquerque. Spanish was their first language. They learned English at school, or later at work. As some of these speakers said:

(11) a. *pa' mí era muy duro, porque yo lo que aprendí a hablar- inglés lo aprendí trabajando cuando ya había jalido a trabajar con los gringos ahi* (NMCSS#115)
'for me it was very hard, because whatever English I learned I learned working, after I had gone out to work with the *gringos*'

b. *Cuando después que me casé, mi esposo sabía muy bien la idomia inglés, y él, y de él aprendí...* (NMCSS#20)
'When after I got married, my husband knew the English language very well, and he, and from him I learned'

c. *hasta que tenía como doce años yo no sabía una palabra en esp- en inglés* (NMCSS#76)
'Until I was about twelve years old I didn't know one word in Spa- in English'

Some of the phonetic features in this group of speakers are eth deletion, word-initial /s/ aspiration as in *salido – jalido* (example (a) above), aspiration of /f/ as in *fui – jui*, weak intervocalic /y/ and /y/ epenthesis as in *creo – creyo*, and paragogic /-e/, as in *trabajar – trabajare*. There are borrowings such as *el bos* 'the bus' and calques such as *atender escuela* 'attend school'. Code-switching in this corpus is mostly limited to single-word switches, as in *hicieron* "parade" 'they did a parade' (NMCSS#10) or *una pregunta muy* "easy" 'a very easy question' (NMCSS#115). Most frequently switched are dates, for example, *era en el* "eighteen eighty one" 'it was in...' (NMCSS#162) and names of cities or states. Also common are discourse markers such as "so" and "you know". Examples from NMmon will be cited by NMCSS tape number.

1.5.3.2 *New Mexico bilingual* (NMbil)

The bilingual group has 15 speakers. Three are interviews from the NMCSS, most of the remainder are recordings I made between 1995 and 1998.[13] All speakers in this group received an interviewer rating of 5 for Spanish and a 4 or 5 for English. They were all born between 1930 and 1945, with the exception of one younger speaker. All but two have lived over 20 years in Albuquerque. These speakers regularly use both languages. Phonetic features and borrowings are the same as in NMmon. An important difference is the extent and type of code-switching, especially intrasentential switching which is considered to be characteristic of bilinguals proficient in both languages (Poplack 1982). As one person said,

> (12) *Cuando menos pienso estoy hablando en español y tengo la mania de que, cuando no la pienso,* **I start talking in English** (NMbil/ Joe)
> 'When I'm not even thinking about it I am speaking in Spanish and I have the habit, when I don't think about what I am doing, ...'

Examples from NMbil will be cited by the first letters of the speaker's name.

1.5.3.3 *New Mexico transitional bilingual* (NMtb)

This group has 9 speakers, all but three born after 1975. One is from the NMCSS, the remainder are from interviews I conducted between 1995 and 1998. All rated 3 or less in Spanish, 5 in English. Unlike speakers in the NMmon group, who use mostly Spanish, and speakers in NMbil, who regularly use both languages, these speakers use Spanish only when absolutely necessary, either with their grandparents or in Spanish class.

1.6 Summary

In short, this is a study of grammaticization, variation, and language contact. We may group our findings into three broad sets.

(13) Diachronic paths in the evolution of *-ndo* constructions:
    a. *-ndo* constructions originate as locative and motion expressions. The mechanism of change is semantic reduction, with loss of spatial features of meaning.
    b. In parallel, *-ndo* constructions undergo reductive changes in form.
    c. Both formal and semantic reduction are linked to construction frequency increases.
    d. *Estar* + *-ndo* has increased in relative frequency with respect to motion verb *-ndo* constructions.
    e. *Estar* + *-ndo* has generalized to a broader range of main verbs and to compatibility with habitual contexts.

(14) Synchronic variation in present-day Spanish:
    a. The distribution of auxiliaries in *-ndo* constructions with respect to cooccurring main verbs, locatives, and time expressions reflects their original lexical meaning, in support of the retention hypothesis. Specific features of meaning follow from the original uses of the source constructions.
    b. At the same time, semantic reduction is manifested in overlapping uses and layering in the domain of progressive aspect.
    c. Particular high frequency auxiliary — gerund combinations have become routines or fixed expressions, as in *estar hablando* 'be (located) talking', *ir creciendo* 'be (go) growing', and *andar buscando* 'be (go around) looking for'.
    d. Newer habitual uses of *estar* + *-ndo* have an experiential meaning component, which follows from the locative origins of the construction.
    e. The frequency and distribution of *-ndo* constructions depends on register factors.

(15) Spanish — English language contact:
    a. The token frequency of *estar* + *-ndo* among bilinguals is the same as in comparable (oral, popular) monolingual varieties, in which the simple Present is also increasingly restricted to non-progressive uses.
    b. *Estar* is displacing *ir* but not *andar* among bilingual speakers. This is evidence against contact-induced simplification and for

the acceleration of an internal, diachronic process of specialization in favor of *estar*.

c. The major dividing line falls between transitional bilingual speakers and all other speakers — both monolingual and proficient bilingual. Transitional bilinguals show weakening of pragmatic constraints on habitual uses of *estar* + *-ndo*.

Notes

1. "Grammaticalization" is now more common than "grammaticization" (cf. Lehmann (1995: 9–11), but following Bybee et. al (1994: 4, note 2) I will use the shorter term.

2. See King 1992 for a comprehensive endeavor to represent all uses of each Spanish verb form in terms of binary features.

3. As we will see in Chapters 3 and 4, *ir* + *-ndo* may specify that a continuous situation develops gradually. In example (1c) though, given the economic situation at the time, it is likely that even as the speaker was saying *va subiendo* the U.S. dollar was indeed rising with respect to the Mexican peso, making the example more of a true progressive!

4. In example (2a), *está cuidando televisión* 'he is wathcing television' is the speaker's answer to my question about her husband's location. The converse is also true, that is, that a location response may be given to an *estar* + *-ndo* question. For example,

    – *Y entonces, ¿en qué está trabajando []?*
    – *Pues está...pues en en una fábrica, ¿verdad?* (UNAM 1976: 173)
    – So then, what kind of work is she doing?
    – Well, she is in a factory, right.

    These examples belie the view that in combination with a gerund *estar* may be interpreted only as an auxiliary (Olbertz:1998: 300–1).

5. I have used standard orthography in most of my transcriptions of oral data. Some of the NMCSS (New Mexico Colorado Spanish Survey) transcriptions are from Ysaura Bernal, to whom I am very grateful; these give some indication of phonetic features.

6. The tradition among Hispanists is to discuss *estar* + *-ndo* and the motion verb constructions together, as in Spaulding (1926), Keniston (1936), Gili Gaya (1964), Roca Pons (1958), Coseriu (1968), Hamplová (1968), Luna (1980), Solé (1990), and Arjona (1991). Nevertheless, many Spanish grammars written for English speakers either have nothing to say about motion verb *-ndo* constructions (e.g. Lunn and DeCesaris 1992; Whitley 1986) or mention them separately from *estar* + *-ndo* (e.g. Butt and Benjamin 1994: 230ff.).

7. See, for example, Heine (1993: 3–26) for definitions of auxiliaries in different linguistic schools; Dietrich (1983: 35–93) for a summary of views on Romance auxiliaries; Luna Traill (1980: 141–65) for definitions of Spanish "perífrasis verbales".

8. Expected future uses of the English Present Progressive are apparently on the rise, though I am not aware of studies indicating their frequency (cf. Mair and Hundt 1995: 118).

Introduction 29

9. I owe the discussion of the English Passive to Alan Hudson.

10. The figures in Clegg and Rodríguez (1993) do not always add up. For Table 3, I subtracted the number of gerunds alone from the gerund total to arrive at the number of gerunds with an auxiliary.

11. Speakers in the Chih'97 corpus are (i) unskilled manual urban or rural laborers; (ii) semi-skilled workers, trained workers currently employed in manual labor, small business owner-operators (*taquerías, cafeterías*), policemen, housewives not employed outside the home; and (iii) labor union representatives, individuals actively involved with a political party, school teachers, writers, and others with (at least some) university education or who are subject to "linguistic market" pressures (Sankoff and Laberge 1978).

12. Mougeon and Beniak (1991: Ch.6) propose that changes originating in child language may become part of adult vernaculars under conditions of language shift. Lipski (1990: 47–8) also raises the possibility that semi-speaker usage may modify a dialect.

13. Thanks to Esteban Hernández for suggesting English "how much" as the inspiration for *jamachear*. "Intensive" use of the 3rd person dative pronoun *le* as in *ahi le jamacheo* is a feature of Mexican Spanish found in both the Chihuahua and New Mexico data (cf. Torres Cacoullos and Hernández 1999). This example from Chih'97 is very similar to the NMmon example in (10). In both cases the *le* + verb construction means just managing to do something.

> *Sí fíjate, es que [ ] con la computadora. Pero no aprendo, nada. [ ] Ahi no más **le** pico. Ahi no más **le** pico*...(Chih 97#12b)
> 'Yes you see, [ ] with the computer. But I haven't learned, anything. [ ] I just press the keys (I just mess with it)...'

14. The NMbil group includes four speakers recorded by students taking a phonetics course at the University of New Mexico.

Chapter 2

Formal reduction in grammaticization

Diachronic changes in the form of *-ndo* constructions

Cross-linguistic studies by Bybee (1985) and Dahl (1985) have shown a high correlation between tense-mood-aspect categories and types of expression. Types of expression are ways that two or more semantic elements may be combined. These range on a continuum from tightly fused to loosely connected combinations, including lexical, derivational, inflectional, periphrastic, and syntactic expression (Bybee 1985: 11–12). For example, in *mostrar* 'show', the two semantic components *hacer* 'cause' and *verse* 'to be seen' are combined into a monomorphemic word, in an instance of lexical expression. In derivational *enseñar* 'show', these two semantic components are expressed in separate morphemes. Inflectional expression is the same as derivational, except that inflections are obligatory (Bybee 1985: 81), for example, the synthetic future suffix in *enseñaré* 'I will show'. At the end of the continuum is syntactic expression, where there is no fusion and two independent words combine freely, as in *exponer a la vista* 'expose to view'. Periphrastic or free grammatical expression is somewhere in between inflectional and syntactic, in that two semantic components are expressed in separate words, but one of these is grammatical and has a fixed position, as in the *ir* + *a* + Infinitive periphrastic future, for example, *voy a enseñar* 'I am going to show'.

The idea that expression type may be semantically determined is not new (cf. Sapir's 1921: 101 classification of concepts), but actual cross-linguistic surveys provide striking results. For example, Dahl (1985: 185) found that 75% of inflectional categories express one of three grammatical meanings: past, perfective – imperfective, or future. On the other hand, progressives overwhelmingly — in 85% of all cases surveyed — tend to have periphrastic expression, most often by means of auxiliary constructions (Dahl 1985: 91). This is the case with *-ndo* constructions in present-day Spanish.

From a diachronic perspective, Bybee, Perkins and Pagliuca (1994) have shown that a concomitant of grammaticization of function is grammaticization of form. This is known as the "parallel reduction hypothesis": reduction in meaning is paralleled by reduction in phonetic substance. If *-ndo* constructions evolved from free combinations of independent lexical items to periphrastic expressions of aspect, we would expect to observe some changes in form between Old Spanish and present-day varieties. Bybee et al. (1994: 106ff.) identify two types of formal change that accompany semantic reduction in grammaticization: phonetic reduction and loss of autonomy.

Unfortunately, phonetic reduction in the form of loss of segmental or suprasegmental features is difficult to show in the case of Old Spanish *-ndo* constructions, since we must depend on written data. For example, it is likely that one reductive change was the loss of stress on erstwhile locative *estar* in combination with a stressed *-ndo* form, so that *estar* + *-ndo* constructions were left with one main stress, now on the *-ndo* form. A case for phonetic reduction in *estar* + *-ndo* may be made from *ta* + verb-stem constructions, for example, *yo 'ta habla(ndo)*, in Afro-Hispanic creoles and vernacular Dominican Spanish (cf. Lipski 1993b; 1994: 30–1). But a change such as loss of stress on *estar* would not be reflected in Old Spanish manuscripts.

A more promising way to operationalize the parallel reduction hypothesis in written texts is to look for indices of loss of autonomy and increasing fusion of the auxiliary with the gerund. In this chapter I look at four indices of formal reduction:

1. first, the positional fixing of the two elements in the construction — to an auxiliary first, gerund second, order;
2. second, the decline of multiple gerund constructions, in which one auxiliary is associated with two or more gerunds;
3. third, the reduction in the amount of material intervening between the auxiliary and the gerund;
4. and fourth, clitic climbing frequencies, which show a tendency for object pronoun clitics to be preposed to the auxiliary.

Sections 2.1–2.4 review this series of reductive changes. In Section 2.5, we will see that these changes are linked to frequency increases of auxiliary-plus-gerund sequences. It will turn out that both absolute token frequency (the average occurrence of *-ndo* constructions in running text) and relative fre-

Formal reduction in grammaticization 33

quency (the proportion of gerunds in construction with an auxiliary) are important in evaluating frequency effects in reductive change. Section 2.6 examines synchronic variation in construction frequency, based on differences of register. Finally, Section 2.7 looks at bilingual data in light of diachronic patterns and register differences.

2.1 From positional variation to positional fixing

In the 12th century poem *Poema de mio Cid* (PMC) there is positional variation between *-ndo* forms postposed and preposed to the auxiliary. The following examples illustrate. In (1a) *catando* 'watching' is postposed to *estar*, in (1b) it is preposed. In (2a) *pesando* 'dismaying' follows *ir*, in (2b) it precedes *ir*.

(1) a. *Tornaua la cabec'a & **estaua los catando*** (0002)
'he turned his head and stood looking at them' (Hamilton and Perry 1975)
b. ***Catando estan** a myo c'id q<u>a'ntos ha en la cort* (3123)
'everybody in the court was gazing at My Cid' (Such and Hodgkinson 1987)

(2) a. *Alos vnos plaze & alos otros **va pesando*** (1837)
'Some of them were pleased, and others dismayed' (Such and Hodgkinson 1987)
b. *Hya va el mandado por las t<ie>rras todas*
***Pesando va** alos de monc'on & alos de huesca* (940)
'News of this raid spread through the country round about, filling the inhabitants of Monzon and Huesca with dismay' (Hamilton and Perry 1975)

The average number of preposed *-ndo* forms in the PMC, as in the (a) examples above, is 20% for *estar* and *seer* 'be (seated)' combined and 35% for *ir*. It is interesting that preposing seems to be a routine with certain main verbs. For example, all three cases of *passando* 'passing' are preposed to *ir* (verses 323, 544, 1826), as in *Passando ua la noch* 'night passes' (verse 323). Three of five cases of *tornando* 'turning' are preposed to *ir*, including both cases of the expression *tornando va la cabeza* 'turns his head' (verses 377, 943, 1078, 2429, 2783). Despite routinized preposing with certain expressions, in most cases there seems to be no pattern, as in examples (1) and (2). The variable position of the gerund with respect to the auxiliary in the PMC indicates that these two elements were combining freely as independent lexical items.

The results for positional variation are summarized in Table 5.

Table 5. Positional variation: -ndo forms preceding ESTAR, IR

Old Spanish text*	-ndo preceding ESTAR N	Proportion	-ndo preceding IR N	Proportion
PMC (1140/1207)	2(2)**	20%	22	35%
Apol (c.1250)	0	0	0	0
EE1 (1270–1284)	0	0	0	0
LBA (1330/1343)	0	0	0	0
Luc (1335)	0	0	0	0
Corb (1438)	5	17%	2	17%
C01 (1499)	4	13%	0	0
OldSp total	13	8%	24	9%
MexPop	0	0	0	0

* For list of Old Spanish texts, see Chapter 1 (Section 1.5.1) and Appendix II.
** Figures in parentheses are for *seer + -ndo*.

After the PMC, there are no tokens of preposed gerunds in the other medieval texts surveyed, with the exception of the 15th c. *Corbacho* (Corb) and *Celestina* (C01). Preposing averages 17% for *estar* and *ir* in Corb and 13% for *estar* in C01. We might attribute the relatively high proportion of preposed *-ndo* forms in the PMC to the preservation of older forms in that text. On the other hand, preposing in Corb and C01 might be part of the more stylized prose in parts of these texts (see Section 2.6).

The position of the gerund with respect to the auxiliary was pretty well fixed by the end of the Old Spanish period. Keniston (1937a: 105) reports that preposing is rare in 16th century prose. In the popular Mexico City (MexPop) corpus, there are no preposed gerunds at all, that is, postposing is categorical. As free combinations of lexical items become periphrastic expressions, the elements of the emerging grammatical morpheme come to have a fixed position. The change from a variable to a fixed position for the auxiliary with respect to the gerund may be taken as one index of loss of autonomy (cf. Bybee et al. 1994: 110).

2.2 The decline of multiple gerund constructions

Another measure of loss of autonomy and fusion is the decline in multiple gerund constructions. In what I am calling multiple or parallel gerund constructions, two gerunds are conjoined with an explicit *y* (*e*) 'and' or *o* 'or', as in examples (3a) and (3b) below, or without a conjunction, as in examples (3c) and (3d).

(3) Old Spanish multiple *estar* + *-ndo* constructions (i) With a conjunction
- a. *E estaua **fabla<n>do** ante tod el pueblo **& falagando** los.*(EE1 74v32)
 'And he was **speaking** before all the people **and flattering** them.'
- b. *A cabo de algunos días, unos omnes estavan **riendo e trebejando** e escribían todos los omnes que ellos conosçían, cada uno de quál manera era, e dizían:* (Luc, Ex. XX, p.153)
 'In a few days' time men were **laughing and joking** about the matter and decided to write down a list of the names of all the people they knew together with their qualities' (Keller and Keating 1977: 91)

(4) Old Spanish multiple *estar* + *-ndo* constructions (ii) Without a conjunction
- a. *Com<m>o ladron venjste de noche a lo escuro estando nos **dormjendo yaz'jendo** nos sseguro* (LBA, 1192)
 'You came like a thief in the night, in the dark, while we were **asleep** and were **reposing** free from care' (Willis1972: 324)
- b. *Siempre están **fablando, librando** cosas agenas* (LBA, Segunda parte, Cap. XII, p.195)
 'They are always **gabbling** and **poking** their noses into other people's business' (Simpson1959: 153).

In counting multiple gerund constructions I included cases where the gerunds are separated by a location or manner adverbial, for example (3a) above, or by an NP subject or object, for example (6) below.[1]

Whether the two are linked by a conjunction, as in the examples in (3), or the second appears to be more of a modifier of the first, as in examples in (4), these gerunds are symmetrically coordinated or parallel, in that each one could be construed as being in construction with the auxiliary. This is reflected in Willis's (1972) use of the Progressive *be* + *-ing* construction, 'were reposing', in the English translation of the parallel gerund *yaziendo* in example (4a). What is important is that in multiple gerund constructions there is not a one-to-one relationship between an auxiliary and an *-ndo* form, since the same auxiliary appears to be in construction with two or more gerunds, each one vying for a connection with the auxiliary. The lack of a one-to-one relationship between the auxiliary and the *-ndo* form detracts from their identification as a fused unit.

Table 6 shows the number of multiple gerund constructions in Old Spanish texts. In the *Estoria de España* (EE1) alone, 13% (5/39) of *estar* + *-ndo* tokens are multiple gerund constructions, either with or without an explicit conjunction. For *ir* + *-ndo* the average is 11% (13/114), and for *andar* + *-ndo*, 17% (12/64). In the Old Spanish corpus overall, the average occurrence of these multiple gerund constructions is 13% (21/167) for *estar* and 10% (28/274) for *ir*. That is, of all auxiliary-plus-gerund sequences, 13% in the case of *estar* and 10% in the case of *ir* have a second (if not third) gerund parallel to the gerund immediately following the auxiliary.

Table 6. Multiple gerund constructions in Old Spanish

	All *-ndo* constructions ESTAR	All *-ndo* constructions IR	Multiple *-ndo* constructions ESTAR*	Multiple *-ndo* constructions IR**	Proportion of all *-ndo* constructions ESTAR	Proportion of all *-ndo* constructions IR
PMC	20	63	1	10	5%	16%
Apol	2	26	1	0	50%	0%
EE1	39	114	5	13	34%	11%
LBA	22	22	1	1	5%	5%
Luc	24	18	1	0	4%	0%
Corb	29	12	8	2	28%	17%
C01	31	19	4	2	13%	11%
OldSp (total)	167	274	21	28	13%	10%

*   PMC 1566; Apol. 121; EE1–5v15, 7r30, 74v32, 79r26, 144r7); LBA 1192; Luc. p.153; Corb. p.118, 148, 194 (2), 222, 227, 228, 299; C01 19v23, 35v14, 37v20, 61v4
** PMC 323, 377, 607, 758, 1046, 1078, 1513, 2344, 2804, 2871; EE1–2v72, 4v52, 6r4, 42v8, 45r71, 57v59, 63v23, 75v84, 139v91, 141r99, 144r99, 168v6, 176r30; LBA 723; Corb. p. 132, 182; C01–21r23, 58r9

In contrast, as shown in Table 7, there are only two multiple *estar* + *-ndo* tokens in the MexPop corpus (UNAM 1976: 16, 126), less than 1% of all

Formal reduction in grammaticization 37

tokens of *estar* + *-ndo*. There are two examples for *ir* + *-ndo* (UNAM 1976: 138, 422), only about 1%. Even the following is not a very good example of a multiple gerund construction, since *subir y bajar* 'go up and (go) down' may be said to form a routine unit, i.e., 'go up and down'.

(5) *la presión que se siente en...de que ha de estar **subiendo y bajando*** (UNAM 1976: 16)
'the pressure you feel in...that you have to be **moving up and moving down**' (when you play center position in soccer).

A better present-day example of a parallel gerund construction is (a) from the NMmon corpus, or (b) from MexPop.

(6) a. *Y ahi está uno **cortando** pedazos **y comiendo** carne.* (NMmon/ NMCSS#4)
'And there you are **cutting** pieces **and eating** meat.'
b. *Pues el chofer se jalaba, y aquellos se iban hasta **riendo**, **comiéndose** los tamales.* (UNAM 1976: 422)
'Well the driver would start the bus and they would go off **laughing, eating up** the tamales.'

Table 7. Multiple gerund constructions in present-day corpora

| | All -*ndo* constructions || Multiple -*ndo* constructions || Proportion of all -*ndo* constructions ||
	ESTAR	IR	ESTAR	IR	ESTAR	IR
MexPop	338	146	2	2	< 1%	1%
NMmon	42	14	4	1	10%	7%*
NMbil	144	6	3	0	2%	0%
Essays	67	101	5	10	7%	10%**

* The proportion of multiple gerund constructions is higher in NMmon than in MexPop (z = 4.3794, p = .0000) and in NMbil (z = 2.2294, p = .0258) for *estar*, though not for *ir*. Differences between NMbil and MexPop are not statistically significant.
** The proportion of multiple gerund constructions is significantly higher in Essays than in MexPop, for both *estar* (z = 3.9423, p = .0000) and *ir* (z = 3.0660, p = .0011).

The decline in the proportion of multiple gerund constructions between OldSp and MexPop is statistically significant, for both *estar* + *-ndo* and *ir* + *-ndo* (z = 6.0764, p = .0000 and z = 3.3534, p = .0004, respectively, in a one-sided chi-square test for equality of proportions).[2] What we see instead in MexPop is a tendency to repeat the auxiliary for each *-ndo* form. The redundant use of *ir* and *estar* as in the following examples may itself be taken as an indication of the grammaticization of the constructions as aspectual markers (cf. Bybee et al. 1994: 8). Example (7) is a description of shoe sewing; the subject of the series of *ir* + *-ndo* constructions is a needle.

(7) *O sea que **va** agarrando y **va**...enudando en cada pisada. **Va** enudando así, ¿entiende? O sea **va** agarrando así, lo **va** dejando...* (UNAM 1976: 39)
'**It goes** taking hold and **it goes**...knotting at every step. **It goes** knotting like this, see? You know, **it goes** taking hold like this, **it goes** leaving it...'

(8) *Además, en cualquier época, pues **estar** trabajando y **estar** estudiando, no se puede.*(UNAM 1976: 253)
'Also, it's always been the case, well, to **be** working and to **be** studying, it can't be done.'

Let us now look at the results for the New Mexico corpora in Table 7. Multiple gerund constructions average 10% (4/42) and 7% (1/14), respectively, for *estar* and *ir* in the monolingual group (NMmon). The higher proportion of parallel gerunds for *estar* in NMmon than in MexPop may reflect the retention of older forms in traditional New Mexican Spanish. On the other hand, the bilingual data (NMbil) is virtually identical to MexPop in the proportion of multiple-gerund constructions, with 2% for *estar* and none for *ir*.

2.3 Reduction of intervening material

2.3.1 *Diachronic changes*

A strong indication of fusion is the quantitative change in both the amount and kind of material intervening between the auxiliary and the gerund. In the case of *estar* + *-ndo*, we find that some item intervenes between *estar* and the gerund in 65% of all tokens in the *Poema de mio Cid* and 51% of all tokens in the *Estoria de España*.

The tokens in the EE1 with intervening material break down as follows: 15% (6/39) closed class items, 28% (11/39) open class items, and 8% (3/39) cases of two intervening items. Closed class items are subject or object pronouns. Open class items include three cases each of a manner or time expression and two cases each of a subject or locative word or phrase. Two intervening items (constituents) include a temporal plus a locative expression. Examples in (9) and (10) illustrate.

(9) *Estar* + *-ndo* with intervening open class material in EE1
 a. *E abaxo luego la cabec'a contra aq<ue>llos q<ue> lo estauan **assi** loando & dixo les.* (EE1 74v32)
 'And then he bowed his head to those who were **thus** lauding him and said.'
 b. *% Estaua **un dia** cantando enel teatro. & tremio la tierra assoora.* (EE1 75v35)
 'He was **one day** singing in the theater. And the earth suddenly trembled.'

(10) *Estar* + *-ndo* with two items intervening in EE1
 a. *% Este rey Viterigo seyendo **un dia a su mesa** comiendo; uinieron omnes q<ue> dieron en el grandes feridas & mataron le.* (EE1 166v32)
 'This king Viterigo being (sitting) **one day at his table** eating, there came some men who inflicted great wounds on him and killed him.'
 b. *E tan grand miedo auie dalgunos quel dizien q<ue>l andauan assechando por lo matar maguer no era uerdat. q<ue> quiso por ende muchas uezes dexar ell Jmpe-rio. [%] E el q<ue> estaua **una uez en el te<m>plo** faziendo sacrificio. fallaro<n> cabo del un omne q<ue> tenie un bullon.* (EE1 73v101)
 'And he was so afraid of some people who he was told were after him to kill him even though it was not true, that for this reason he tried many times to leave the empire. And he was **once in the temple** offering a sacrifice, they found next to him a man holding a stud.'

Table 8. Intervening material in ESTAR + -NDO

	None	Closed Class	Open Class	Two Items	Total N
PMC	35%	50%	10%	5%	20
EE1	49%	15%	28%	8%	39
LBA	64%	4%	4%	27%	22
Luc	71%	12%	8%	8%	24
Corb	59%	17%	17%	7%	29
C01	71%	6%	13%	10%	31

	N	%	N	%	N	%	N	%	Total N
OldSp (total)	96	**58%**	27	**16%**	25	**15%**	17	**10%**	165
MexPop	292	**86%**	25	**7%**	18	**5%**	5	**1%**	340
NMmon	33	79%	3	7%	5	12%	1	2%	42
NMbil	135	94%	1	<1%	6	4%	2	1%	144

* Closed class items counted were mostly subject and object pronouns, open class items were mostly subject NPs, locatives, temporals, and manner adverbials, and "two items" were cases of two open class items.

** The difference in the proportion of cases with no intervening material between OldSp 58.2% and MexPop 85.9% is significant: $\chi^2 = 47.88648$, p = .0000. Also significant is the difference in the proportion of cases with intervening open class items (combining the 3rd and 4th column) between OldSp 25.4% and MexPop 6.8%: $\chi^2 = 34.60185$, p = .0000.

As shown in Table 8, cases of intervening open class items drop by two-thirds, from 15% in the Old Spanish corpus overall to 5% in the Mexico City data. Even more striking is the drop in two-item intervening material. Cases of *estar* + [x] + [y] + *-ndo* in the Old Spanish corpus, as in examples (10) above, number 17 or 10% of the total. There are only five cases in the Mexico City corpus, equal to 1% of the total. Adding together cases of one and two items, the difference between OldSp and MexPop in the average of open class items intervening between *estar* and the gerund, at 25% as opposed to 7%, is highly significant ($\chi^2 = 34.60185$, p = 0.0000).

The results for *ir* + *-ndo* are similar. As shown in Table 9, the average occurrence of *ir* + *-ndo* constructions with intervening open class items, combining cases of one and two items, decreases from 22% in OldSp to 8% in MexPop ($\chi^2 = 13.98921$, p = .0002). There were no cases at all of two intervening items in MexPop, compared with 8% in OldSp.

Formal reduction in grammaticization 41

Table 9. Intervening material in IR + -NDO

	None		Closed Class		Open Class		Two Items		Total N
PMC	87%		11%		2%		0		63
Apol	50%		8%		23%		19%		26
EE1	60%		16%		16%		8%		114
LBA	64%		0		14%		23%		22
Luc	89%		0		11%		0		18
Corb	58%		0		42%		0		12
C01	68%		0		21%		10%		19
	N	%	N	%	N	%	N	%	Total N
OldSp (total)	187	**68%**	27	**10%**	39	**14%**	21	**8%**	274
MexPop	130	**89%**	5	**3%**	11	**8%**	0	**0**	146

* The difference in the proportion of cases with no intervening material between OldSp 68% and MexPop 89% is significant: $\chi^2 = 22.69926$, p = .0000. Also significant is the difference in the proportion of cases with intervening open class items (combining the 3rd and 4th column) between OldSp 22% and MexPop 8%: $\chi^2 = 13.98921$, p = 0.0002.

Viewed from the opposite perspective, the proportion of *estar + -ndo* and *ir + -ndo* **not** separated by any kind of intervening material (zero) increases from 58% to 86% and 68% to 89%, respectively. The lower probability of intervening open class items indicates a higher degree of fusion between an emerging grammatical morpheme and the verb it attaches to in the construction (Bybee et al. 1994: 113).

There is an important difference between *ir + -ndo* and *estar + -ndo*, however. In the Old Spanish corpus the proportion of cases with no (zero) intervening material is higher for *ir + ndo* (68%) than for *estar + -ndo* (58%) (z = 2.0812, p = .0187). This may be taken as one piece of evidence in favor of the hypothesis that *ir + -ndo* had already grammaticized to a (greater) extent by the time the earliest available Old Spanish texts were written. On the other hand, although the proportion of cases with intervening open class material decreases between OldSp and MexPop for both *ir* and *estar*, the change appears to be greater for the latter. The drop from 22% to 8% for *ir + -ndo* represents slightly less than a threefold decrease, while for *estar + -ndo* the decrease is nearly fourfold, from 25% to 7%. Thus, even though *ir + -ndo* seems to have gotten a head start on the grammaticization path, *estar + -ndo* has caught up if not outpaced it, at least with respect to the average occurrence of intervening material. We will see that *ir + -ndo* shows a slower pace of change than *estar* + *-ndo* with respect to other indices as well, such as cliticclimbing (Section 2.4, below). I return to this point and relate the asymmetries between *estar* and *ir* to differences in frequency increases in Chapter 4 (Section 4.5).

For *andar* + *-ndo*, a partial count limited to the EE1 suggests that *andar* + *-ndo* not only has a higher average of intervening open class items but also a fair number of cases of more than two intervening items or constituents. The proportion of *andar* + *-ndo* with intervening open class items (including two items) is a high 48%, or 33 of 69 tokens. There are also seven cases of more than two items intervening, as in the following example, where there is an intervening sequence of a subject and two prepositional phrases, *por* 'around' and *con* 'with' (three PPs if we count *en* 'on').

(11)   *E q<u>a'ndo sopieron en Roma cuemo era muerto; tan grand alegria ouo tod el pueblo. q<ue> andauan **todos por la cibdat co<n> guirlandas en las cabec'as**. faziendo muy gra<n>d fiesta. por q<ue> eran salidos de poder de tan mal sennor.* (EE1 79r64)
'And when they found out in Rome how he had died all the people were so happy that they went around **all of them around the city with garlands on their heads** making a great celebration because they had escaped from the power of such a bad master.'

Examples like this were not included in the count of *andar* + *-ndo*, to facilitate comparison with *estar* + *-ndo* and *ir* + *-ndo*, for which there were only one or two such cases in the Old Spanish corpus.

Present-day examples of *andar* + *-ndo* with intervening material are (12) from MexPop and (13) from NMbil. In both examples we also have a parallel gerund (a code-switch to English in (13)).

(12)   *Empecé a andar **de…en el campo, de pastor**, trabajando en un… en el campo, laboreando las huertas, los terrenos, todo eso* (UNAM 1976: 78).
'I started to go around… **in the countryside, as a herdsman**, working in a… in the countryside, working the vegetable gardens, the fields, all that'

(13)   *Y que él andaba **allá** tirando [ ] y que e e resisting arrest, yo no sé qué tanto.* (NMbil /Joe)
'And that he was going around **there** making trouble and "resisting arrest" and who knows what all else.'

Over time intervening material decreases for *andar* + *-ndo*, as with the other auxiliaries. In MexPop, open class intervening material averages 10%, or 9 of 89 tokens. This is still a higher average than for *estar* + *-ndo* or *ir* + *-ndo*, and may be taken as an indication that *andar* + *-ndo* is less grammaticized than the other two. I return to this point in Chapter 4 (Section 4.6).

2.3.2 English interference?

It is important that the change from Old Spanish to present-day Spanish is primarily quantitative. That is, it is still possible for open class items to appear between *estar* or *ir* and the *-ndo* form. The following popular Mexico City examples show an intervening subject (a) and manner adverbial (b).

(14) a. *Allá (es)tán **las muchachas** haciéndolo.* (UNAM 1976: 289)
 'There (they) are **the girls** doing it.'
 b. *No se puede estar **completamente** cuidando al chiquillo.*
 (UNAM 1976: 344)
 'One can't be **completely** watching the little one.'

For *estar* + *-ndo*, most frequently occurring intervening open class items in the Mexico City corpus are subjects (6 cases), locatives (4), temporals, and manner adverbials (3 cases each). In comparison, in the Old Spanish data, most frequently intervening between *estar* and the gerund are locatives (8 cases), followed by temporals (5), manner words *as(s)í* 'thus' and *mucho* 'much' (4), and subjects (3). For *ir* + *-ndo*, most frequently occurring intervening open class items in MexPop are manner adverbials (4 cases) and the subject word *uno* (3). In the Old Spanish data, most frequently intervening are locatives (12 cases), manner adverbials (10), objects (5) and subjects (4). It is interesting that the main difference between MexPop and OldSp, besides the quantitative drop in the overall frequency of intervening open class material, is the decrease in intervening locatives. We return to the decline in cooccurring locatives in Chapter 3.

While these findings are what we would expect from the perspective of grammaticization, scholars investigating the effects of language contact have concluded that the presence of intervening material between *estar* and *-ndo* in Spanish is a manifestation of English interference. In her study of educated San Juan, Puerto Rico Spanish, for example, Vásquez (1989: 219) considers examples such as *estoy **actualmente** cogiendo varios cursos* 'I am **currently** taking a number of courses' a case of syntactic transfer from English since, as she states, Spanish rejects intervening adverbials of this type (see Chaston (1991: 308) for a similar view in a study of Texas bilinguals). However, a closer look at her data does not support the English transfer hypothesis. First, the relative frequency of *estar* + *-ndo* with intervening open class items in the San Juan data is 3%, or 12 of 443 tokens, which is still less than that found in the Mexico City corpus, at 5% (18/340).[3] Indeed, oral Spanish varieties show an average of about 5% cases of *estar* + *-ndo* with an intervening element (Clegg n.d.). Second, the type of intervening material is very similar: most frequently subjects (3 cases) and temporals (7), including three cases of *todavía* 'still', as in *estamos todavía viviendo la etapa del paternalismo* 'we are still living through the stage of paternalism' (Vásquez 1989: 217). More likely than an explanation based on English to Spanish transfer is the one offered here: cases with intervening open class items reflect an earlier stage of the language; their decreased relative frequency indicates grammaticization of *-ndo* constructions.

Data from New Mexican Spanish speakers is very similar to the Mexico City data with respect to the type of intervening material.[4] Open class items intervening between *estar* and the gerund in NMmon and NMbil are NP subjects (4 cases), locative (4) and temporal expressions (2), and one case of *¿cómo?* 'how, what' as the speaker tried to find a word. This distribution of types of intervening items is virtually identical to MexPop. As shown in Table 8 above, the average occurrence of intervening open class items is 12% (5/42) in the monolingual group (NMmon) and 4% (6/144) in the bilingual group (NMbil), compared with 5% in MexPop (18/340). None of the differences is statistically significant.

Contrary to what might be expected if intervening items were the result of contact with English, it was the oldest and probably most monolingual speaker in the NMmon data, a woman born in 1898, who provided this example. Here *estar* and the gerund are separated by a predicative adjective and a locative.

(15) *No pues, como te digo yo estoy impuesta a estar* **muda en el telar** *bailando el día [entero?]. Y no me gusta que me molesta naiden.* (NMCSS #219, 1A)
'Well, like I said I'm used to being **silent at the loom** spinning all day. And I don't like for anyone to bother me.'

So far we have seen evidence for a diachronic process of formal reduction in

Formal reduction in grammaticization

-ndo constructions, based on three indices: positional fixing (Table 5); a decrease in multiple gerund constructions, which means an increased probability that a gerund is associated with an auxiliary in a one-to-one relationship (Tables 6 and 7); and a sharp drop in intervening open class items (Tables 8 and 9). All these indicate tighter fusion between the two elements in the construction. In the next section we examine clitic climbing as another index of reductive change in *-ndo* constructions.

2.4 Clitic climbing as an index of formal reduction

Since object pronoun clitics first appeared in Romance, the tendency has been toward fixing the position of the clitic with respect to the verb. In Old Spanish there was variation between proclitic and enclitic objects for both finite and non-finite forms, for example, *me dijo* 'me told' as well as *dijome* 'told me'. In present-day Spanish, postposition with finite forms other than Imperative occurs, if at all, only in certain written registers (Gili Gaya 1964: 236, §177). However, there is still variation in clitic position for non-finite forms in periphrastic constructions. The variable position of clitics in periphrastic constructions was studied by Silva-Corvalán (1994: 127) as a change in progress that is more advanced among Spanish-English bilinguals.

A generally accepted idea is that clitic climbing in periphrastic constructions indicates semantic bleaching. Lenz (1925, §247) and Keniston (1936: 163) had proposed that object clitic position may be used to distinguish grammatical from lexical uses of a verb that is in construction with another. More recently, Myhill (1988a, 1988b) compared frequencies of clitic climbing in Spanish periphrastic constructions to study the variation between main verb (lexical) and auxiliary (grammatical) uses of the same verb. He found that preverbal clitic position was most strongly favored when the verb conveys epistemic, future, or progressive meaning, that is, meanings which languages tend to express by means of bound morphology (Bybee 1985). The following examples illustrate clitic climbing (CC) and lack of clitic climbing (non-CC) in *estar* + *-ndo*:

(16) a. Clitic climbing = CC
Me estoy   cansando
1SG.REFL am-1SG get tired-GERUND
'I'm getting tired'

b. No clitic climbing = Non-CC
... *toda la cosecha de cebada estaba asoleándose*
was-3SG
lie-in-sun-GERUND.3SG.REFL
en el solar
'...the whole barley harvest was lying in the sun in the yard'

Myhill (1988b: 239) proposed that CC is disfavored in (b) because *estar* retains more of its original locative meaning, whereas in (a) the locative sense is bleached and *estar* contributes only progressive meaning.

In this section we look at evidence that supports a reformulation of the relationship between clitic climbing and grammaticization proposed by Myhill. First, the Old Spanish data indicate that "mechanical" factors related to cooccurring items as opposed to semantic considerations best account for the position of the clitic in *-ndo* constructions. Second, the comparison of Old Spanish and popular Mexico City data suggests that clitic climbing frequencies have increased in tandem with other indices of formal reduction. Rather than directly reflecting semantic bleaching, clitic climbing develops as part of the series of reductive changes in the form of *-ndo* constructions. That is, the increase in clitic climbing does not reflect a direct correspondence between the occurrence of clitic climbing and the meaning of the periphrastic expression — grammatical versus lexical — in any given example, but rather the conventionalization of auxiliary-plus-gerund sequences as units whose components are increasingly fused.

2.4.1 Clitic position in Old Spanish

I will start by looking at clitic position in Old Spanish *-ndo* constructions. Given the flexible word order in Old Spanish, the label "clitic climbing" can actually be misleading, with respect to both terms. Rivero (1986) provides evidence that Old Spanish "clitics" have the same distribution as independent words, unlike their modern counterparts, which are more like bound morphemes. For example, non-tonic object pronouns in Old Spanish may be separated from the verb by open class intervening material, as in *quien te* **algo** *prometiere* 'the one who would to you something promise', in which *algo* 'something' separates dative *te* from the verb *prometiere* (Rivero 1986: 777). Even more relevant is Rivero's (1986: 783) observation that in Old Spanish, not only non-tonic object pronouns, but full-blown NPs could "climb" in periphrastic expressions. The next set of examples (from Rivero) with *querer* 'want' + Infinitive illustrates:

(17) a. *quando...Jesuchristo **las sus divinales bodas** quisyiere celebrar* (Corb)
'when Jesus **his sacred wedding** would wish to celebrate'
b. *antes que **la** quería complir* (Corb)
'before **it** he wanted to fulfill'

Nevertheless, I will use the now-traditional term "clitic-climbing" (CC) for *-ndo* constructions to refer to the positioning of an unstressed object pronoun preposed or postposed to the auxiliary, as opposed to postposed to the gerund, to make my results more readily comparable to those of other studies.

Object clitics appear in one of three positions in Old Spanish *-ndo* constructions. Following familiar formal syntax terminology, possible "landing sites" for clitics that have "climbed" from a verb to the right to a verb to the left are preposed to the auxiliary and postposed to the auxiliary, that is, midway between the auxiliary and the gerund. A third possibility is for the clitic to "remain" postposed to the gerund, that is, to the verb whose original argument it seems to be.[5] The following examples illustrate.

(18) Old Spanish *-ndo* construction clitic positions
    a. Preposed clitic climbing
*Desque el negro esto dixo, otro que **lo** oyó dixo esso mismo, e assí **lo** fueron diziendo...*(Luc, XXXII, p.216)
'once the Negro had said this, another person who heard it said the same thing, and soon everyone [**it**] was saying it ...' (cf. Keller and Keating 1977: 132–3).
    b. Midway clitic climbing
*E [...] estávan**le** esperando a media legua de aquella su casa.* (Luc. XVIII, p.144)
'And those who were to kill him were [**for him**] waiting for him a half a league from his house' (cf. Keller and Keating 1977: 85)
    c. No clitic climbing
*...esta diziendo **le** alla su corac'on...* (C01- 32r28, Act IV).
'...his heart is telling **him** there'

Table 10 shows the positioning of clitics in Old Spanish texts for *estar + -ndo*.

In the PMC, 70% of all clitic climbing cases for *estar* + *-ndo* and *seer* + *-ndo* are of the (b) type (verses 154, 1058, 1746, 2305 for *estar*, and 122, 1840, 2239, 2532, 3553 for *seer*). In the Old Spanish corpus as a whole, 39% (11/28) of all cases where clitic climbing was possible were cases of clitic climbing to the midway position between *estar* and the gerund.

Table 10. Clitic climbing (CC) in ESTAR + -NDO in Old Spanish

	No CC		Midway CC		Preposed CC		Overall CC*	
	N	%	N	%	N	%	N	%
PMC	0	0	7	70%	3	30%	10	100%
EE1	2	25%	2	25%	4	50%	6	75%
LBA	0	0	0	0	1	100%	1	100%
Luc	1	50%	1	50%	0	0	1	50%
Corb	1	50%	1	50%	0	0	1	50%
C01	4	80%	0	0	1	20%	1	20%
OldSp (total)	8	29%	11	39%	9	32%	20	71%
MexPop	12	10%	4	3%**	99	86%	103	90%

*   Overall CC combines preposed and midway CC.
** Midway CC in MexPop is limited to cases of Infinitive *estar* + *-ndo*.
The difference between OldSp and MexPop in preposed CC is significant (χ^2 =35.4477, p = 0.0000). So is the difference in overall CC (χ^2 = 6.157023, p = 0.0131).
Location of possible CC cases in OldSp corpus: PMC verse 2,154,1058, 1746, 2305 / 122, 1840, 2239, 2532, 3553; EE1 folio/line 5v15, 18v25, 74v32, 75v72, 85v29, 111v15, 116r61, 144r79; LBA verse 811; Luc Ejemplo XVII, LI; Corb Primera parte — XXXVII; C01folio/line (Act) 32r28 (IV), 38r26 (VI), 61v4 (IX), 73r22 (XII), 75v12 (XII)

In contrast, midway clitic position is limited to Infinitive *estar* plus gerund in the Mexico City corpus, as in the following example.

(19) *Entonces, se bajan de la cama descalcitos o sucios; lo que sea, tengo que estarlos mirando.* (UNAM 1976: 430)
'Then they get out of bed barefoot or dirty; whatever the case, I have to be [**them**] watching them.'

There were only four examples of midway CC in MexPop, or 3% of all cases where clitic climbing was possible.

In addition to CC to midway position, 32% (9/28) of possible clitic climbing cases were clitic climbing preposed to *estar* in OldSp. In MexPop, preposed clitic climbing averages 86% (99/115). The difference in the proportion of CC preposed to *estar* between the Old Spanish corpus and the Mexico City corpus is highly significant ($\chi^2 = 35.4477$, p = 0.0000). Now, if we add cases of preposed and midway position, we have an overall clitic climbing total of 71% in OldSp and 90% in MexPop. The difference in this overall proportion of CC to non-CC is also significant ($\chi^2 = 6.157023$, p = 0.0131). In short, not only has overall CC frequency in the *estar* + *-ndo* construction increased over time, but there has been a change in "landing site" from variation between midway and preposed position to categorical preposing for finite forms of *estar*. This result may be taken as an indication of increasing fusion of *estar* with *-ndo* in the construction.

Table 11 shows the results for *ir* + *-ndo*. These are similar in the decline of clitic climbing to midway position. The Old Spanish data show a 40% frequency of the midway position, while the Mexico City data show only 7%, limited again to cases of Infinitive *ir* + *-ndo*. For preposed clitic climbing OldSp shows 57%. This frequency increases to 86% in the Mexico City data, a significant increase ($\chi^2 = 13.04807$, p = 0.0003).

Table 11. Clitic climbing (CC) in IR + -NDO in Old Spanish

	No CC		Midway CC		Preposed CC		Overall CC*	
	N	%	N	%	N	%	N	%
PMC	1	4%	6	26%	16	70%	22	96%
Apol	0	0	3	43%	4	57%	7	100%
EE1	1	4%	18	69%	7	27%	25	96%
LBA	0	0	3	50%	3	50%	6	100%
Luc	0	0	0	0	6	100%	6	100%
Corb	0	0	2	40%	3	60%	5	100%
C01	0	0	0	0	6	100%	6	100%
OldSp (total)	2	3%	32	40%	45	57%	77	97%
MexPop	4	7%	4	7%**	49	86%	53	93%

* Overall CC combines preposed and midway CC.
** Midway CC in MexPop is limited to cases of Infinitive *ir* + *-ndo*.
The difference between OldSp and MexPop in preposed CC is significant ($\chi^2 = 13.04807$, p = 0.0003). However, the difference in overall CC is not ($\chi^2 = 1.579956$, p = 0.2088).

However, two interesting differences between *estar* and *ir* are apparent. First, preposed CC is preferred with *ir* + *-ndo* even in the Old Spanish corpus, with a 57% average (the EE1 is one exception), while preposed CC with *estar* +

-ndo in OldSp averages only 32%. *Estar* + *-ndo* clitics are more evenly distributed across the three positions, with a slight preference for midway CC. Here we may have another piece of evidence in favor of the earlier grammaticization of *ir* + *-ndo*. Second, the diachronic difference between OldSp and MexPop in overall CC frequency is significant for *estar* + *-ndo* (from 71% to 89%) but not for *ir* + *-ndo* (from 97% to 93%). At the same time, the synchronic difference between *ir* + *-ndo* and *estar* + *-ndo* in overall CC frequencies in MexPop (93% and 89%, respectively) is also not significant. Thus, even though *ir* + *-ndo* may have gotten a head start on the grammaticization path, *estar* + *-ndo* has "caught up", which implies that the pace of change has been faster. This is the same pattern we observed with intervening material (Section 2.3). We return to the asymmetry in the pace of change for these two constructions in Chapter 4.

A striking fact about the Old Spanish data is the low number of possible cases of clitic climbing that is, the low number of *-ndo* constructions with any clitics at all. There were only 28/165, or 17%, such cases for *estar* + *-ndo*, and 79/275, or 29%, for *ir* + *-ndo*. In the Mexico City corpus these frequencies double for *estar* + *-ndo*, with 115/338, or 34%, and increase by a fourth for *ir* + *-ndo*, with 57/146, or 39%.

One source for the increased frequency of clitics and clitic climbing in *-ndo* constructions may be verbs that have become reflexive over time. In Old Spanish, we find many examples where the reflexive pronoun's host may be either the main verb or the auxiliary.

(20) & *come<n>c'o el toro a dar grandes bramidos & cayo a soora en tierra muerto. % E sant siluestre q<ue> uio aq<ue>l-lo. fizo much adur callar todas las gen-tes q<ue>* **se estauan** *mucho* **marauillando** *daq<ue>l fecho & dixo les.* (EE1–116r61)
'And the bull started to give great bellows and fell suddenly to the ground dead. And Saint Silvestre who saw all of this silenced with great difficulty all the people who [**se**] **were marvelling** at this happening and said to them.'

(21) *Míranse las manos con tantas sortijas e* **vanse** *los beços* **mordiendo** *por los tornar bermejos, faziendo de los ojos desgaires, mirando de través, colleando como locas, mirándose unas a otras, sonriendo e burlando de quantos e quantas ven e pasan.* (Corb, Parte II, Cap. VIII, p.182)

'She looks at her hands all covered with rings, and chews her lips [literally: they **go** [se] their lips **chewing**] to make them red, casting her eyes about, looking sideways, wriggling her bottom like mad, looking at the others, and smiling and making jokes about all the men and women she passes.' (Simpson 1959: 140)

In the first example, is the 3rd person singular reflexive clitic *se* part of *estarse* 'be located, be standing' or part of *maravillarse* 'marvel'?[6] In the second example, is it part of *irse* 'go, depart' or part of *morderse* 'chew'? It is likely that this ambiguity of reflexive pronoun clitics promoted the change in favor of clitic climbing by adding to the frequency of apparent clitic climbing constructions (cf. Labov 1994: 588ff. on probability matching by language learners).

2.4.2 Factors in clitic climbing

Let us now see whether our data support the idea that clitic climbing correlates with grammatical uses of *estar* + *-ndo*, that is, uses where the meaning of *estar* is more bleached. Three factors that seem to disfavor clitic climbing in the OldSp data are the presence of a locative expression, intervening open-class material, and a parallel gerund.[7] First, of the 28 cases in which clitic climbing was possible, 8 had a co-occurring locative. None of these had preposed clitic climbing, 3 (37.5%) had clitic climbing but only to midway position, and 5 (62.5%) had no clitic climbing at all. Second, of three cases with intervening open class material, two have no CC (both in C01, 38r26 and 61v4) and one has an ambiguous reflexive pronoun.

These "mechanical" factors related to items surrounding the construction may override semantic considerations. The next set of examples is interesting because the main verb is the same, *catando* 'watching, looking at', yet in each case the object clitic has a different position. In (a) it is preposed to *estar*, in (b) it is in midway position, and in (c) it is postposed to the main verb. In both non-preposed cases we have a multiple gerund construction, *catando ... cuidando* 'looking at...thinking', in (b) and *catando & maravillando* 'looking at and marveling', in (c). In the latter we also have the subject pronoun *él* 'he' intervening between *estar* and the first gerund.

(22) a. *E ataron le al cuello una muela de brac'o & echaro<n> lo de la puente en el rio. & ando gra<n>d piec'a sobrel agua fablando con lo[^s] q<ue> **lo(^s)** estaua<n> catando.*(EE1 111v15)

'And they tied a stone to his neck and threw him from the bridge into the river. And he walked for a long while on the water speaking to those who [**him**] were (stood there) watching him.'

b. *e quando cesar la uio estudo* **la** *cata<n>do gra<n>d piec'a cuydando.* (EE1 5v15)
'and when Cesar saw her he remained (stood there) [**her**] looking at her for a long while, thinking'

c. *E estando el catando* **los** *& marauillando se dellos; dixol aq<ue>lla uirgen.* (EE1 144r79)
'And while he was (stood there) looking **at them** and marveling at them, that virgin said to him:'

The meaning seems to be just as ambiguous between a more or less bleached *estar* + *-ndo* in all three examples, that is, either the subject is (merely) watching or the subject is (located) watching. It is not at all apparent that parallel gerunds as in (b) and (c) are compatible with lexical rather than grammatical uses of *estar* + *-ndo*, or with less bleached rather than more bleached *estar* in the construction.

Support for the idea that mechanical factors related to cooccurring items provide a better explanation than meaning differences for the position of the clitic comes from the next set of examples, all from the *Celestina*. It is interesting that this text has the lowest clitic climbing frequency for *estar* + *-ndo*, since it is the latest Old Spanish text. There is only one case of clitic climbing from a total of five where clitic climbing was possible. The lack of clitic climbing is explainable in light of the factors we have been discussing. Two non-CC cases have intervening open class material as well as a parallel gerund, as in the following example.

(23) *E como ella* **estuuiesse** *suspensa:* **mirando me** *espantada del nueuo me<n>saje: escucha<n>do fasta ver quien podia ser: el que assi por necessidad d<e> su palabra penaua. o quien pudiesse sanar su lengua: en no<m>brando tu nombre: atajo mis palabras dio se enla frente vna grand palmada:* (C01–38r26, Act VI)
'And while she **was** hanging on my words, **looking at me**, frightened at my strange message, and trying to guess who it was who could be cured in that fashion, I mentioned your name. Whereupon she gave herself a great slap on the forehead...' (Simpson 1955: 69)

'And as she **stood looking at me** in amazement, surprised at this message and waiting to discover the name of the sufferer who could be cured if she but spoke — when, sir, I named your name, she cut my discourse sharply off, gave herself a great slap with the palm of her hand on her forehead...' (Singleton 1958: 100)

In this example the relationship between *estar* and the gerund *mirando* 'looking at' is not tight at all. *Estar* appears to be more in construction with the intervening descriptive adjective *suspensa* 'hanging, amazed' than with *mirando* 'looking at', which in turn appears to be more linked to the parallel gerund *escuchando* 'listening', as in "looking and listening." Thus, e*star* and *mirando* barely appear to form a unit. However, even though this is a non-CC case, aspectual meaning is not precluded, that is, the looking is viewed as being in progress for a brief period until the offending name is named. This meaning is reflected in the use of "while" and "as" in the English translations by Simpson (1955) and Singleton (1958).

The other two cases in the *Celestina* where clitic climbing fails to occur have cooccurring locatives. It is important, however, that locative meaning does not preclude temporal (aspectual) meaning. The following example illustrates how *estar* + *-ndo* may have both a locative and a temporal sense. Here *estar* + *-ndo* clearly has a locative dimension, as indicated by the motion verb *voy* 'I (will) go' in the main clause and the cooccurring locative *allá* 'there'. That is, the speaker will go to where the person represented metonymically by "his heart" is physically located: *está...allá* 'is...there'. At the same time, *estar* + *-ndo* has progressive meaning, that is, the action referred to by the gerund is in progress at speech time, as indicated by *se me figura que* 'I imagine that'. In fact, both Simpson's (1955) and Singleton's (1958) translations omit the locative meaning.

(24) *Yo voy co<n> tu cordon tan alegre: que **se me figura** que esta diziendo le alla su corac'on la merced que nos heziste: & que le te<n>go de hallar aliuiado.* (C01- 32r28, Act IV)
'**I will** at once **go** with the cord, and go so happily that **I can almost imagine** I hear his heart **is telling him there** of the great favor you have done us' (cf. Singleton 1958: 87, Simpson 1955: 58)

The one case of clitic climbing in the *Celestina* is reproduced below. The meaning does not seem to be more progressive here than in the previous example, where clitic climbing does not occur. What is different is the lack of a locative to which *estar* might be connected, or a parallel gerund to which the first might be connected, or intervening material separating the two. These kinds of cooccurring items pull *estar* and the gerund apart, making for a less tight connection between the two and detracting from the identification of *estar* + *-ndo* as a unit. As we have seen, both multiple gerund constructions and intervening material have declined over time. In the following chapter we will see that cooccurring locatives decline as well.

(25) *Pero como soy cierto d<e> tu limpieza d<e> s(e)[a]ngre & fechos:* **me estoy remirando** *si soy yo calisto a quie<n> tanto bien se le haze.* (C01–73r22, Act XII)
'but now that I am certain of your pure intentions [1SG REFL.**me**] **I am wondering** whether I am really Calisto for whom such glorious things have been done!' (Simpson 1955: 132)

Loss of internal constituent structure is common in grammaticizing constructions (Bybee and Thompson 1997; Heine, Claudi, and Hünnemeyer 1991). In generative syntax, clitic climbing (or clitic promotion) has been analyzed as the result of a structure-reducing transformation in the complement clause (e.g. Rivero 1970; Luján 1980) or as a restructuring rule that reanalyzes a series of verbs into a single verbal complex, thus transforming two underlying clauses into one (e.g. Rizzi 1982). The change in clitic climbing frequencies between Old and present-day Spanish shows a downgrading of constituent boundaries from two clauses to one, as locative *estar*, directional motion *ir,* or non-directional-motion *andar*, go from being "full-blown" verbs with a verbal complement to becoming more auxiliary-like, and the gerund becomes more tightly attached to these auxiliaries. Thus, we may view clitic climbing as an index of reductive change.

In summary, there has been a series of diachronic changes in the form of *-ndo* constructions — the fixing of the position of the auxiliary with respect to the gerund, the decline of multiple gerund constructions, and the decrease in intervening open class material — all contributing to the tighter fusion between the auxiliary and the gerund. The claim here is that the diachronic increase in the frequency of clitic climbing is part of this series of formal changes that contribute to the emergence of *estar* + *-ndo* as a unit. That is, the increase in clitic climbing is not due to semantic bleaching of *estar* alone, so that there is a direct correspondence between clitic climbing and aspectual, as

Formal reduction in grammaticization

opposed to locative, meaning in any given example. Rather, over time the string (locative) + *estar* + (x) + (y) + *-ndo* (+ *-ndo*) has been conventionalized as the *estar* + *-ndo* construction, increasingly without cooccurring locatives (Chapter 3), without intervening material (Section 2.2), and without a parallel or close-by gerund (Section 2.3), all of which detract from the identification of *estar* plus *-ndo* as a unit. As *estar* + *-ndo* emerges as a unit in and of itself, the clitic is increasingly preposed to *estar*, as is categorically the case with finite verb forms in present-day Spanish.

$$(\text{locative}) + estar + (x) + (y) + \text{-}ndo\ (+\ \text{-}ndo)$$
$$\Downarrow \qquad\qquad \text{decline of} \begin{cases} \text{cooccurring locatives} \\ \text{intervening material} \\ \text{multiple gerunds} \end{cases}$$
$$estar + \text{-}ndo$$

→ object clitics preposed to unit

Figure 2. Emergence of ESTAR + -NDO unit

2.5 Construction frequency

So far the comparison of Old Spanish and present-day data shows that CC frequencies have increased as part of a series of formal changes contributing to the emergence of *-ndo* constructions as fused units. Recognizing the important role of repetition in language, Bybee (forthcoming) proposes a new definition of grammaticization, more traditionally defined as "the process whereby lexical items and constructions come in certain linguistic contexts to serve grammatical functions…" (Hopper and Traugott 1993:xv). Based on a review of the effects of token and type frequency in semantic, phonological, and morphosyntactic change, she characterizes grammaticization as "the process by which a frequently-used sequence of words or morphemes becomes automated as a single processing unit" (Bybee, forthcoming). The increase in CC frequencies points to precisely this kind of process of automatization for *-ndo* constructions.

In this section we will see that reductive changes in form are linked to an increase in the token frequency of auxiliary-plus-gerund sequences. We will also see that token frequency has increased in tandem with an increase in the proportion of gerunds in construction with an auxiliary: that is, there has been an increase in the frequency of gerunds preceded by an auxiliary relative to those gerunds that are lone-standing (as adverbials or relatives) or in multiple gerund constructions. This double frequency change — absolute and relative token frequency — has contributed to the emergence of -*ndo* constructions as more fused and more automatized units.

Let us look first at the dramatic increase in the token (or text) frequency of -*ndo* constructions. Table 12 shows token frequency as the average number of tokens per 10,000 words of running text.

Table 12. *Diachronic increase in token frequencies of -ndo constructions (tokens per 10,000 words)*

Corpus	Word count	ESTAR	IR	ANDAR	Other	Total -*ndo* constructions
PMC	30,044	6.6	20.7	0.7	1.7	29.9
EE1	279,504	1.4	4.1	2.5	0.5	8.4
LBA	58,195	3.8	3.8	3.1	2.4	13.0
Luc	84,500	2.8	2.1	1.2	0.7	6.9
Corb	74,100	3.9	1.6	0.7	0.8	7.0
C01	53,428	5.8	3.5	1.5	2.0	12.9
OldSp total	579,771	2.9	4.7	2.0	0.96	**10.6**
MexPop	172,699	19.7	8.4	5.1	1.97	**35.3**
16th c. prose	(300,000)	3.1	3.6	1.0	0.43	**8.3**
Early 20th c. prose	(600,000)	5.1	6.3	0.5	4.5	**16.4**

* In the PMC and EE1, the token count for *ESTAR* includes cases of *seer + -ndo*. MexPop total does not include 39 cases of *seguir + -ndo*, of which there was only one token in the entire OldSp corpus.

** Figures for the 16th c. are calculated from the frequencies given in Keniston (1937a: 469), assuming a 300,000 total word count (30 units @ 10,000 words each; see Keniston 1937a:xiv-v). Figures for the early 20th c. are calculated from the frequencies given in Keniston (1937b: 207), assuming a 600,000 total word count (60 units @ 10,000 words each; see Keniston 1937b: 6). The high figure in the "other" category in this corpus is largely due to *seguir*, at 2.3.

The token frequency of -*ndo* constructions has increased over time, from an average of 10.6 occurrences per every 10,000 words in OldSp to 35.3 in MexPop. In other words, these constructions occur three times more frequently in the Mexico City than in the Old Spanish corpus. True, some of the frequency difference between the Mexico City and the Old Spanish corpora may be attributed to differences between conversational data and written texts in any given period, however much Old Spanish works like the *Corbacho* and the *Celestina* reproduce popular speech of the time. However, figures from

Keniston (1937a, 1937b), who studies comparable corpora of 16th and early 20th century prose, leave no doubt that there is a diachronic side to the increase in text frequency. These figures show that the token frequency of -*ndo* constructions has doubled, from 8.3 occurrences per 10,000 words of text on average in the 16th century, to 16.4 occurrences per 10,000 words of text in the early 20th century.[8]

Concurrent with the increase in the token frequency of -*ndo* constructions is a shift in the proportion of -*ndo* forms in construction with an auxiliary. Spanish gerunds not in construction with an auxiliary may be used as manner adverbials, as in *Se pasan la mañana **hablando** por teléfono* 'They spend the morning **talking** on the phone'. This use describes more than half the tokens of lone-standing gerunds in a corpus of present-day educated Mexico City Spanish; overall, adverbial uses of -*ndo* forms, including manner, temporal, conditional, and concessive uses, add up to 84% of all tokens (Luna 1980: 95–119). Spanish gerunds may also be used as nonrestrictive relatives referring to the subject or, with certain predicates, the direct object of the finite verb, as in *¿A dónde hay mayor porcentaje de mujeres trabajando?* 'Where is there a bigger percentage of women **working**? (Luna 1980: 108). In Old Spanish (and some present-day varieties) there was also the *en* + -*ndo* construction, more or less equivalent to present-day Spanish *al* + Infinitive or English *(up)on* + -*ing*, as in **endurmiendo**. *apareciol el nuestro sennor ih\<es\>u xp\<rist\>o* (EE1–112r) '**upon falling asleep** appeared before him our lord Jesus Christ'. I subsume all these uses under the label "lone-standing gerunds", in opposition to -*ndo* constructions, as defined in Chapter 1.[9]

Table 13 shows that the proportion of gerunds in construction with *estar*, *ir*, *andar*, or another auxiliary has increased, from about 20% in the Old Spanish corpus to 66% in the popular Mexico City corpus. Conversely, the proportion of -*ndo* forms standing alone has decreased, from 80% to 34%. The increase in the frequency of -*ndo* constructions relative to lone-standing gerunds is highly significant. Again, part of the difference must be attributed to register differences, but Keniston's (1937a, 1937b) figures for 16th and 20th century prose, which show a 10% increase in the proportion of -*ndo* constructions with respect to lone-standing gerunds, confirm that there is a diachronic side as well.

Table 13. Diachronic increase in proportion of gerunds in construction with an auxiliary

Corpus	-ndo Constructions N	Proportion	Lone-standing -ndo N	Proportion	Total -ndo N	Average -ndo per 10,000 words
PMC	90	52%	82	48%	172	57.2
Apol	36	49%	38	51%	74	NA
EE1	235	19%	1025	81%	1260	45.1
LBA	76	28%	193	72%	269	46.2
Luc	58	17%	289	83%	347	41.1
Corb	52	9%	534	91%	586	79.1
C01	69	23%	233	77%	302	56.5
OldSp (total)	616	**20%**	2394	**80%**	3010	50.6
MexPop	609	**66%**	316	**34%**	925	53.6
16th c. prose	248	**14%**	1579	**86%**	1827	60.9
Early 20th c.	987	**24%**	3135	**76%**	4122	68.7

* Auxiliaries included in the count of *-ndo* constructions are *estar, ir, andar, venir, salir* (17 in OldSp, 1 in MexPop), and *quedar(se)*. Not included here in the MexPop count are 39 tokens of *seguir*. These figures were obtained with a manual count; the gerund total for MexPop is from Clegg and Rodríguez (1993).
** Figures for 16th and 20th c. prose were calculated from Keniston (1937a: 469, 552–7; 1937b: 207–8, 239–42).
The proportion of gerunds in construction with an auxiliary is significantly higher in MexPop (66%) than in OldSp (20%): z =25.5616, p = .0000. Also in early 20th c. prose (24%) than in 16th c. prose (14%): z = 9.0974, p = .0000.

In his study of emerging English auxiliaries, Krug (2000) uses the term "string frequency" to refer to the frequency of the sequence of a verb (e.g. *want* or *got*) followed by *to* plus Infinitive, and finds that string frequency is related to indices of grammaticization, specifically to contraction of forms (e.g. *wanna* and *gotta*). However, "string frequency" is not readily applicable to *-ndo* constructions. First, *-ndo* constructions are composed of a discontinuous string, auxiliary + verb stem + *-ndo*. In other words there is an open class verb slot between the auxiliary and the *-ndo* suffix, so there is not really a single string to count, as in the case of *want to*. Second, auxiliaries *estar, ir* and *andar* participate in other constructions, for example, the resultative *estar* + Past Participle construction or the future *ir* + *a* + Infinitive construction. We could, of course, calculate transitional probabilities (cf. Saffran, Newport, and Aslin 1996). This means counting the number of times *estar*, for example, is followed by a gerund as opposed to something else, that is, the number of times *estar* participates in an *-ndo* construction as opposed to a resultative or other construction, or the number of times it is used as a lexical verb. This would be informative about the expansion of *estar* to a growing number of constructions and contexts, but it is not clear what this would tell us about *-ndo* constructions.

In this case, it seems appropriate to measure "string frequency" backwards, from the perspective of *-ndo* rather than the auxiliary, since the only constructions *-ndo* participates in are with *estar, ir, andar* and maybe a few other verbal auxiliaries. That is, we can count the tokens of *-ndo* preceded by *estar* or another auxiliary as compared with the number of tokens of lone-standing *-ndo*. We can think of it in terms of transition probabilities in reverse, or right-to-left instead of left-to-right transition probabilities. As we have seen, the proportion of lone-standing gerunds declines between the Old Spanish and the Mexico City data, from 80% to 34%. The decrease in the proportion of lone-standing gerunds means an increase in the probability that a gerund will be in construction with an auxiliary as opposed to standing alone.

There is another important change in the distribution of gerunds. Concurrent with the decrease in lone-standing gerunds is the decrease in multiple-gerund constructions (Section 2.2). Taken together, these distribution changes mean an increased probability that a gerund and auxiliary are not only associated in a construction, but also are in a one-to-one relationship, as opposed to multiple gerunds competing for ties to the auxiliary. In other words, we see an increase in the probability that *estar, ir,* or *andar* and *-ndo* are bound in a one-to-one construction.

We may call the increase in the token frequency of auxiliary-plus-gerund sequences, in combination with the decrease in the proportion of lone-standing gerunds and multiple-gerund constructions, an increase in *-ndo* "construction frequency". It is important that construction frequency is calculated not only by counting tokens of the auxiliary-plus-gerund sequence but also the tokens of gerunds **not** in such sequences. Increased construction frequency makes for a higher probability that a gerund is indeed tied to an auxiliary. The tighter connection between the auxiliary and *-ndo* means that increasingly the sequence is identified as a fused unit.

The significance of construction frequency as we have defined it based on the present data is that loss of autonomy (Bybee et al. 1994: 110) may affect both elements of an emerging construction. Not only does the auxiliary lose autonomy but so does the *-ndo* form, as shown by the decline in lone-standing gerunds. In other words, it is increasingly likely that when a gerund appears it is associated with an auxiliary. Thus, rather than characterizing the process as the "morphologization" of auxiliaries (cf. Hopper and Traugott 1993: 130), the formal change is better described as the fusion of both elements, the auxiliary and the gerund, or, in Bybee's (forthcoming; cf. Haiman 1994) terms, their automatization as a single processing unit.

The idea of construction frequency is also the key to our reformulation of the relationship between clitic climbing and grammaticization. The Old Spanish evidence does not contradict Myhill's (1988a, 1988b) conclusion that CC frequencies correlate with semantic bleaching of the auxiliary in periphrastic expressions. But in showing that clitic climbing is part of a series of reductive changes in the form of *-ndo* constructions, we put forward a stronger statement about the role of form and its relationship to meaning in grammaticization. The difference lies in the role attributed to construction frequency. Specifically, the diachronic evidence shows that higher clitic climbing frequencies correspond to higher construction frequencies.

2.6 Register differences in construction frequency

Beside the diachronic side to frequency effects in formal reduction, another dimension, one that has received scant — if any — attention, is the role of register. In this section we look at Old Spanish and present-day evidence for register variation in the frequency of *-ndo* constructions.

Halliday (1988: 162) defines register in terms of cooccurrence patterns, as "a cluster of associated features having a greater-than-random [ ] tendency to cooccur." Biber (1986 and elsewhere) has shown that the distribution of linguistic features in English (for example, contractions, passives, nominalizations) patterns along certain textual characteristics or "dimensions" rather than a written/spoken dichotomy. Specifically, he found that fiction is closer to conversation than to academic prose or planned speeches along the dimension identified as "abstract vs. situated content", which corresponds to formal vs. colloquial style (Biber 1986: 396, 399). It turns out that *-ndo* construction frequency is stratified similarly along a formal vs. informal division. I use the term register here in a broad sense to refer to situational variation (cf. Biber and Finegan 1994), including stylistic variation, whether defined in terms of attention to form (Labov 1972a) or audience design (Bell 1984).

Let us look first for evidence from within the Old Spanish corpus for

Formal reduction in grammaticization 61

frequency differences based on register. The texts with the lowest construction frequency, combining absolute token frequency (Table 12) and the proportion of gerunds in construction with an auxiliary (Table 13), are *Estoria de España*, with 8.4 and 19%; *Lucanor*, with 6.9 and 17%; and *Corbacho*, with 7.0 and 9%. In comparison, the OldSp average is 10.6 and 21% (the high frequency of *ir* + *-ndo* in the PMC stands out as an exception). These works may be said to be more formal along the dimensions of genre and topic: the *Estoria de España* is a chronicle, *Lucanor* is a collection of didactic exempla, and *Corbacho* has extensive sermon passages (cf. Deyermond 1971).

Especially striking is the low relative frequency of *-ndo* constructions in the *Corbacho*. This is a work that includes both more pedantic and more colloquial language (D. Alonso 1958: 135; Gerli 1975). Using sentence length as a measure of formality, San Román (1987) found a significant difference between Part One, with an average of 42.96 words per sentence, and Part Two, with an average of 26.86. Not surprisingly, Part Two has more passages written in direct speech than Part One. To see if the distribution of *-ndo* constructions follows the same pattern as sentence length, I did a count for each Part. Table 14 shows the results. The absolute token frequency of *-ndo* constructions, measured as an average per 100 printed pages of text, is nearly double in Part Two, at 30 occurrences, compared with 15.4. Part Two also has double the proportion of gerunds in construction with an auxiliary, at 12%, compared with 6%. In other words, construction frequency is nearly twice as high in Part Two than in Part One. This result is consistent with San Román's (1987) finding on sentence length. The uneven distribution of *-ndo* constructions in the *Corbacho* provides additional evidence for a register effect on construction frequency.

Table 14. Distribution of -ndo constructions in the "Corbacho"

	Pages	*-ndo* constructions N	Frequency*	Proportion	Lone-standing *-ndo* N	Proportion	Total *-ndo* N
Part I	78	12	**15.4**	**6%**	177	94%	189
Part II	60	18	**30**	**12%**	136	88%	154

* Average frequency per 100 pages of text

The *Celestina* also indicates the stylistic and social stratification of *-ndo* constructions. 52% (16) of all tokens of *estar* + *-ndo* occur in dialogue, or rapid exchanges. Another seven occur in extended speech (more than five lines) and eight in stage instructions. The distribution of *estar* + *-ndo* by the social status of the speaker seems to favor the servant class: 14 tokens are in the speech of Sempronio, Parmeno, Tristan, Areusa, and Lucrecia; Celestina has four, Calisto five. The association of progressives with informality may extend cross-linguistically. For example, Strang (1982: 438, 452), discusses the use of *be* + *-ing* to portray social class and personal characteristics in an 18th c. epistolary novel. Frequency increases of the English Progressive have been correlated with informality (Mair and Hundt 1995) and intimacy (Arnaud 1998).

Let us now look at present-day register variation. The Essays corpus includes essays, formal speeches, and scholarly writings by Mexican authors (see Chapter 1, Section 1.5.2). This corpus represents a formal as opposed to colloquial style in the sense of Biber (1986: 396, 399). As shown in Table 15, the average occurrence of *-ndo* constructions in Essays is 7.6 per 10,000 words. This figure compares with 33.9 tokens on average per 10,000 words in HablaCulta, a corpus of educated Spanish spoken in major cities (Clegg and Rodríguez 1993; cf. Lope Blanch 1986) and 23.5 in Madrid, a corpus of the educated variety spoken in Madrid, Spain (Olbertz 1998; cf. Esgueva and Cantarero 1981). The popular Mexico City corpus (MexPop) average is 37.5. These results indicate that *-ndo* constructions are between three and five times more likely to appear in conversation than in formal texts!

Table 15. *Token frequencies of -ndo constructions in present-day corpora (per 10,000 words)*

Corpus	Word count*	*-ndo* constructions N	*-ndo* constructions Average frequency**
Essays	376,300	278	**7.4**
HablaCulta	1,300,000	4409	33.9
Madrid	148,200	349	23.5
MexPop	172,700	648	37.5
NMmon	34,900	76	21.8
NMbil	49,700	145	29.2

* For word counts, see Appendix I. All tokens of *estar, ir, andar, venir, quedarse, seguir* (only 1 token in OldSp), *continuar* (no tokens in OldSp), *salir* (only 1 token in MexPop) plus a gerund were counted. NMmon and NMbil figures are based on 15 and 11 speakers, respectively. Figures for HablaCulta are from Clegg and Rodríguez (1993), for Madrid from Olbertz (1998).

** Tokens per 10,000 words.

These results are not really surprising, given that the distribution of verb forms is highly "genre-dependent" (Givón 1990: 963). For example, in about 110 pages of academic prose (Canclini, ed. 1993: 86–196), there were 13 *-ndo* constructions in the words of the authors (*ir* 7, *seguir* 3, *estar* 2, *venir* 1), but 15 in quotes from oral interviews (*estar* 7, *ir* 3, *seguir* 3, *andar* 1, *venir* 1), even though these made up only a small portion of the text. The high proportion of stative verbs and the kinds of things talked about in formal registers explains, at least in part, the low token frequency of *-ndo* constructions, since these constructions generally express progressive or continuous (durative) aspect. That is, there may be good "functional" motivations (in the sense reviewed in Labov 1994:547 ff.) for the low token frequency of *-ndo* constructions in these texts.

What is striking about the Essays corpus is the low occurrence of clitic climbing. As shown in Table 16, clitic climbing frequencies are at a low 68% for *estar* + *-ndo* and 45% for *ir* + *-ndo*, compared with 90% and 93% in MexPop.

Table 16. Clitic climbing (CC) in present-day corpora

	ESTAR + -NDO				IR + -NDO			
	CC		Non-CC		CC		Non-CC	
Corpus	N	%	N	%	N	%	N	%
Essays	15	68%	7	32%	15	45%	8	55%
MexPop	103	90%	12	10%	53	93%	4	7%
NMmon	8	100%	0	0%				
NMbil	23	85%	4	15%				

* Differences between Essays and MexPop in CC are significant for both *estar* (χ^2 = 7.069016, p = .0078) and *ir* (χ^2 = 42.93175, p = .0000).
** Differences between NMmon, NMbil, and MexPop are not significant.

Functional reasons, however, do not help explain the low frequency of clitic climbing. Even if there are fewer *-ndo* constructions because of what is talked about, why should the proportion of CC cases be lower?

The low figures in Essays point to the stylistic stratification of clitic climbing. The status of clitic position as a stylistically stratified variable is confirmed in statements by various Hispanists. Spaulding (1926: 274), for example, observed that postposed position is found, "not [ ] in [19th and early 20th century] writers like Galdós, Alarcón or Valera, but in rhetorical stylists like Tamayo, or Valle-Inclán." Lenz (1925, §247) wrote that "es muy posible que la inclinación del lenguaje literario a añadirlo al final del infinitivo o gerundio se deba a reflexión gramatical" — 'it is very possible that the inclination in literary language to postpose [the object clitic] to the infinitive or gerund is due to grammatical reflection'. Anecdotal reports of school teachers' remarks about correctness (e.g., Silva-Corvalán 1994: 128, note 18) are also in line with an awareness of clitic position as a mark of formality.

It is important that the low occurrence of CC in the Essays corpus is concurrent with low construction frequency for auxiliary-plus-gerund sequences in these texts. Not only is token frequency lower than in MexPop (Table 15) but the proportion of gerunds in construction with an auxiliary is also considerably lower, at 28% compared with 70% (Table 17).

Table 17. Proportion of gerunds in construction with an auxiliary in present-day corpora

	-ndo Constructions		Lone-standing -ndo		Total -ndo
	N	Proportion	N	Proportion	N
Essays	133	**28%**	340	72%	473
MexPop	648	**70%**	222	30%	925
NMmon	76	**61%**	49	39%	125
NMbil	145	**78%**	41	22%	186

* Differences are significant at p < .01: MexPop > Essays (28%) (z = 14.9407, p = .0000); NMbil (78%) > NMmon (61%) (z = 3.2713, p = .0005). Differences are significant at p < .05: NMbil (78%) > MexPop (70%) (z = 2.1758, p = .0148); MexPop > NMmon (61%) (z = 2.0988, p = .0179).

In addition, multiple gerund constructions average 7% and 10% in Essays for *estar* and *ir*, respectively, in contrast with less than 2% in MexPop (Table 7). On the one hand, then, is MexPop with higher construction frequency and higher CC, and on the other is Essays, with lower construction frequency and lower CC. Thus, we find again that clitic climbing frequency corresponds to construction frequency.

A question that deserves further study is, by what mechanism does frequency have an effect on clitic climbing? Construction frequency may operate by means of a parallel structure or "birds of a feather" effect in clitic climbing. A well-known effect in psycholinguistic studies is the priming of lexical items by semantically or phonetically similar items. Sociolinguistic studies have shown that priming and parallel structure effects also apply to

Formal reduction in grammaticization 65

syntax. Thus, Weiner and Labov (1983) found that agentless passives in English are most strongly favored following another agentless passive and that coreferential subjects tend to appear in the same syntactic position. Scherre and Naro (1991) found that agreement markers in Brazilian Portuguese are subject to a parallel processing effect in that explicit marking is followed by explicit marking and lack of marking is followed by further lack of marking. Spanish clitic climbing may be showing the same kind of effect. Since clitics are categorically postposed to lone-standing gerunds, the relatively high proportion of such forms in formal texts may encourage a parallel structure in the much smaller proportion of gerunds that are in construction with an auxiliary (Torres Cacoullos 1999b).

2.7 Clitic climbing in the New Mexico corpus

Let us now look at the New Mexico data, to see if we can find further support for construction frequency effects. Table 16 in the previous section shows that clitic climbing frequencies for *estar* + *-ndo* in the monolingual group (NMmon) and the bilingual group (NMbil), with a combined average of 89% (31/35), are virtually the same as in MexPop (90% = 103/115).

As we would predict based on the diachronic link between CC and construction frequency, the New Mexico corpora line up with the popular Mexico City rather than the Old Spanish corpus, both in the absolute token frequency of *-ndo* constructions and their frequency relative to lone-standing gerunds. First, the average occurrence of *-ndo* constructions is 21.8 per every 10,000 words in NMmon, 29.2 in NMbil, and 37.5 in MexPop (Table 15, above). These figures contrast with a token frequency of 10.6 in OldSp (Table 12, Section 2.5). Second, the proportion of gerunds in construction with an auxiliary lies well above 50% in all three corpora, at 61% in NMmon, 78% in NMbil, and 70% in MexPop (Table 17), in contrast with 20% in OldSp (Table 13).

It is interesting that the New Mexico bilingual group does not show higher clitic climbing frequencies in *estar* + *-ndo* than the monolingual group. In contrast, Silva-Corvalán (1994: 129–30) found higher CC frequencies in second generation than first generation speakers in Los Angeles, in support of the hypothesis that language contact situations accelerate language change. Two reasons might account for the discrepancy. First, both the New Mexico and Los Angeles data are very limited, with only 27 and 20 tokens, respectively, so we cannot really be confident of either result. Second, I did not include in the calculation of clitic climbing percentages cases with ambiguous reflexives (though these, three in total, would only raise CC in NMbil to 87%).

Cases in which the clitic is part of *estarse* 'stay' were not included in the CC count. In the following example, the *se* preposed to *están* clearly "originated" there, since the gerund *paseándose* 'strolling around' has its own *se*. Also, the speaker has just used the verb *estarse* in a locative construction with *allá arriba* 'up there'.

(26) – *Sí, yo no fui. Las muchachas sí fueron. Se fueron el vienes y no vinieron hasta el martes. **Se estuvieron allá** arriba.*
– *Mm, ¡qué bonito! ¿Qué tanto hacen allá?*
– *Allá **se están paseándose**, mirando para allá.* (NMmon/ NMCSS#10)
– 'Yeah, I didn't go. The girls, they went. They left on Friday and didn't get back until Tuesday. They **stayed** up **there**.'
– Mm, how nice! What all do they do there?
– They [se] **stay** there **strolling around**[se], looking around'

There were also cases in the NMbil data in which it was not clear whether the *se* preposed to *estar* had "climbed" from the gerund or was part of *estarse*. I did not include ambiguous cases like these in the CC count either.

(27) *Y luego aquí **se estaban esperando** a que hiciera la cena ya les daban ansias.* (NMbil/Edwin)
'And then they [se] **would be waiting** here for me to make dinner, they'd already be hungry.'

(28) *Aquí viene y trae sus papeles, aquí **se está haciendo** su trabajo.* (NMbil/Vig)
'She comes here and brings her papers, she [se] **stays** here **doing** her homework'

The presence of locative *aquí* 'here' in these examples would weigh in favor of viewing *se* as part of *estarse*. At the same time, *esperar* may alternate with *esperarse*, as in the Imperative form, *espera–espérate*, both glossed as 'wait'. The same is true of *hacer su trabajo–hacerse su trabajo* 'do her work'. The ambiguity of reflexive pronoun clitics in periphrastic expressions arises because of the diachronic tendency for verbs to become lexicalized reflexives, which may be more advanced in some varieties of Spanish, including northern Mexican and U.S. Southwest varieties (cf. Silva-Corvalán 1994: 122).

Such ambiguous reflexive pronouns may account, at least in part, for the higher CC frequencies which have been observed among bilinguals. That is, the occurrence of seeming cases of CC as in the above examples make for an overall appearance of higher CC frequencies, which in turn encourages more actual CC (cf. Labov 1994: 588ff.), as we suggested with respect to diachronic changes in clitic position (Section 2.4.1).

Although in we did not find differences between the bilingual and monolingual groups in clitic climbing frequencies, remember that we did find a difference in the proportion of *estar + -ndo* with parallel gerunds (Section 2.2), so that on this measure of reductive change the bilingual group seems to be more advanced than the monolingual group. We have seen that an important mediating mechanism in formal reduction is construction frequency. It turns out that construction frequency is also involved in differences between NMbil and NMmon. As shown in Tables 15 and 17, both absolute token frequency and the proportion of gerunds in construction with an auxiliary are higher in NMbil than in NMmon, i.e. *-ndo* construction frequency is higher in NMbil.

The mediating role of construction frequency does not explain, of course, why there are differences in construction frequency in the first place. The ordering of the corpora with respect to token frequency and the proportion of gerunds in construction with an auxiliary is:

(29)   MexPop   > or <   NMbil   >   NMmon

(the reason for the "or" is that MexPop > NMbil in absolute but not relative frequency).

In studies of Spanish in the United States the privileged explanation for frequency differences has been convergence with English (e.g. Klein 1980; see Section 1.4.1, Chapter 1). We have confirmed, however, that there is a diachronic dimension to frequency differences. Part of the explanation, then, for lower construction frequency in NMmon than in MexPop may well be the retention of older or archaic patterns in traditional New Mexican Spanish. Given the isolation of the region it is not surprising to find archaisms, many of them common in rural varieties across the Spanish-speaking world, in lexical, phonetic, and morphological variants (e.g. Espinosa, Jr. 1975). Additional support for archaism in this variety is continued use of the auxiliary *salir* 'go out', with 2% of all *-ndo* constructions, about the same average as in OldSp, while there was only one token in MexPop (see Section 4.7).

There is also a register dimension to frequency differences. It is likely that part of the difference between NMbil and NMmon in *-ndo* construction frequencies is register-related. Studies of phonological variation in Puerto Rican Spanish indicate that group interviews show more nonstandard forms than individual interviews (Cameron 1996: 80; Medina 1996: 214, 217). On the other hand, it is well known from sociolinguistic studies that narratives of personal experience, especially around topics such as fear, surprise, or humor, favor vernacular speech (Labov 1984: 32–5). I do not undertake here a detailed analysis, but it is important to point out that there are differences between the New Mexico corpora along such stylistic dimensions. The NMCSS recordings, which make up the entire NMmon corpus, were mostly individually conducted interviews and included a substantial dialectology questionnaire (Vigil and Bills 1993). On the other hand, half the NMbil recordings were conversations including at least three participants and (except for three) did not include a formal questionnaire component.

Synchronic differences between formal and informal varieties in the frequency of *-ndo* constructions and clitic climbing suggest that register may be an important factor in evaluating changes in language contact. What may appear to be loss due to language contact may simply be a deviation from prescriptive or idealized notions of standard usage, as suggested in Poplack's (1997) study of the French subjunctive. The purportedly high frequencies of *estar + -ndo* found in Puerto Rican and Southwest Spanish may reflect the oral and popular features of the varieties studied, rather than convergence with English. If we had taken the Essays corpus as the baseline monolingual variety, we too would have found higher token frequencies. Instead, we find that *-ndo* construction frequencies in the bilingual NM corpus are not higher than in the popular Mexico City corpus, which represents a sociolinguistically comparable variety.

Register considerations may also be part of the explanation for differences in clitic climbing frequencies. If higher clitic climbing frequencies are found in contact varieties, as suggested by the results in Silva Corvalán (1994: 129–30), these could be encouraged by the lack of normative pressure and the lack of exposure to formal registers. In other words, the acceleration of change in language contact might be an indirect reflection of register variation rather than a direct effect of bilingualism.

2.8 Summary

To conclude, we may summarize the main findings of this chapter as follows: First, we found support for the parallel reduction hypothesis (Bybee et al. 1994). Positional fixing, the decline of multiple-gerund constructions, the reduction of intervening open class material, and clitic climbing are indices of reductive formal change, all contributing to the emergence of auxiliary-plus-gerund sequences as fused units. Second, this diachronic series of reductive changes is linked to construction frequency increases. In calculating construction frequency it is important to count not only tokens of auxiliary-plus-gerund sequences, but the tokens of gerunds not in construction with an auxiliary. Third, higher clitic climbing frequencies correspond to higher construction frequencies, rather than directly reflecting the degree of semantic bleaching of auxiliaries. Fourth, construction frequency and clitic climbing is subject to register variation. And finally, the New Mexico data are consistent with diachronic patterns of formal reduction and with synchronic patterns of register variation, both with respect to overall construction frequencies and with respect to formal changes.

Notes

1. I did not include cases where the two gerunds have different subjects in the count of multiple gerund constructions, for example, *Estando él **sufriendo** este dolor e **teniendo** el físico el fígado en la mano* (Luc p. 108).
2. I use the chi-square test for equality of proportions to check for significant differences. In the tables I report the significance (p) level, as well as the chi-square (χ^2) value or z value (for one-sided tests).
3. Vasquez (1989: 217) reports 13 cases of *estar + -ndo* with intervening material, but only lists 12 examples. In calculating the relative frequency of these cases, I subtracted one example from her total, *me estaba él diciendo*, since I count subject pronouns separately as closed-class items.
4. For the material I transcribed, I did not include pauses as intervening material.
5. "Clitic climbing" as traditionally defined is impossible in cases where the gerund is preposed, as in *Catandol sedie la barba q<ue> tan aynal crec'iera* (Cid, verse 2059). I excluded these cases from the clitic climbing count, since all the examples I saw were like the one above, with the clitic attached to the gerund.
6. Keniston (1937: 104–6; cf. Spaulding 1926: 267) also includes the occurrence of a stressed word before the construction as a factor in clitic position.

7. The "ambiguous" reflexive pronoun in example (20) was counted as a case of clitic climbing because *maravillarse* appears as a reflexive later on in the same text (see 22c).

8. Keniston's 16th c. data are from a corpus of forty prose texts, totaling 300,000 words (1937a:xiv). Over half the texts "contain a more or less literary version of actual conversation" (Keniston 1937a:xxi). The 20th c. data are from sixty 1900–1933 prose texts totaling 600,000 words (1937b: 7), and again, "over half the materials studied represents a literary version of conversational style" (1937b: 6). Based on Keniston's statements and the breakdown of text types, I assume that register has been as much as possible controlled for, so that differences can be attributed to diachronic change.

9. On uses of lone-standing gerunds in 16th century prose, see Keniston (1937: 552–7).

Chapter 3

Evidence for semantic reduction

Changing patterns of cooccurring locative and temporal expressions

As the token frequency of *-ndo* constructions increases, the contexts in which they occur are generalized. In the next chapter we will see that *estar* + *-ndo* expands to new semantic classes of verbs, more tenses, and inanimate subjects. Concomitant with use in more contexts is semantic generalization (reduction, bleaching), or loss of specific features of meaning. In particular, spatial — locative or movement — meaning is lost.

We may group competing hypotheses on the grammaticization mechanism of progressives into two main sets: (1) the space-time metaphor hypothesis, and (2) the locative origin-semantic reduction hypothesis. A widely held view is that the development of expressions of tense and aspect from lexical sources is a metaphorical change from the spatial to the temporal domain (Anderson 1973; Claudi and Heine 1985; Sweetser 1988; Traugott 1978). In the space-time metaphor hypothesis, spatial expressions serve as structural templates for temporal expressions and the change involves a metaphorical shift. On the other hand, in the semantic reduction or generalization hypothesis, the development of progressives is explained as the gradual loss of locative meaning (Bybee et al. 1994: 133–7).

In this chapter I describe quantitative and qualitative changes in locative and temporal expressions cooccurring with *-ndo* constructions and adduce support for the view that semantic reduction is the primary mechanism of change for progressives. The competing accounts make different predictions about cooccurring locative and temporal expressions. The metaphor hypothesis would predict an increase in cooccurring temporal expressions over time. That is, we would expect to find that *-ndo* constructions initially do not occur

with a temporal reading but that later they may appear in two different kinds of context, both in a new temporal domain and in an older, but persisting, locative domain. In contrast, the reduction hypothesis predicts a decrease in cooccurring locatives. The expectation is that we will find both a spatial and a temporal dimension from the beginning but that the locative component is gradually reduced (Bybee et al. 1994: 291–2). In short, we will test the following predictions:
1. Cooccurring locatives will decrease, temporals will increase (metaphor)
2. Cooccurring locatives will decrease, temporals will remain constant (reduction)

Our data provide evidence for semantic reduction. We will see that *-ndo* constructions occur with temporal readings from their earliest uses, as shown by cooccurring temporal expressions in Old Spanish. On the other hand, cooccurring locatives decline over time. As locative meaning is lost, temporal meaning accordingly gains preponderance, and it becomes less necessary to express specific temporal or aspectual senses lexically. Thus, not only is there no increase in cooccurring temporal expressions, as turns out to be the case with *estar + -ndo* and *andar + -ndo*, but there may be a decrease, as occurs with *ir + -ndo*. Expressions such as *ya* 'already' and *desde* 'since', indicating inceptive meaning, and *poco a poco* 'little by little', for gradual development meaning, are highly associated with *ir + -ndo* from the earliest Old Spanish texts. Over time their use declines, suggesting that inceptive and gradual development meaning has largely been absorbed by this construction from such frequently cooccurring expressions.

We will be looking at Old Spanish data (OldSp), present-day Mexico City data (MexPop), and New Mexico data (NMmon and NMbil). Section 3.1 describes changing patterns of cooccurring locatives. In Section 3.2, I propose a non-metaphor account of the uses of *estar + -ndo* with mental verbs such as *pensando* 'thinking'. Sections 3.3, 3.4, and 3.5 look at temporal expressions for *estar, ir, andar + -ndo* and the development of specific aspectual meanings for each of these constructions. Section 3.6 compares New Mexico and Mexico City data. Finally, in Section 3.7 I return to a discussion of usage effects in the conventionalization of aspectual meaning.

3.1 Semantic retention and reduction in the distribution of locatives

3.1.1 *Counting cooccurring locatives*

In looking at cooccurrence patterns, we must decide what to count as a cooccurring locative. A first decision was to include only locative expressions that occur in the same clause as the *-ndo* construction. But in many cases the "scope" of the locative is ambiguous: does it encompass the auxiliary-plus-gerund sequence as a unit, or is either the auxiliary or the main verb alone in its orbit? A second decision was to count all locatives, including those that may be taken to modify either the auxiliary or the main verb. For example, included in the count of locative expressions for *andar + -ndo* are cases like (1), as well as cases like (2).

(1) ...*del qui<n>to fijo de Japhet q<ue> ouo nombre thubal donde uinieron los espannoles. so linage daq<ue>l* **andudieron por muchas tierras buscando logar** *pora poblar de q<ue> se pagassen.* (EE1 3v78)
'...from the fifth son of Japhet who was named Thubal whence the Spaniards came; under his lineage they **went around many lands looking for a place** to settle which would satisfy them.'

(2) *Ya oyestes desuso cuemo Caco fue uenc['']udo. y hercules segudol fasta moncayo o el solie morar. e* **anda<n>dol bus-cando por aq<ue>lla tierra** *semeiol muy buena.* (EE1 6r51)
'You have already heard above how Caco was defeated. And Hercules followed him up to Moncayo, where he usually resided. And as he **went looking for him all around that land**, the land seemed to him very good.'

In the first example *por muchas tierras* 'around many lands' appears to refer to *andar* rather than to *buscar* 'look for', since the locative is positioned immediately after *andar* and *buscar* has as its own direct object the NP *lugar* 'place'. In contrast, in the second example, *por aquella tierra* 'all around that land' appears to refer to *buscar* rather than to *andar*, since the locative is positioned immediately after *buscar* and *buscar* has as direct object the pronoun *lo*, which, furthermore, is enclitic to *andar*. In cases such as these, then, the locative expression could be taken to modify either the auxiliary or the main verb, or both.

Cases of ambiguously referring locatives are included in the count since, even if the locative is taken to refer to the main verb, it must be consistent with the meaning of the particular *-ndo* construction. That is, the distribution of locatives follows particular auxiliary plus *-ndo* combinations rather than just main verbs. In the following set of examples, the main verb is the same, *catando* 'watching', but the locatives are different. Each locative is consistent with the meaning of the respective *-ndo* construction: an *en* 'in' + LOC(ATION) locative for *estar* + *-ndo*, but a *por* 'along' + LOC(ATION) locative for *ir* + *-ndo*.

(3)   *E Nero **estaua en somo duna torre catando** cuemo ardie. & dizie q<ue> se alegraua mucho con la grand fermosura de la llama.* (EE1 77r69)
'And Nero **was on (in) top of a tower watching** how it burned. And he said that he was much cheered by the great beauty of the flame.'

(4)   *e siempre **yuan catando por la ribera** o fallarien buen logar o poblassen una grand cibdat.* (EE1 5r31)
'and they always were (literally: **went**) **watching along the shore** for where they would find a good place to found a great city.'

A first view of the data in Table 18 shows that the distribution of locatives in the Old Spanish corpus is noticeably skewed. *En* 'in' + LOC locatives tend to cooccur with *estar* + *-ndo*, with 8.4% (14/167) of all *estar* + *-ndo*. Also pairing up with *estar* + *-ndo* are deictics *aquí* 'here' and *allí* 'there' and *con* 'with' + PERSON expressions. On the other hand, *por* 'along' + LOC, the most frequently occurring locative type in the Old Spanish corpus with 47 tokens, is evenly split between *ir* + *-ndo* and *andar* + *-ndo*. These motion-verb constructions, however, do not have the same spread with respect to locatives. One-fifth or 19.7% of all *andar* + *-ndo* sequences have a cooccurring *por* 'along' + LOC. *Ir* + *-ndo* has a wider spread: 9.3% of all tokens cooccur with *por* 'along' + LOC, 3.6% with *a* 'to' + LOC and another 4% with *de* 'from' + LOC.

Evidence for semantic reduction 75

Table 18. *Cooccurring locatives in -ndo constructions*

	ESTAR + -ndo		IR + -ndo		ANDAR + -ndo		Totals	
	OldSp	MexPop	OldSp	MexPop	OldSp	MexPop	OldSp	MexPop
	%	%	%	%	%	%	N	N
Deictics *aquí, allí*	6.6	10	.8	7.7	3.4	7.9	17	52
ai 'around there'		2		4		5.6	0	18
en 'in' LOC	8.4	3.5	.8	1.4	.8	7.9	17	21
con 'with' PERS	4.2	3.2	1.6*	0	2.6	2.2	14	13
donde 'where'	3.6	1.8	.8	2	0	0	8	9
a 'to' LOC	1.7	0	3.6	0	2.6	0	15	0
por 'along' LOC	.6	0	9.3	1.4	19.7	7.9	47	9
de 'from' LOC	0	0	4	0	3.4	0	14	0
Other**	4.2	.6	7.3	4.1	4.3	1.1	30	9
Total locatives	**30%**	**21%**	**28%**	**20%**	**37%**	**33%**		
Locatives N	49	72	70	30	43	29	162	131
Construction N	167	338	248	146	117	89	532	573

* Three of four OldSp cases of *ir* + *-ndo con* + PERSON occurred in the PMC.

** Other locatives with *ir* + *-ndo* are: *pora* or *para* LOC (5), two cases each of *en pos, fasta* LOC, *contra (tierra)*, and one each of *alent, delant, a derredor, ante, entre, ribera de la mar, el rio abaxo*. Other locatives with *andar* + *-ndo* are: *cabo de una pinaça* (Apol 121c), *en torno* (Corb. p. 281), *entre los de la otra huest* (EE1,147r52), *tras* (Corb. p.281), *sobre mar* (EE1, 78v36).

Differences between OldSp and MexPop in the average of locatives cooccurring with *ir* + *-ndo* are significant at p <.05 if cases of *ai* in MexPop are dropped from the count (χ^2 = 5.98752, p = 0.0144), otherwise, p = 0.0908. For *andar* + *-ndo* differences are not significant, whether *ai* is included or not.

These distribution differences support the hypothesis that grammaticizing constructions retain features or nuances of meaning of their source construction, known as the retention (Bybee and Pagliuca 1987) or persistence (Hopper 1991) hypothesis (see Chapter 1, Section 1.1.2). I return to this point in the ensuing discussion. At the same time, we see evidence for a diachronic process of semantic reduction. In comparing the OldSp data with the MexPop data, two results are most striking. One, there has been a decline in the average number of cooccurring locatives from 30% to 21% for *estar*, 28% to 20% for *ir*, and 37% to 33% for *andar* + *-ndo* constructions. These results indicate loss of locative meaning. Two, deictic *aquí* 'here' and *allí* 'there' locatives are now fairly evenly distributed among *-ndo* constructions, pointing to semantic reduction in the same direction.

3.1.2 *Estar* + *-ndo* locatives

Locatives cooccurring most frequently with *estar* + *-ndo* are consistent with the locative origin of the construction, "being located in a specific place doing something." The most frequent locative type is *en* 'in' + LOC, with names of cities, in 4 cases (PMC 1243, 1566; EE1 86v17; Corb. p. 276); or an NP indicating a location with a definite article, demonstrative, or possessive pronoun, in 6 cases (EE1 73v101, 74r36, 75v35; Corb. pp. 223, 244, 299); or an NP with an indefinite or no article, in 4 cases (EE1–77r69, Luc pp. 117, 157; C01–11v30). An indication of the strong association between *estar* + *-ndo* and *en* + LOC in the Old Spanish corpus is the proportion of *en* + LOC cooccurring with *estar* as opposed to any other auxiliary: 82% (14 of 17) of all tokens are with *estar* + *-ndo*. *En* + LOC indicates a specific place, as in the following example.

(5) % *Estaua un dia cantando **en el teatro**. & tremio la tierra assoora. & estremeciosse el teatro todo. de guisa q<ue> se espantaro<n> todos qua<n>tos y estauan* (EE1 75v35)
'He was one day singing **in the theater** and the earth suddenly trembled and the entire theater shook so that all who were there were frightened.'

Table 19. ESTAR + -NDO locatives in Old Spanish texts

	PMC N	EE1 N	LBA N	Luc N	Corb N	CO1 N	OldSp total N	MexPop N
deictics *aquí, y, allí, allá*	1	3	2	1		4	11	34
ai								7
en 'in' + LOC	2	5		2	4	1	14	12
con 'with' + PERSON	1	1		1	1	3	7	11
o / donde 'where'		6					6	6
a 'at' + LOC	1	1		1			3	
Other*	2	3	1		2		8	2
Total locatives	7	19	3	5	5	10	49	72
Average	35%	49%	14%	21%	17%	32%	**30%**	**21%**

* "Other" locatives in OldSp: *ante* person(s) (EE1 2, LBA), *entre* persons (EE1, C01), *adelant* (PMC), *cabe la puerta* (C01), *por las finiestras* (PMC)
** The difference in the average of locatives between OldSp and MexPop is significant at p < .05 (χ^2 = 4.277415, p = .0386).

Evidence for semantic reduction

As shown in Table 19, after *en* + LOC and deictic *aquí* 'here', *allí* 'there' locatives, the third most frequent locative type cooccurring with *estar* + *-ndo* is *con* 'with' + PERSON. 4% (7/167) of all *estar* + *-ndo* tokens cooccur with *con* 'with' + PERSON. An obvious question is, why count *con* + PERSON expressions as locatives? Lyons (1977: 693) shows that an entity may refer to the space it occupies, as in *I'll meet you at the car* = "at the place where the car is". The Old Spanish data reveal that *con* + PERSON expressions actually range on a continuum from more comitative to more locative. In some cases the *con* phrase appears to unambiguously modify the main verb alone as a comitative. In the first example below it could be argued that *con quien* 'with whom' refers more directly to main verb *hablar* 'speak' than to *estar*. But *con* + PERSON may refer more directly to a physical location, as in the second example, where *conmigo* 'with me' refers to *aquí* 'here'.

(6) *entrare a ver* **con quie<n>** *esta* **habla<n>do** *mi sen~ora.*(C01 62v13–Act X)
'I will go up and see **with whom** my mistress **is talking**' (cf. Singleton 1955: 114)

(7) *Aun agora* **estava conmigo fablando***; agora se partió de mí; aun agora le vi pasar por* **aquí** *sano e alegre, e fabló conmigo, aun agora salió de su casa...* (Corb. Quarta parte, Cap. I, p. 244)
'Even just now he **was with me chatting**; just now he took leave of me; just now I saw him pass by **here** healthy and happy, and he chatted with me, just now he came out of his house...'

Rather than draw an arbitrary line between comitative and locative uses, I counted all cooccurring *con* + PERSON tokens (except for *consigo* 'with him/herself').

A stronger reason to count cases of *con* + PERSON as locatives is that they follow a consistent pattern of cooccurrence with *estar* in preference to *ir* or *andar* + *-ndo*. Con + PERSON does not occur with *ir*, with the early exception of three cases of *ir* + *-ndo con...* in the PMC (verses 565, 1052, 1057). In the Old Spanish corpus, *con* words or phrases are associated in particular with *estar hablando* 'be (located) talking', with 7 tokens of *hablando con* from a total of 18 *estar hablando* tokens (examples (6) and (7) above; also, Luc. I, p.74, 75; Corb. II/XII p.194; C01 61v19, 79r3). More generally, main verb *hablando* pairs up with *estar*, with 11% of all *estar* + *-ndo*. On the other hand there are only 7 tokens of *ir hablando* (less than 3% of all *ir* + *-ndo*), very unevenly distributed, with 6 cases all in the C01 (see Chapter 4, Sections 4.2 and 4.4). The one other example of *ir hablando* occurs in the PMC (2229), *Alos yfantes de carrion minaya va fablando* 'Minaya addresses the Infantes of Carrión'. It is interesting that in this example *ir* + *hablando* cooccurs with an *a* + PERSON rather than a *con* + PERSON phrase, in keeping with the association of *a* 'to' phrases with *ir* + *-ndo*.

The association of *estar* + *-ndo* with *con* + PERSON locatives continues to the present day, as shown by the MexPop data, with 3% (11/338) of all *estar* + *-ndo*. These are not limited to *hablando* or *platicando* 'chatting' but also occur with *ayudando* 'helping' (UNAM 1976: 56), *llevando* 'taking' (UNAM 1976: 55, 56), *jugando* 'playing' (UNAM 1976: 120), *tomando* 'drinking' (UNAM 1976: 456), and *trabajando* 'working' (UNAM 1976: 56, 82). The following example illustrates.

(8) ...*menos de un año estuve* **con ella** *trabajando*. (UNAM 1976: 56)
'less than a year I was **with her** working'

Of 13 *con* + PERSON tokens in MexPop, 85% (11/13) cooccur with *estar*, none with *ir*, and only 15% (2/13) with *andar* + *-ndo*, following the OldSp pattern. On the other hand, in a change from OldSp, *en* + LOC locatives are now divided between *estar* + *-ndo* and *andar* + *-ndo*, with 57% (12/21) and 33% (7/21), respectively.

Deictic locatives *aquí* 'here' and *allí* (or *y*) 'there' are the second most frequent locatives cooccurring with *estar* + *-ndo* in the OldSp data, with 7% (11/167). I return to these in Section 3.1.5. Like *en* + LOC and *con* + PERSON, *aquí* and *allí* refer to a single, relatively narrowly confined or bounded location. In this they contrast with *por* + LOC and other motion verb locatives.

3.1.3 *Ir* + *-ndo* locatives

In contrast to *estar* + *-ndo* locatives, *ir* + *-ndo* locatives are consistent with physical motion, either **from** someplace (*de* + LOC), or **to** someplace (*a* + LOC) or **along** some extended location (*por* + LOC). In the OldSp corpus, *a* + LOC and *de* + LOC expressions each average about 4% of all *ir* + *-ndo*, with 9 and 10 tokens, respectively. *Por* + LOC tokens number 23, or 9%. There are another 18 cases, or 8%, of "other" locatives, such as *para* 'toward' and *hasta* 'until' phrases. Overall, *ir* + *-ndo* has a cooccurring locative 28% of the time

(Table 18). Included in the count are locatives that may be said to refer more directly to the main verb than to *ir*, as in cases of *ir entrando por* 'go entering via', for example, *fuero<n> entra<n>do **por la tierra** despa<n>na la mayor* 'they went entering by the land of Spain' (EE1-14v93). Not included are cases of a direct object NP indicating location, such as *las sierras* 'the mountains' in *Passando van las sierras & los montes & las aguas* 'They go on, crossing mountains, woods and rivers' (PMC 1826).

A particular expression found to cooccur with *ir* + *-ndo* is *de...en...* 'from...to...'. In some cases it is more clearly a locative, as in the first example below, in others it is less clearly so, as in the second example.

(9) &' como **fueron uiniendo de tierra en tierra** uenciendo muchas batallas & conquiriendo muchas tierras fasta q<ue> llegaron a espanna (EE1 2v72)
'and how they (literally) **went coming from land to land** winning many battles and conquering many lands until they reached Spain.'

(10) E entendio aq<ue>ste fecho un assiriano. & desi **duno en otro fueron sabiendo** todos. q<ue> aq<ue>l linage dombres presto era pora toda cobdicia. (EE1 82v41)
'And an Assyrian understood this happening and then **from one to an other** everyone (literally): **went finding out** that those men were disposed to all kinds of greed.'

Nevertheless, even those uses of *de...en...* that are more clearly locative have a temporal component, indicating a gradually developing situation. In the first example, the conquering is a step-by-step process, not occurring in one fell swoop but rather *de tierra en tierra*, one territory at a time. In the second example, the knowledge spreads gradually, *de uno en otro*, from one person to another.

Like *de...en*, *por* + LOC may also be consistent with a gradually developing situation. In examples such as *fue yendo por la mar hasta que llegó...* 'he traveled by sea until he reached...', the subjects move along a fairly extensive location-path before reaching their destination. Movement along or through an extensive dimension must be gradual, it cannot be instantaneous.

(11) Despues q<ue> esto ouo fecho. coiosse con sus naues e **fue yendo por la mar** fasta q<ue> llego al rio Bethis q<ue> agora llaman guadalquiuir. e **fue yendo por el** arriba fasta q<ue> llego al logar

o es agora Seuilla poblada. (EE1–5r27, 5r29)
'After he had done this, he took his vessels and went (literally: **went going**) **along the sea** until he reached the river Bethis which they now call Guadalquivir. And he went (literally: **went going**) **along it** upstream until he reached the place where Seville is now.'

(12) *E depues **fueron uiniendo por la mar** fasta q<ue> llegaron a espanna a aquel logar o es agora bayona.* (EE1–8v6)
'And afterwards they came (literally: **went coming**) **along the sea** until they reached Spain, at that place where Bayona is now.'

As with *de...en...*, the idea of gradual development with *por* + LOC may extend to non-physical movement situations. In the next example, the subject will be working to convince his victim little by little as they proceed along the road.

(13) *V el conseiando por el camino q<ue> fable & no quiera morir. & si uieres q<ue> te cree & te respondiere; descabec'a lo luego.*(EE1–89v74)
'**Go counseling him along the way** that he should speak to avoid death. And if you see that he believes you and gives you an answer, then cut off his head'

As shown in Table 18, *por* + LOC declines over time with *ir* + *-ndo*, with only two cases in the MexPop data, where this locative type is most closely associated with *andar* + *-ndo*. Indeed, *a* + LOC and *de* + LOC locatives also decline, with no cases at all. The most frequent *ir* + *-ndo* locatives in the MexPop data are *aquí, allí*, just as with *estar* + *-ndo*, a point we return to shortly.

3.1.4 Andar + -ndo locatives

Andar + *-ndo* has the highest average of cooccurring locatives in OldSp, with 37%, compared to 30% for *estar* + *-ndo* and 28% for *ir* + *-ndo*. Not included in the count are 23 cases of the cooccurring word *tierra* 'land' in the *Estoria de España*, of a total of 69 cases of *andar* + *-ndo* in this text. These were not included in the count of locatives, for results to be comparable to those for *ir* + *-ndo*, where NP objects of main verbs were excluded. Inclusion of *tierra* would raise the average of *andar* + *-ndo* locatives even further. It is interesting

Evidence for semantic reduction 81

that even though *tierra* indicates a single location, it is quite an extended one. Furthermore, 14 of 23 *tierra* cases are with a "conquering" main verb, as in *andauan destruyendo toda la tierra* 'they went around destroying the entire land' (EE1 104r30, 104r39, 104v44, 107v57, 125r86, 126r14, 126r75, 127v92, 131r67, 131v78, 143v71, 156r86, 160r38, 192v5). *Tierra* and conquering both imply big expanses. The cooccurrence of *tierra* with *andar* + *-ndo* and the use of *andar* with "conquering" main verbs provide evidence that *andar* retains features of its lexical "go around" meaning. The association of *andar* with *tierra* is not limited to the EE1, as shown by the following example from the LBA:

(14) *dende andare la tyerra / dando a muchos materia* (LBA, 1312d)
'from there I will travel over the land and will give to many people the wherewithal [for tales of love]' (Willis 1972: 354)

Most frequently cooccurring with *andar* + *-ndo* in the OldSp corpus is *por* + LOC, with 23 cases. The association of this locative type with *andar* + *-ndo* is the strongest of any of the locatives with *-ndo* constructions. One-fifth or 20% (23/117) of all cases of *andar* + *-ndo* have a *por* + LOC expression! *Por* + LOC is highly congruous with the "going around" meaning of *andar*. A difference between the *por* + LOC tokens occurring with *ir* + *-ndo* and those occurring with *andar* + *-ndo* is that for *andar*, the location is often multiple places, indicated by plural NPs. In the EE1, for example, of 21 *por* + LOC locatives, 8 have a plural NP and 3 more are of the type *por todo…* 'around or along the entire…', as in *andar corriendo por toda la casa* 'go running around the whole house' (EE1–118r70). An additional 3 tokens have the locative *a todas partes* 'to all places'.

Multiple locations are consistent with frequentative meaning, that is, that the situation is repeated frequently. If someone "goes around" places doing something, it may be inferred that this "doing" is repeated. In the first example below, *por los portales* indicates multiple locations. Frequentative aspect is made explicit by the expression *a menudo* 'often' in a preceding clause. In the second example, *poro* (*los portales*) again indicates multiple locations, and *solie* 'was accustomed to' is a lexical frequentative or habitual.

(15) *Despertauasse much a menudo quando durmie. assi q<ue> el su dormir numqua era mas q<ue> tres oras de la noche. & con enoio de yazer **andaua por los portales llamando** al dia.* (EE1 72r9)

'He would often awake from his sleep so that he would never sleep more than three hours at night, and annoyed at having to lay down he **would go around the halls calling** to the day.'

(16) *E desq<ue> entendio por cierto q<ue> era uerdadera la sospecha. & se llegaua el tiempo en que auie mester de se guardar; fizo **en los portales poro solie andar folgando** departimientos en las paredes duna piedra q<ue> a nombre phingites.* (EE1 86v4)

'And ever since he became sure that the suspicion was founded and that the time was approaching when he would need to be on his guard, **in the halls around which he used** to rest (literally: was accustomed **to go around resting**), he made divisions in the walls of a stone which is called "phingites".'

One important difference between the Old Spanish and the Mexico City data is the quantitative and qualitative reduction of *por* + LOC locatives. *Por* + LOC continues to be associated with *andar* in MexPop at 8% (7/89), but this average is less than half of that for the OldSp data. Furthermore, *por* + LOC in MexPop is mostly *por aquí* 'around here' and *por allá* 'around there', which are less specific than *por* NP, indicating a vague location that may be more or less distant from the speaker. Another difference between the corpora is the increasing association of *en* + LOC locatives, previously limited to *estar* + *-ndo*, with *andar* + *-ndo* (Section 3.1.2 above). It is interesting, though, that the *en* + LOC expressions cooccurring with *andar* refer to general (generic) or extensive locations, such as *en la calle* 'in the street' or *en el campo* 'in the fields', as opposed to the *en* + LOC expressions cooccurring with *estar* + *-ndo*, which refer to more confined spaces, such as *en la casa* 'in the house'.

3.1.5 Loss of locative features

The skewed distribution of locatives in OldSp just reviewed, with *en* + LOC and *con* + PERSON associated with *estar* + *-ndo*, *a* + LOC, *de* + LOC, *por* + LOC with *ir* + *-ndo*, and *por* + LOC(s) (multiple places) with *andar* + *-ndo*, shows that all three constructions retain features of their original lexical meaning. A striking difference between the OldSp and MexPop data is the overall increase in *aquí, allí* locatives, from 3% (17/532) of *-ndo* constructions (combining *estar*, *ir*, and *andar*) to 9% (52/573). The frequency of deictic locatives may be higher because the MexPop data are conversational. However, a second difference between the OldSp and MexPop distribution of locatives which cannot be attributed to differences in discourse type is that *aquí, allí* are now more evenly distributed among all three auxiliaries. *Aquí, allí* cooccur with 10% of *estar* + *-ndo*, 7.7% of *ir* + *-ndo*, and 7.9% of *andar* + *-ndo* (Table 18). This is one piece of evidence pointing to parallel bleaching, or semantic generalization in the same direction, so that the auxiliaries may now be interchangeable, at least with respect to cooccurring *aquí, allí*.

That all three auxiliaries have lost specific features of locative or motion meaning is also shown by the sharp drop in specific locatives in the "other" category, such as *entre* PERSONS for *estar* + *-ndo* or *para* LOC for *ir* + *-ndo* (Tables 18 and 19). Their total drops from an average of 5.6% (30/532) in OldSp, to 1.6% (9/573) in the MexPop data, a significant decrease ($z = 3.6856$, $p = .0001$). There is a concomitant rise in the *ai* locative, again distributed over all three auxiliaries. *Ai* itself is a reduced variant — both semantically and formally — of *allí*, and may convey a vague location, as in (17), or really no location at all, as in (18).

(17) - ¿*Y la siguen plantando allá, en Contreras, o ya no?*
- *Pues...este...ya poco, porque no...tienen su raiz...este...muy pequeña. Y...tiene que estar regando muy seguido. Como **ai se ha ido escaseando el agua**...* (UNAM 1976: 141)
'- And are they still cultivating it there, in Contreras, or not any more?
- Well...uhm...now just a little, because they don't...their roots are...uhm...very small. And...you have to be watering very often. And since **around there the water's been getting scarcer**...(literally: has been going getting scarcer)'

(18) *Yo y él nos conocimos en la escuela. Digamos...él tenía...unos diez años; yo tenía unos doce años o trece. En la escuela. Digamos...ya con el tiempo, pues...ya nos llegamos a conocer, a comprender. Agarramos esta arte — como dicen — de la guitarra. Pues **ai le vamos siguiendo** poco a poco, ¿no?* (UNAM 1976: 233)
'We met each other at school. Let's see...he was...around ten years old; I was around twelve or thirteen. At school. Lets see...after a while, well...then we got to know each other, understand each other. We took up this art — as they say — of the guitar. Well [*ai*] **we're keeping it up** little by little, right? (literally: there we go continuing)'

The drop in specific locatives, the more even distribution of *aquí, allí* locatives, and the use of *ai* with all three auxiliaries, all point to loss of specific features of locative and motion meaning.

Quantitative evidence also shows semantic reduction or bleaching. The average of cooccurring locatives declines significantly for *estar + -ndo*, from 30% to 20%, even if we include cases of grammaticizing *ai* in the count (χ^2 = 4.277415, p = .0386, see Table 19)[1]. Differences between OldSp and MexPop in the average of locatives for *ir + -ndo*, from 28% to 20%, are significant if cases of *ai* are dropped from the count (χ^2 = 5.98752, p = .0144, see Table 18). For *andar + -ndo* the decline from 37% to 33% is not significant either way (Table 18).

The drop in the average of cooccurring locatives for *estar + -ndo* supports a locative origin for the construction, and bleaching as its fate. However, there is no need to invoke a space > time metaphor in the evolution of locative to aspectual meaning. As we will see in following sections, a temporal-aspectual component has always formed part of the meaning of *-ndo* constructions. A comparison of OldSp and MexPop data with respect to cooccurring temporal expressions will show that the average cooccurrence of temporal expressions has remained constant over time, in support of a semantic reduction account of the evolution of *-ndo* constructions. What happens is that, as the locative component is lost, time remains as a more prominent feature of meaning. But first, let us take on the case of *estar* + mental verb.

3.2 Analogy in the extension of *estar + -ndo* to mental verbs

A good candidate for the metaphor hypothesis are cases of *estar* + mental verb + *-ndo* + *en* 'in' NP, where NP is not a location, for example, *estar pensando en algo* 'be thinking of something'. Other mental activity verbs in this string are *comedir* 'ponder', *cuidar* 'think', *dudar* 'hesitate', *parar mientes* 'think', *remirar* 'wonder'.

Cases of *en* + NP (non-LOC) are not included in the count of locatives since they do not refer to a physical place. However, *estar* + mental verb + *en* NP strings are interesting because they are parallel in form to *estar* + (activity) verb + *en* LOC strings, as can be seen by comparing the following example to example (5), repeated here as (20) (cf. Bouzet 1953: 49).

Evidence for semantic reduction

(19) *De que se assentaron, estavan parando mientes **en quáles libros** avían de començar. E estando ellos **en esto**, entraron dos omnes* ...(Luc Ex XI, p.118)
'As soon as they were seated they began considering **[en] which books** to read first. Now while they were engaged **in this**, two men appeared at the door...(cf. Keller and Keating 1977: 69)

= ESTAR + V_{mental} + *-ndo* + *en* NP (non-LOC)

(20) % *Estaua un dia cantando **en el teatro***. (EE1 75v35)
'He was one day singing **in the theater**'

= ESTAR + $V_{activity}$ + *-ndo* + *en* NP (LOC)

More generally, *estar en* NP, where the NP does not refer to a physical location, as in *estar en coyta* 'be in sorrow', *estar en dubda* 'be in doubt', *estar en pena* 'be in pain', seems to have been a fairly frequent construction in Old Spanish. An idea of the frequency of *estar en* NP strings, including non-location as well as location NPs, is given by the frequency of *estando en NP* expressions in the *Estoria de España*. In this text, 40% (31/78) of *estando* tokens cooccur with an *en* NP phrase. Furthermore, the expression *estando en esto* 'while in the middle of this', as in example (19) above, appears to have been a common formula, with 10% (3/31) of *estando en* NP tokens.

Estar en NP was often combined with a gerund, so that the resulting string was *estar en* NP *-ndo* (Yllera 1980: 28). In the following example, the gerund *llorando* 'crying' appears to be in construction with the entire *estar en oración* 'be in prayer' string rather than with *estar* alone.

(21) *E el **estando en oracion llorando** antell sepulcro dell apostol san Pedro; assi como a la media noche. uino una grand luz del cielo a colpe & alumbro toda la eglesia.*(EE1 174r28)
'And **while he was in prayer crying** before the tomb of the apostle Saint Peter, right around midnight, a great light suddenly came from the sky and illuminated the entire church.'

Mental verbs occur in construction with *estar* from the earliest texts, adding up to about 10% of all main verbs in the Old Spanish data (Chapter 4, Section 4.2). One hypothesis is that *estar* + mental verb + *-ndo* rises through a space — time metaphor, so that location in space becomes location in time. Yllera (1980: 28–30), essentially following Menéndez Pidal (1964), attributes a location in time meaning of "permanecer en un estado o acción" 'to remain in a state or activity' to *estar* plus adjective, participle, or gerund. The assumption seems to be that *estar en* a location becomes *estar en* an activity or state via a metaphorical shift. This could be represented schematically as follows:

(22) be located in a location > be located in a situation

Crosslinguistically progressives are associated with morphemes used to indicate "location at or in" (Anderson 1973: 15ff.; Comrie 1976: 98–105). Bolinger (1971), for example, points to parallels between "He is at prayer" and "He is praying". However, this association need not involve a metaphorical shift.

An alternative account of the development of *estar* + mental verb + *-ndo* is based on the frequent cooccurrence of *estar* with *en*. As we saw from the distribution of locatives (Section 3.1.2, Table 18), *en* pairs up with *estar* rather than with the motion verb auxiliaries. On the other hand, mental verbs in construction with *estar*, as opposed to those in construction with *ir*, also cooccur frequently with *en*. 44% (7/16) of *estar* mental verbs have an *en* + NP phrase (EE1–143v23; LBA 640b, 640c, 833a; Luc p.118; Corb p.277; C01–61v4). It is likely that mental verb + *en* NP strings (NP = non-location) are associated with *estar* + *en* NP strings (NP = location) because of formal parallelism.

Table 20 shows cooccurring locatives by the semantic class of the main verb (gerund). Evidence for the hypothesis that these mental verb non-physical location *en* + NP phrases are associated schematically with *en* + LOC "true" locatives is the striking result that, of all semantic classes of main verbs in *estar* + *-ndo*, mental verbs have **no** cooccurring locatives. As shown in Table 20, cooccurring locative averages for all other main verb classes range from 25% for verbs in the "watching" class to 54% for verbs in the "waiting" class. This result suggests that the absence of true locatives for mental verbs is made up for by *en* + NP phrases.

Evidence for semantic reduction 87

Table 20. ESTAR + -NDO locatives by semantic class of main verb in Old Spanish texts

	PMC	EE1	LBA	Luc	Corb	C01	OldSp (totals) N loc's	% loc's	N tokens
Watching	2	2					4	25%	16
Waiting	1		1	2		2	6	54%	11
Talking	1	2	1	2	2	5	13	29%	45
Bodily activities	1	7					8**	22%	36
Physical activities		3		1	1	1	6	35%	17
Mental activities							**0**	**0%**	**15**
General activities		3	1				4	29%	14
Other*	1				2	2	5		11
Total locatives	6(7)	17(19)	3	5	5	10	49	30%	165

* See Table 29 (Chapter 4) for an explanation of main verb classes. Other includes location (2 locatives / 4 tokens in class), listening (2/4), emotion (1/2), and aspectual (0/1). The totals for PMC and EE1 are different from those shown in Table 19 because three cases of two locatives per *-ndo* construction are omitted; see also note 1.
** 4 of 8 are a "donde" clause with an "eating" main verb, as in *o seye comiendo* (EE1 78v47, 160r32, 194r32, 194r38).

In short, one schema emerging from the distribution of locatives associates *estar* (+ *-ndo*) with *en* + LOC locatives. Another schema associates certain mental verbs with *en* + NP. Finally, a schema emerging from the formal parallelism between them associates *en* + NP with *en* + LOC. Given the string (mental) verb + *-ndo en* NP (NP = location or non-location), the choice of auxiliary must be *estar*. These schematic associations could be diagrammed as in Figure 3.

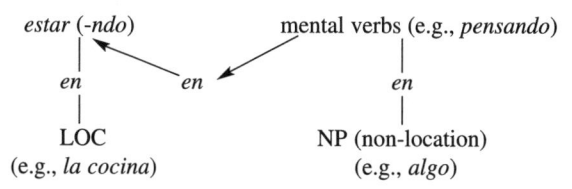

```
    estar (-ndo)          mental verbs (e.g., pensando)
        |                         |
        en        en              en
        |                         |
       LOC              NP (non-location)
    (e.g., la cocina)        (e.g., algo)
```

On the left hand side, *estar* (*-ndo*) is directly associated through a syntagmatic relationship with *en* + LOC, for example, *estar (cocinando) en la cocina* 'be (cooking) in the kitchen'. On the right hand side, certain mental verbs are directly associated with *en* + NP (non-location), for example, *pensando en algo* 'thinking of [literally: in] something'. *En* links the two sides: mental verbs are associated with *estar* via *en*.

Figure 3. ESTAR + mental verb: Schematic associations based on "en"

Thus, the expansion of erstwhile locative *estar* + *-ndo* to use with mental verbs typically not associated with location appears to have occurred by analogical extension, from true *en* locatives to *en* NP phrases:

(23) *Estaua un dia cantando **en el teatro*** (example 20)
ESTAR   V$_{activity}$ + *-ndo* EN + NP (LOC)
↓

*estavan parando mientes **en quáles libros*** (example 19)
[auxiliary]   V$_{mental}$ + *-ndo* EN + NP (non-loc)
⇓
ESTAR

Since metaphor is not involved in the broader evolution of *-ndo* constructions into aspectual expressions, an account based on analogy via association with *en* phrases seems preferable to a space-time metaphorical shift account as a special case for mental verbs.

3.3 *Estar* + *-ndo* temporal expressions: Expansion to present habitual uses

In the next three sections we look at cooccurring temporal adverbials. Temporal adverbials include both one-word or lexical adverbials (for example, *siempre*) and phrasal adverbials, such as noun phrases (*un dia* 'one day'), prepositional phrases (*dende un poco* 'in a little while'), and subordinate clauses (*quando me firió* 'when he wounded me'). We will begin with *estar* + *-ndo*. As shown in Table 21, in the Old Spanish corpus there were a total of 42 cases with a cooccurring temporal adverbial or 25% of all tokens of *estar* + *-ndo*. In the popular Mexico City corpus there were 102 cases, or 30%. The difference between OldSp and MexPop in the average occurrence of temporal adverbials is not statistically significant. This result counters a space > time metaphor hypothesis, since there is no shift in the frequency of temporal expressions.

Evidence for semantic reduction 89

Table 21. ESTAR + -NDO: Coocccurring temporal adverbials

	locating	cuando "now"	ya	durative	"while"	"always"	frequentative	N*	%
OldSp 8% (N = 167)	3%	1%	0	3%	3%	4%	0.5%	42	25%
MexPop 5% (N = 338)	3%	7%	6%	2%	0	2%	3%	102	30%

Locating	=	e.g. *un día* 'one day', *luego* 'then', clock times
cuando	=	a cooccurring *cuando* 'when' clause, in OldSp, or in a *cuando* clause, in MexPop
"now"	=	*ahora* 'now', *ahorita* 'now-diminutive', *apenas* 'scarcely'
durative	=	e.g. *un grand tiempo* 'a long time', *dos o tres horas* 'two or three hours', *un año* 'one year'
"while"	=	e.g. in *mientras* 'while' or *entre tanto (que)* 'while' clause
frequentative	=	e.g. *cada rato* 'every so often', *diario* 'daily', *seguido* 'often'
"always"	=	*siempre* 'always' or *todos los días* 'every day'-type

* The total N of cooccurring temporal expressions includes "since" tokens, 3 in Old Spanish and 8 in Mexico, and 1 case of *después (que)* in OldSp.
** The difference in the average number of cooccurring temporal expressions between the Old Spanish (25%) and Mexico data (30%) is not significant, $\chi^2 = 1.38616$, p = .2391.

There are, though, differences in the distribution of temporal adverbial types. In the Old Spanish corpus most frequent were "locating" adverbials (Smith 1991: 155), or adverbials that answer the question "when?". The average occurrence of locating adverbials is about 11% (18/167), including 5 cases of *un día* and 5 cases of a cooccurring *cuando* 'when' clause. In the following example, *estar + -ndo* has progressive meaning, as the situations occur simultaneously with the punctual action referred to by the *cuando* clause.

(24) *Aunque ay algunos que dizen: "¡Oh cuitado! ¡O cuitada! este mal, esta ocasión, este daño que me vino, pues yo non me lo procuré, nin fui causa dello; que descuidado estava quando me vino;* **durmiendo estava quando** *me contesçió;* **rezando estava quando** *me dio;* **labrando estava quando** *me firió; non fazía mal a ninguno cuando me acaesçió; pues ¿cómo me dizen agora que la persona es causa de su mal, porque él o ella se lo procura o busca; pues si lo buscó e falló que se lo tenga? (Corb, Quarta parte, Cap. III, p. 299–300)*
'Although there are some who say: "Oh wretched me! This bad thing, this happening, this harm that came upon me, I did not bring it on, nor did I cause it. I was off guard, when it came upon me; **I was sleeping when** it happened to me; **I was praying when** it

struck me; **I was laboring when** it hit me; I wasn't doing anybody any harm when it befell me; so, how can they now tell me that a person is responsible for their woe, because he or she brings it on or seeks it; that if the person sought it and found it, well, let them have it?'

A big difference between the Old Spanish and the Mexico City data is the increased use of what I call "now" expressions. There were only two cases in the Old Spanish corpus, *ahora* 'now' (Corb, p.244) and *hoy día* 'this day, in present times' (EE1–158v6). The one example from the EE1 is quite exceptional on three counts: one, the cooccurring "now" expression *hoy día* itself; two, an inanimate subject, *Affrica* (which, however, is metonymic for human subjects); and three, an "aspectual" (or stative) main verb, the only one in the Old Spanish data, *perseverar* 'persevere', which in the context seems to mean 'continue' (or 'remain').

(25) % &' esto fue quando se cumpliero\<n\>. nouaenta & siete annos que los vuandalos entraron en Affrica. &' dalli adelante finco siempre en poder de los Romanos fasta la uenida de Mahomat el falso p\<ro\>ph\<et\>a. que por la su art & la su sabiduria fue toda toruada & ensuziada & tornada a la su mala secta en la qual ***oy dia esta perseuerando*** por sus malos peccados. % (EE1 158v6)
'And this was when ninety seven years had passed since the Vandals entered Africa. And from then on it remained permanently under the power of the Romans until the arrival of Mohammed the false prophet; through his skill and knowledge it was all vilified and sullied and converted to his evil sect in which to **this day it continues** (literally: is continuing) to its great misfortune.'

In contrast, "now" expressions total 13% (44/338) of all *estar* + *-ndo* tokens and 43% (44/102) of *estar* + *-ndo* temporal adverbials in the MexPop data, with 20 cases of *ya* 'already', 14 of *ahorita* 'now- diminutive', 6 of *ahora* 'now' and 4 of *apenas* 'just, barely'. This may be partially attributed to the higher frequency of Present-tense forms in the MexPop corpus, as we would expect in conversational data.

Another difference between the OldSp and the MexPop data sets, this one not so easily dispensed with as an epiphenomenon of differences in the distribution of tenses, is the increase of frequentative or "frequency" (Smith 1991: 159) adverbials. These include *diario* 'daily', *seguido* 'very frequently',

Evidence for semantic reduction 91

and expressions such as *cada rato* 'every now and then', *en las noches* 'at night, on nights', *varias veces* 'several times'. Frequentative adverbials indicate frequentative aspect, a situation that is repeated frequently but not necessarily on one occasion, as in iterative aspect, nor as a customary or usual situation, as in habitual aspect (Bybee et al. 1994: 317). There was only one case that might be taken as a frequentative in the entire Old Spanish corpus.[2] In contrast, frequentative adverbials add up to 3% (11/338) of all *estar + -ndo* tokens and 11% (11/102) of temporal adverbials in the MexPop data, as in the following example.

> (26) ...*le dan treinta pesos a la semana, cuando va a la escuela; y **ahorita** que **está yendo diario**; le dan cincuenta.* (UNAM 1976: 258)
> '...he gets 30 pesos a week, when he goes to school; and **now** that **he is going every day**; they give him 50.'

The dramatic increase of frequentative adverbials indicates that *estar + -ndo* has become compatible with frequentative or even habitual situations, at least in the Present tense.

Notice in (26) that *ahorita*, a "now" adverbial, and *diario*, frequentative, cooccur. This example suggests that the high number of "now" expressions in MexPop compared with their scarcity in OldSp is more than a simple by-product of the preponderance of Present-tense forms and the use of deictic expressions in conversational data, but may itself be an indication of the semantic generalization of *estar + -ndo* to habitual, albeit new and noteworthy, situations. I return to habitual uses in Chapter 5.

Cases of *siempre* 'always' and expressions with *todo*, such as *todo el tiempo* 'all the time' were counted separately, since in construction with *estar + -ndo* these may express a subjective speaker attitude toward the situation.[3] There were 7 cases of *siempre* or *todo* expressions in the Old Spanish corpus. Two of these are the defunct expression *(siempre) estar callando* 'always be silent', both in 13th century texts (*los peces son los huéspedes, que siempr' están callando* 'the fish are the guests, who are always silent' Apol. 506c; *Las 'mas uezes siempre estaua callando porq<ue> auie la fabla muy uagarosa*, 'Most of the time he was always silent because his speech was very slow' EE1–69v45). I found no subsequent cases of *estar callando* in the Old Spanish corpus (but *yremos calla callando* 'we will go there very quietly') appears in the LBA, 864–4, and *torna callando* 'turn and go back quietly' appears in the *Celestina*, C01–74v6, Act XII). The remaining 5 cases of *siempre + estar + -ndo*, one from the LBA and four from the *Corbacho*, express a certain speaker attitude, just like present-day uses. This "emotional coloring", in Jesperson's (1931: 180) words, conveys reproof or displeasure, as in the following examples.

(27) *% Dixo el abutarda loca sandja vana*
syenpre estas chirlando *locura de man~ana*
no<n> q<u>i'ero tu conssejo vete p<ar>a villan~a
dexame esta vegada tan fermosa & ta<n> llan~a (LBA 750)
'Said the bustard: 'Crazy, foolish, empty-headed bird,
you are always chirping nonsense early in the morning;
I don't want your advice; away with you for a stupid peasant;
Leave me in this field which is so lovely and so flat' (Willis 1972: 200)

(28) *E demás, por mucho que tengan* **siempre están llorando e quexándose** *de pobreza: "Non tengo; non alcanço; non me preçian las gentes nada; ¿Qué será de mí, cuitada?"* (Corb, Segunda parte, Cap. I, p.148)
'Moreover, however much they have, **they are always crying and complaining** of their poverty, and they say: "I haven't got anything; I can't get anything; the people despise me. What is to become of me, poor wretch?"' (Simpson 1959: 103)

(29) **Todo el día e toda la noche están regañando***, dando maldiciones a quien los sirve;* (Corb, Tercera parte, Cap. IX, p. 228)
'...and **day and night they quarrel** and curse their servants.' (Simpson 1959: 195)

Negative attitude is evident from the main verbs *chirlando locuras* 'chirping nonsense', *llorando* 'crying', *quexándose* 'complaining', and *regañando* 'scolding'. It is interesting that all cases of *siempre* or *todo... + estar + -ndo* in the *Corbacho* refer to women! This is not surprising, since the work is meant to be a "treatise against the sin of lust" (Deyermond 1971:142).

In summary, most frequently cooccurring with *estar + -ndo* in OldSp are locating adverbials such as *un día* 'one day' and *cuando* 'when' clauses. In MexPop there is a sharp increase in frequentative adverbials and "now" expressions. On the other hand, *siempre + estar + -ndo* has been used to express a negative speaker attitude since the time of the earliest available texts.

3.4 *Ir* + *-ndo* temporals: Inceptive-continuative and gradual development

Table 22 shows four major differences between *ir* + *-ndo* and *estar* + *-ndo* with respect to temporal adverbials in the Old Spanish data:
- *ya* 'already';
- *desque* 'since' and *hasta que* 'until' clauses;
- *después* 'afterwards'; and
- *poco a poco* 'little by little'

cooccur with *ir* + *-ndo*, but not with *estar* + *-ndo*. The first three types are related to inceptive and continuative uses of *ir* + *-ndo*, while *poco a poco* is related to gradually developing uses.

Table 22. IR + -NDO: Cooccurring temporal adverbials

	locating	cuando	ya	después	"since"	hasta que	poco a poco	N*	%
OldSp (N = 248)	1%	2%	5%	4%	7%	6%	6%	79	32%
MexPop (N = 146)	3%	0.5%	3%	1%	2%	1%	5%	32	22%

"Since" adverbials = *desque* clause, *dantes, de ahí, desde…* ; *hasta que* = 'until' clause. Only *hasta* NP in MexPop

* The total N of cooccurring temporal expressions includes "other" tokens, 4 in OldSp (2 durative, 1 "while", and 1 "always") and 6 in MexPop (1 durative, 2 in *cuando* clause, 1 frequentative, and 2 "always").
** The average number of cooccurring temporal expressions is greater in OldSp (32%) than in MexPop (22%): z = 2.1176, p = .0171.

3.4.1 Inceptive and continuative

First, there were 12 cases of cooccurring *ya* 'already'. 8 of these occur in the earliest text examined, the *Poema de mio Cid* (verses 1036, 1238, 1247, 2262, 2429, 2985, 3568, 3603). The following examples illustrate.

(30) *Q<u>a'ndo esto oyo el conde yas[e] yua alegrando* (PMC 1036)
'En oyendo esto el conde empezó a alegrarse' (Bolaño e Isla 1976: 67)
'Al oirlo Don Ramón mucho que se fue alegrando' (Salinas 1963: 85)

'When the count heard this **he began to recover his spirits**.' (Hamilton and Perry 1975: 77)

(31) *Hyas*[e] *yuan partiendo aq<ue>stos ospedados* (PMC 2262)
'Comienzan a partir los huéspedes' (Bolaño e Isla 1976: 67)
'Ya todos aquellos huéspedes de Valencia van marchando' (Salinas 1963: 161)
'**Now** the guests **were going on their way**' (Such and Hodgkinson 1987: 175)

(32) *Assis*[e] *yran vengando don eluira & dona sol* (PMC 3187)
'empiezan a ser vengadas doña Elvira y doña Sol' (Bolaño e Isla 1976: 179)
'que os iremos vengando, doña Elvira y doña Sol' (Salinas 1963: 215)
'thus **will** Doña Elvira and Doña Sol **be avenged**' (Such and Hodgkinson 1987: 229)

In these examples, *ir* + *-ndo* has inceptive meaning, or that the dynamic situation begins, as shown by the modern Spanish and English translations. Inceptive meaning is contributed by *ya* in the first two examples. The third example has no *ya* or other temporal adverbial to which we might attribute inceptive meaning.

Yllera (1980: 59) attributes inceptive meaning in examples such as the third above to the reflexive main verb, in this case, *vengarse* 'be avenged'. It is well known that Spanish reflexive pronouns may function aspectually to convert durative or stative situations into punctual or inceptive, for example, *durmió* 'she slept' versus *se durmió* 'she fell asleep' (Arce-Arenales, Axelrod, and Fox 1993: 6; cf. Maldonado 1999: 353 ff.). But it is likely that the reflexive form of *ir* itself, *irse* 'to go, to depart', also contributes inceptive meaning. In the first and third example it is not clear whether the *se* pronoun "originates" with main verbs *alegrar(se)* and *vengar(se)*, appearing preposed to *ir* as a result of clitic climbing, or whether it originates with *ir(se)*. The second example supports the second option. In *Hyas[e] yuan partiendo* it is highly unlikely that main verb *partir* 'depart', an intransitive motion verb, is reflexive, and *se* must be attributed to *ir(se)*. *Irse* or leaving includes the idea of ending one thing and starting another and in the appropriate context may imply inceptiveness.

However, it is important that *ir* + *-ndo* may convey inceptive meaning without a cooccurring temporal adverbial or reflexive pronoun, as in the following example.

(33) **Comiendo va** *el conde dios q<ue> de buen grado [...]*
Con estos dos cauall<er>os a p<r>i'essa **va ia<n>tando**
Pagado es myo c'id q<ue> lo esta aguarda<n>do (PMC 1052–1058)
'**empieza a comer**, Dios, y con qué buen apetito! [...]
Con presteza **empiezan a comer** él y los dos caballeros;
el Cid que los está mirando se pone contento,' (Bolaño e Isla 1976: 69)
'the Count **started eating** with great zest. [...] and with the two knights he speedily **set about his meal** [...] to the delight of the Cid, who sat watching him. (Hamilton and Perry 1975: 79)

Here inceptive meaning in *va comiendo* and *va yantando* (literally, goes eating) is inferable from the immediate lexical context (the count eats with great appetite, eats hurriedly), the grammatical contrast with *estar + (aguarda) + -ndo* (he eats while the Cid is — standing still, immobile — watching him), and from the pragmatic context (he has just requested water to wash his hands). The translations by Bolaño e Isla (1976) and Hamilton and Perry (1975) show an inceptive reading.

The cooccurrence of *ya* with *ir + -ndo* declines over time, with only two cases in EE1, and one each in LBA and C01. Indeed, in the MexPop data, *ya* tends to cooccur with *estar + -ndo* rather than *ir + -ndo* (Tables 21 and 22).

A second difference between OldSp *ir + -ndo* and *estar + -ndo* temporal adverbials is with what I call "since" expressions and *hasta que* 'until' clauses. "Since" adverbials cooccur with 7% (17/248) of all *ir + -ndo*. These include *dallí* or *daquí adelante* 'from then on' (EE1–108v76, 141r12) or, more frequently, *ir + -ndo* inside a *desque* (*desde que*) 'since' clause. There were also 6% (14/248) cases of *hasta que* 'until' + finite verb or *hasta* 'until' + Infinitive. Both "since" and *hasta que* show a decline over time, and in the MexPop corpus they make up only 3% (5/146) combined.

Let us look at the uses of these Old Spanish "since" expressions and *hasta (que)* clauses. In the *Estoria de España*, cases of *ir + -ndo* in a clause headed by *desque* add up to 9% (10/114) of all tokens. Notice in the first example below that the inanimate subject precludes a physical motion in space reading, so that we have a clear temporal — aspectual use in this 13th c. text (cf. Lenz 1925: 384, §247).

(34) *% E **desque** aquella puebla **se fue acreciendo**. touo por bien dido que ouiesse otro nombre por que sopiesse<n> las gentes que los de tiro la poblaran.(EE1–24v21)*
'And (ever) **since** that settlement **began to grow** (literally: went (on) growing) he considered it good that it should have another name so that people would know that it had been settled by people from Tiro.'

(35) *% Luego de comie<n>-c'o fue gloton. & de grand luxuria. & muy cobdicioso. mas iualo come<n>c['Jando poc[ ]a poco & encubierta mientre. assi q<ue> cuydauan los omnes q<ue> lo fazie con yerro demancebia.*
*% Mas **des que lo fue usa<n>do** bien semeiaua q<ue> auie de natura todos aq<ue>llos malos uicios.* (EE1–76r17)
'Forthwith he became a glutton and greatly excessive and very greedy but he began this (literally: went (about) beginning) little by little and concealingly so that people thought that he was doing it as a youthful error. But (ever) **since he began to practice this** as a custom (literally: went practicing) he clearly appeared to have all those bad vices by nature.'

In these examples *desque* + *ir* + *-ndo* has inceptive meaning (began to grow, began to practice) and causal meaning at the same time (see Traugott and König 1991: 194 on English *since*). Contributing to inceptive meaning is the reflexive pronoun *se* in the first example, and the lexical inceptive *comenzando* 'beginning' in the second.

Another 7% (8/114) of all *ir* + *-ndo* tokens in the EE1 have a cooccurring *hasta que* 'until' clause, which implies that an action begins and continues until some culminating point. The next two examples show the inceptive use of *ir* + *-ndo* + *hasta que*. In the first example, the idea that the port "begins to and gradually widens" is conveyed by the temporal adverbial *después* (at the entrance the port is narrow and "then" it widens), by the reflexive pronoun *se* (it widens "itself"), by the lexical change-of-state process verb ("become" wide), and by the *hasta que* clause itself (the widening process "culminates").

(36) *por que era aquel puerto tenido por el meior de toda affrica por estar y nauios en todo tiempo. sin periglo de se p<er>der por tempestad. Y el puerto daquellas fozes era en manera de lengua. ca enell entrada era estrecho e **depues yuas ensanchando fasta que***

passaua por la uilla. (EE1–32r87)
'Because that port was considered the best in all of Africa, since there were always ships stationed there, without danger of being lost in bad weather. And the port of those parts was in the manner of a tongue, since at the entrance it was narrow and **then began to widen** (literally: went widening) **until** it stretched along the town'

(37) *E comenc'aron de poblar por aq<ue>llos logares que fueran poblados. e por q<ue> aquel mal q<ue> uiniera a espanna dizien que fuera cuemo gafedat, la primera uilla q<ue> poblaron de nueuo fue entrel mar occident y el rio guadalquiuir. e pusieron le nombre lepra. ala q<ue> oy dia llaman niebla. E **fueron assi poblando fasta q<ue>** llegaron alas torres de los dos hermanos. e nos atrouieron poblar y por que les semeio logar much esquiuo.* (EE1–8r21)
'And they began to settle along those parts that had been settled. And because that misfortune that had befallen Spain was said to be like a jinx, the first town that they resettled was between the West sea and the Guadalquivir river, and they called it Lepra, which today is called Niebla. And **thus they continued to settle** (literally: went settling) **until** they reached the towers of the two brothers. And they did not dare to settle there because it seemed to them a very unwelcoming place.'

The second example is especially interesting because *ir* + *-ndo* may have both a spatial and a temporal interpretation. That is, "they went (spatial extension) populating *until* (spatial) they reached the towers". Or, "they went on / continued (temporal) populating *until* (temporal) they reached the towers". There seems to be no reason to choose one interpretation over the other, rather, both the spatial and the temporal meanings of *ir* + *-ndo* are present.

It is important that the last four examples may also be interpreted as continuatives, which mean 'keep on doing' (Bybee et al. 1994: 317). *Desque* 'since' and *hasta que* 'until' are both compatible with continuative aspect, since by implication one continues doing something after beginning it or, from the opposite perspective, until some end point. In present-day Spanish, *ir* + *-ndo* may still be used as a continuative, for example *va estudiando* in the sense of 'continues to study' (or as an iterative, especially with punctual predicates, for example, *van disparando*) (Roca Pons 1958: 65). However, there are few, if any, cases of continuative *ir + -ndo* in the MexPop data. The one possible example I found was:

(38) *Por ejemplo, allí se muere el deudor: dicen que se le queda a la familia, y que si no, que **lo vuelven a ir pagando**...* (UNAM 1976: 445)
'For example, the debtor dies: they say it stays with the family, and if not, **they continue paying again**... (literally: they go paying again)'

The decline in continuative uses of *ir + -ndo* may be related to the rise of *seguir + -ndo* in present-day Spanish. *Seguir + -ndo* apparently does not become widespread until the eighteenth century: both Spaulding (1926: 262) and Yllera (1980: 82) report finding no prior examples except for one occurrence in the late 14th century manuscript of *El libro de Calila e Digna*. Indeed, there was only one case of *seguir + -ndo* in the Old Spanish corpus, and that in the 15th c. *Corbacho* (Primera Parte, VII). On the other hand, there are 39 cases of *seguir + -ndo*, or 6% of all *-ndo* constructions, in the MexPop corpus. This suggests that *ir + -ndo*'s continuative uses have largely been taken over by more specific *seguir + -ndo* in present-day Spanish. I describe changes in the territory of *-ndo* constructions in Chapter 4.

Finally, a note on the temporal adverbial *después* 'afterwards, then'. We have seen that *ya*, "since" adverbials, and *hasta que* clauses cooccur with *ir + -ndo* rather than *estar + -ndo*, a distribution difference we have related to inceptive and continuative uses. *Después* also tends to cooccur with *ir + -ndo*. The skewed distribution of *después*, with only one *estar + -ndo* case and ten *ir + -ndo* cases, all in the EE1, may be related to inceptive uses of *ir + -ndo*, as in the example above with the port, ***depues** yuas ensanchando fasta que passaua por la uilla* '**then** it began to widen until it stretched along the town' (EE1–32r87). The example below also illustrates an inceptive use of *despues + ir + -ndo*.

(39) *E el primer anno del su Jmperio; no eran las gentes despagadas del. mas **despues** fue faziendo por quel quisiessen mal.* (EE1–86r9)
'And the first year of his rule people were not unfond of him. But **afterwards he started to act** (literally: went acting) so that they desired him ill.'

The relatively frequent cooccurrence of *después* may also be related to uses in

Evidence for semantic reduction 99

foregrounded narrative clauses, as in the following example. We will see in the next chapter that *ir* + *-ndo* occurs in more Preterite and main clause contexts than the other auxiliaries. Both of these are consistent with foregrounded narrative (Hopper 1979).[4]

(40) *E depues q<ue> esto ouo fecho. fuesse pora guadalquiuir al logar o mandara fazer la ymagen e fallo la erzi-da} e plogol mucho. desi fue adelant alli o mandara fazer la uilla sobre los palos e pusol nombre hyspalis e mandola cercar de muro e de torres e **depues fue assi yendo** ribera dela mar. pobla<n>do los logares q<ue>l semeiaron q<ue> eran de poblaR.* (EE1–6r4)

'And after doing that he went toward the Guadalquivir to the place where he had commissioned the statue and he found it standing and was very pleased. Then he went on to where he had ordered building of the town on the poles and he called it Hyspalis, and he ordered that it be enclosed with a wall and towers. And **then he went** thus (literally: went going) along the shore settling those places he thought should be settled.'

3.4.2 Gradual development

The term "progresiva" as traditionally applied to *ir* + *-ndo* by Hispanists (e.g. Roca Pons 1958: 66; Hamplová 1968: 220; Lorenzo 1971: 123–6; Luna 1980: 206; Dietrich 1983: 210) does not mean progressive as defined by Comrie (1976) but rather progressive in the sense of progressing or advancing. This label corresponds to what we will call the "gradual development" use. The meaning seems to be that of a continuous situation that involves a gradual process or change. Roca Pons (1958: 64) calls this *incoativo*, in the sense of change toward a new state or the increasing or diminishing of an existing state, so that inceptive (inchoative) and gradual meaning often blend in *ir* + *-ndo* (cf. Squartini 1998: 269).

Gradual development may be distributed over different subjects or objects, which invite a "distributive reading" (Espunya I Prat 1996: 296). Thus, Keniston (1936: 172–3) mentions a nuance of successive parts, which we see with expressions like *un a uno* 'one by one', as in *yualos matando **un a uno*** 'he went killing them **one by one**' (EE1–114v96), or *unos e otros* 'some here and others there', as in *fue diziendo a unos e a otros* 'he went around telling people' (Luc. Ex. XX, p.151). Hamplová (1968: 220) refers to a meaning of "desenvolvimiento... entrecortado (de carácer reiterativo)" 'discontinous development (of a repeated character)' as in ...*se ocupan de ir publicando su cuantiosa obra inédita* 'they are concerned with issuing his substantial unpublished work', while Talmy (1991: 493) characterizes *ir + -ndo* as an aspectual type meaning "to V (NP) one after another cumulatively", as shown in the translation of the following example (from Talmy):

(41) *Juan fue aprendiendo las lecciones*
'John learned one after another of the lessons'

Alternatively, the gradual development may be more properly continuous in the sense of "coherente (continuo)" 'coherent (continuous)' (Hamplová 1968: 220) or "cumulative parts" (as opposed to "successive"), in Keniston's (1936: 173) terms. The best example is *va creciendo* 'gradually grows'. According to Solé (1990: 64), it is this sense of "gradual evolutivo" 'evolutional gradual' that allows the cooccurrence of "partitive" adverbials such as *poco a poco* 'little by little'.

The adverbial most frequently cooccurring with *ir + -ndo* is indeed *poco a poco*, with 6% (15/248) of all *ir + -ndo* constructions in the Old Spanish data. Unlike *hasta que* clauses and *después*, which show a disproportionate drop in the Mexico City data, *poco a poco* continues to be associated with *ir + -ndo*, with 5% (8/146) of all *ir + -ndo* tokens in MexPop. *Poco a poco* indicates a gradually developing situation, as in the following example. Other present-day gradual development adverbials with *ir + -ndo* are *cada vez más* 'each time more', *lentamente* 'slowly', *conforme* 'as, accordingly' (Luna 1980: 207; Squartini 1998: 257).

(42) *& fuesse **poc apoco** la cosa cayendo en oluido.*(EE1–118r22)
'And the affair gradually fell (literally: **little by little** went falling) into oblivion'

This example is interesting because the subject is inanimate, *la cosa* 'the thing, the affair' and there can be no sense of physical "falling" motion. However, motion verbs such as *caer* 'fall' and *subir* 'go up' are associated more with *ir* than any of the other auxiliaries, as we will see in the following chapter (Section 4.4.1), and this association carries over to expressions with the same verbs such as *caer en olvido* 'fall into oblivion', *subir en edad* 'grow in age', *subir en las onras* 'rise in honors' which do not refer to physical motion (EE1–84v55, 89r88).

Evidence for semantic reduction 101

It is important, however, that *ir* + *-ndo*'s gradual development use does not depend on the cooccurrence of an explicit expression such as *poco a poco*. In the next example from the *Libro de Buen Amor*, both line c, with *poco a poco*, and line b, without an explicit temporal or manner expression, show the gradual development use of *ir* + *-ndo*.

(43) a. *En q<u>a`nto ella anda / estas oblas fazjendo*
 b. *don carnal el doliente* **yua salud avjendo**
 c. **yuas'e** *poco a poco de la cama (^leuantando)* **yrgujendo**
 d. *penso como fez'jese com<m>o* **fues'e rreyendo** (LBA 1180)
 a. 'While she was moving about doing these works,
 b. the unwell Lord Meatseason was recovering his health;
 c. little by little he was rising up from bed;
 d. he meditated on what to do in order to run away laughing'
 (Willis 1972: 322)

Iba salud habiendo (line b.), literally, 'went having health' is a gradually developing process of regaining health. We know this since the subject is explicitly described as gradually, *poco a poco*, raising himself from bed in the next clause (line c.). Pragmatically, gradually raising oneself from bed doesn't mean slow motion on one occasion, but a gradual process of improving health. In *iba salud habiendo* the idea of gradual development cannot be attributed to the stative predicate *haber salud* but rather comes from the predicate's being in the *ir* + *-ndo* construction.

Line d. of the same example is a case of inceptive use, as shown by Joset's (1990: 500) modern Spanish translation, *pensó cómo hacer para volver a reír* and Singleton's (1975: 115) English rendition, 'He wondered next what he should do — how's woe might be alleviated'. The translations appropriately interpret "beginning to laugh" as "laughing again". Notice that here we have reflexive *se*, which we saw in other examples of inceptive *ir* + *-ndo*.

There are three important differences in linguistic context between the *ir(se)* + *-ndo* of line c. and line d. that give the first a gradual development and the other more of an inceptive interpretation. First, in line c. *se* is offset by *poco a poco*. Furthermore, a strong case could be made that the *se* of line c. originates with reflexive *erguirse* 'rise up' rather than with *irse*. This is not the case for *reir* 'laugh' in line d. Non-reflexive *erguir* 'raise' is transitive, clearly not the meaning intended, while reflexive *reirse* may mean 'laugh at, make fun of', clearly not the meaning intended. Thus line c. is *ir* + *-ndo*, while line

d. is a true *irse + -ndo*. Finally, line d. is in the Preterite, a perfective, which itself has inceptive uses, while line c. is in the Imperfect, an imperfective, very well suited to the idea of an open-ended gradually developing situation.

In summary, temporal adverbials occurring with *ir + -ndo* are of two main kinds. There are those that are consistent with inceptive (and continuative) uses: *ya*, *desque* and other "since" expressions, *hasta que* 'until' clauses, and *después* 'then, afterwards'. On the other hand, *poco a poco* 'little by little' is consistent with gradual development uses. Overall, *ir + -ndo* temporal adverbials have a fairly high average, at 32%, which is about the same as the average of cooccurring locatives, at 28%. We have seen that aspectual (non-locative or motion) uses of *ir + -ndo* are prominent from the earliest texts.

3.5 *Andar + -ndo* temporals: "Going around" in space and time

As with *estar + -ndo*, locating temporal adverbials (those that answer the question "when?") are the most frequent with *andar + -ndo* in the Old Spanish corpus, at 7% (8/117). Locating adverbials include *aquel año* 'that year', *ayer* 'yesterday', *un día* 'one day', and "calendar" time, as in *En la era de trezientos & ochaenta & tres* 'in the time of three hundred eighty three'(EE1 121r36). In the following example, there is both a temporal adverbial, *una uez* 'once', and a locative, *por unos montes* 'around some mountains'. *Andar + -ndo* may be said to have a non-directional motion "going around" meaning and progressive meaning at the same time. The shepherd is literally going around the mountains, but also his watching of the cows is in progress at reference time, the moment at which he notices one of them with a foot cut. "Noticing" is a punctual event.

>(44) *Vn pastor **andaua una uez por unos montes** guardando sus uacas. & uio ell una dellas que traye e[l] pie corto & marauillosse mucho quie\<n\> gelo cortara. & por saber quie\<n\> fiziera tal colpe. tornosse por el rastro de la sangre poro la uaca uiniera.* (EE1-146v18)
>'A shepherd **was (going around) once on some mountains watching** his cows. And he saw one of them, that its foot was short, and he wondered who had cut it. And to find out who had delivered such a blow he went back and followed the trail of the blood along which the cow had traveled.'

Also relatively frequent with *andar* + *-ndo*, as with *estar* + *-ndo*, are durative adverbials, which indicate length of time, or answer the question "for how long?" (Binnick 1991: 300–10; Smith 1991: 156). Examples are *un rato* 'a while' (Corb. p. 289) or "*[tiempo] avie*" 'for a (long) time' (EE1–63r79, 104r30, 126r34).[5] These add up to 8% (9/117), including cases where *andar* + *-ndo* is inside a *mientras* 'while' or a *cuando* 'when' clause. In the following example *andar* + *-ndo* is in a *mientras* clause and refers to a backgrounded situation that is the backdrop for a foregrounded event, the woman's realization.

(45) *Mientre esta cosa **andaua rebolujendo***
Fue la barata mala la duenya entendiendo (Apol, 402)
'Mientras estas cosas ocurrian, la muchacha fue comprendiendo el tráfico vil a que era sometida.' (Manuel Alvar 1976, Vol. 2: 424)
'**While** all this **was (going around) stirring** the woman began to comprehend (literally: went understanding) the despicable transaction'

Similar to *estar* + *-ndo* and distinct from *ir* + *-ndo* is the increase in "now" adverbials and *ya*. In MexPop *ya* cooccurs with *andar* + *-ndo* in 6.7% (6/89) of all tokens and "now" adverbials in 4.5% (two cases each of *ahorita* 'now-diminutive' and *todavía* 'still'). In contrast, there was only one case of *ya* in the Old Spanish corpus, this in the latest text examined, the *Celestina*:

(46) *si por nos otros no fuera **ya andouiera** su alma b(a)[u]scando posada p<ar>a sie<m>pre* (C01 76r17, Act XII)
'If it hadn't been for us, **by this time he'd be looking** for his last resting place!' (Simpson 1955: 138)

As with *estar* + *-ndo*, *siempre* + *andar* + *-ndo* seems to convey a negative speaker attitude, or in Squartini's (1998: 264) terms, "hyperbolic iteration". There were 4 examples in OldSp, two *siempre* (LBA 216, Luc p. 250) and two *todo el día* 'all day' (EE1–107v57, LBA 826). For example,

(47) *veyendo q<u>a'nto dapn~o*
syenpre de ti me vjno / co<n> tu sotil engan~o
***andas vrdiendo s'ienpre** / cobierto s'o mal pan~o* (LBA 216)
'seeing how much harm
has always come to me from you with your subtle trickery;
you always go around plotting, under a mantle of wickedness.'
(Willis 1972: 66)

Aspectually, "always go around verb-ing" is more of a frequentative than a progressive. In Chapter 4 (Section 4.6) we will see that frequentative meaning follows from *andar*'s lexical non-directional motion meaning.

In short, the distribution of *andar* + *-ndo* temporal expressions in the Old Spanish corpus is quite similar to that of *estar* + *-ndo*: most frequently cooccurring are locating-type adverbials and durative or "while"-type adverbials. On the other hand, there are no cases of *después* or *hasta que* clauses, and only two cases of "since"-type adverbials, which we have related to *ir* + *-ndo* inceptive uses. Nor are there any cases of *poco a poco*, which we related to gradual development uses. That is, *andar* is more similar to *estar* than *ir* with respect to temporal adverbials. Overall, the average number of cooccurring temporal adverbials with *andar* + *-ndo* in OldSp and MexPop remains the same, at around 20% (Table 23).

Table 23. ANDAR + -NDO: Coocccurring temporal adverbials

	locating	*cuando*	"now"	*ya*	durative	"while"	"always"	frequentative	N*	%
OldSp (N = 117)	7%	2.5%	0	1%	3%	2.5%	3%	0	25	21%
MexPop (N = 89)	2%	2%	4.5%	6.7%	0	0	2%	1%	18	20%

*   The total N of co-occurring temporal expressions includes "other" tokens, 2 in OldSp and 1 in MexPop.
** The difference in the average number of co-occurring temporal expressions between OldSp (21%) and MexPop (20%) is not significant, $\chi^2 = .03997$, p = .8415.

3.6 Locatives and temporals in New Mexico Spanish

The distribution of locative and temporal expressions cooccurring with *estar* + *-ndo* in the New Mexico corpora, NMmon(olingual) and NMbil(ingual), is very similar to that in the popular Mexico City corpus. First, with respect to locatives, most frequent in all three data sets are deictics *aquí* 'here', *allí* 'there', and *ai* 'around there' with 12% of all *estar* + *-ndo* tokens in MexPop, 19% in NMmon, and 6% to 12% in NMbil, depending on whether we include cases of *aquí en...* 'here in...' in the count. Second most frequent are *en* + LOC expressions, with 3% in MexPop, 7% in NMmon, and 11% in NMbil. The higher percentage of this locative type in NMbil corresponds to the lower percentage of *aquí*, since I counted 8 of 16 cases of *aquí* or *allí en...*, as in the

Evidence for semantic reduction 105

example below, toward the *en* + LOC rather than the *aquí* total.[6] Table 24 summarizes the results.

(48) *...la idioma especialmente aquí en el " ninety two"* **aquí en los Estados Unidos** *se está perdiendo...* (NMbil/NMCSS#21)
'the language, especially here in 'ninety two **here in the United States** is being lost'

Table 24. ESTAR + -NDO locatives in Mexico and New Mexico corpora

Total *estar* + *-ndo*	MexPop N = 338 N	%	NMmon N = 42 N	%	NMbil N = 144 N	%
Deictic *aquí, allí, ai*	41	12%	8	19%	9	6%
en 'in" + LOC	12	3%	3	7%	16	9%*
con 'with' + PERSON	11	3%	1	2%	1	<1%
(de) donde 'where'	6	2%	0	0	2	1%
a 'to' + LOC	0	0	2	5%	2	1%
de 'from' + LOC	0	0	0	0	2	1%
Other	2	<1%	2	5%	1	<1%
Locatives total	72	**21%**	16	**38%**	33	**23%**
No locative	266	79%	26	62%	111	77%

* NMbil *en* + LOC count includes 8 tokens with both an *aquí* and an *en* + LOC locative; "other" locatives in NMmon were *(ahí) afuera* '(there) outside' and in NMbil *patrás y palante* 'back and forth'.

** The proportion of *estar* + *-ndo* with a cooccurring locative is greater in NMmon than in MexPop (z = 2.4332, p = .0075). The NMbil proportion is not different from MexPop, even if cases of *aquí en...* are counted separately, see note 6.

One difference is the cooccurrence of allative *a* 'to'+ LOC expressions with *estar* + *-ndo* in the New Mexico data but not in MexPop. All four cases are with main verb *ir*, as in the following example:

(49) *Ahora* **estuve yendo a Laughlin** *pero-* **estuve yendo** *como tres años* **a las Vegas**, *y me aburrí, y ahora voy a Laughlin. Está más bonito Laughlin, Nevada que Las Vegas.* (NMmon/NMCSS#214)
'Lately **I was going to Laughlin** but- **I was going to Las Vegas** for three years, and I got bored, so now I go to Laughlin. Laughlin, Nevada is prettier than Las Vegas.'

Estar yendo is a newer use. Old Spanish cases of *a* + LOC with *seer* or *estar* + *-ndo* do not involve directional motion and *a* is closer to English 'at' than 'to', as in *a la puerta de la eclegia sediellos sperando* 'was waiting for them at the door of the church' (PMC 2239; also, Luc XVIII, p.144), or *seyendo un dia a su mesa comiendo* 'sitting one day at his table eating' (EE1–160r32). Another difference between the New Mexico and the MexPop data is the cooccurrence of *de* 'from' + LOC expressions, also with a motion verb, with two cases in NMbil, for example,

(50) *Y ahora que ya [ ] ves esto de que están viniendo mucha gente **de otros estados*** (NMbil/Edwin).
'Now that you see this, that a lot of people are coming **from other states**'

We come back to the use of *estar* + *-ndo* with motion verbs in Chapter 5 (Section 5.4).

The overall frequency of cooccurring locatives is higher in NMmon, at 38%, than in MexPop, at 21% (z = 2.4332, p = .0075). Indeed, the proportion of *estar* + *-ndo* tokens with a cooccurring locative is not significantly different in NMmon from the Old Spanish corpus. This result is consistent with archaism or the preservation of older patterns in traditional New Mexico Spanish, as we observed in the last chapter with respect to parallel gerunds (Sections 2.2, 2.7). On the other hand, the overall frequency of cooccurring locatives is virtually the same in NMbil (23%) and MexPop (21%).

Table 25. ESTAR + -NDO temporal adverbials in Mexico and New Mexico corpora

Total *estar* + *-ndo*	MexPop N = 338 N	%	NMmon N = 42 N	%	NMbil N = 144 N	%
"now"	25	7%	3	7%	15	10%
ya	20	6%	1*	2%	9	6%
Locating adverbial	17	5%	3	7%	6	5%
Durative adverbial	6	2%	4	10%	3	2%
in *cuando* 'when' clause	9	3%	0	0	9	6%
"always"	6	2%	3	7%	3	2%
Frequentative adv.	11	3%	1	2%	2	1%
Other**	8	2%	2	5%	1	<1%
Temporals total	102	**30%**	17	**40%**	48	**33%**
No temporal	236	70%	25	60%	96	67%

* Does not include two cases of *ya* with another adverbial (*ya cuando, ya todo el día*). See note 6.
** Other in MexPop is "since" and in NMmon and NMbil *hasta que* 'until'.

With respect to temporal expressions, their overall frequency is not significantly different in MexPop, at 30%, NMmon, at 40%, and NMbil, at 33%. A comparison of *estar + -ndo* temporal expressions is given in Table 25 above. Most frequent in all three data sets are "now" adverbials (*ahora* 'now', *todavía* 'still') and *ya* 'already', with a combined average of 13% in MexPop, 10% in NMmon, and 17% in NMbil. The difference between NMbil and MexPop is not statistically significant at p 0.05, whether we look at the combined "now" / *ya* total or separate out "now" expressions. Second most frequent are locating adverbials, with 5% in MexPop and NMbil, and 7% in NMmon, for example, *después* 'afterwards, then', *luego* 'then', *un día* 'one day', *en el 1950* 'in the year 1950'. A third adverbial type indicates continuous and progressive meaning. In NMmon we have two cases with cooccurring durative adverbials (e.g. *el día entero* 'all day', *como tres años* 'for about three years') and one with *estar + -ndo* in a *mientras* 'while' clause, as in the Old Spanish corpus. In MexPop and NMbil, 3% – 6% of *estar + -ndo* tokens are in a clause headed by *cuando* 'when', as in the example below.

(51)   ...*automaticamente **cuando está printiando** las licencias sale el numbre.* (NMbil/Marg)
'the name comes out automatically **when it is printing** the licenses'

Fourth, frequentative adverbials occur in both NMmon and NMbil, as in MexPop and in contrast with the Old Spanish corpus. In the next example, *estaba yo llorando* 'I was crying' occurs in the midst of a series of simple Imperfect forms and *día a día* 'every day' explicitly indicates a frequently occurring, if not habitual, situation. The use of the first person singular Imperfect Progressive may emphasize the speaker's personal involvement in the "crying"; the simple Imperfect forms are all third person. We return to experiential habitual uses of *estar + -ndo* in Chapter 5.

(52)   *Mi "gran'ma" me acha- mi tía me achaba ajuera, me pegaba y me echaba ajuera, y **día a día 'staba yo llorando** ahi ajuera en el "porch". Y mi marido pasaba de la mina, pasaba por ah', como 'hora aquí el camino, ¿ves? Y- y me miraba él llorando* (NMCSS#60).
'My grandma would send- my aunt would throw me out of the house, she would hit me and send me out, and **every day I would be crying** out there on the porch. And my husband would pass by,

on his way from the mine he would pass by there, like the street here now, right. And he would see me crying.'

On the other hand, cooccurring with *ir* + *-ndo* in the New Mexico corpora are adverbials indicating gradual development, with two cases of *conforme* 'accordingly, as' (NMCSS #219), one of *año tras año* (NMCSS#21) 'year after year', and one with *va creciendo* 'goes growing' in a clause headed by *como* 'as' (NMbil/Marg; see Chapter 4, Section 4.4.3 on *como* clauses). For example,

(53) *luego ya subió a dos reales, luego a treinta centavos. Iban subiendo quizás* **conforme** *iban sacando ellos ganacia, yo creo.* (NMmon/ NMCSS#219)
'then (the price) went up to two *reales*, then to thirty cents. They would raise (go raising) it **accordingly** as their profits went up (went making profit), I think.'

Another *ir* + *-ndo* temporal type in the New Mexico data is "now" and *ya* (NMCSS#245, #346; NMbil/Vig), consistent with inceptive or proximative (Heine 1994b) uses. A nice example of proximative *ir* + *-ndo* is the following:

(54) *Lue'o asperé que creciera, y lue'o me casé con e'a. [...] Y* **ahora vamos cumpliendo** *cuarenta y nueve años, ¿no?* (NMmon/ NMCSS#346)
'Then I waited until she got older, and then I married her. And **now we're about to reach** forty-nine years, right? (literally: we go reaching)'

We also find locating adverbials, such as *antes* 'before', a *luego* 'then' clause (NMCSS#10), and an *esa vez* 'that time' clause (NMCSS#219). Finally, with *andar* + *-ndo* in the New Mexico corpus are four "always" adverbials, two tokens each of *todo el tiempo* (NMCSS#10, NMbil/Fr) and *siempre* (NMCSS#245, NMbil/Nin); three frequentative adverbials, *en vez* 'at times' (NMCSS#162), *a veces* 'sometimes' (NMbil/Bea), *en el verano* 'during the summer' (NMbil/Vig); and two cases in a *cuando* clause (NMCSS#311, #346).

In summary, the distribution of locative and temporal expressions in the New Mexico data is very similar to the Mexico City data. For *estar* + *-ndo*, overall average frequencies are not significantly different in MexPop, NMmon, and NMbil, with the exception of the higher proportion of locatives in NMmon, which we may attribute to archaism. It is important that these results do not support an acceleration of change under language contact hypothesis (e.g. Silva-Corvalán 1994), which is consistent with our findings with respect to formal reduction in the last chapter.

3.7 Usage effects in the conventionalization of aspectual meaning

A striking result of the comparison of Old Spanish and Mexico data was the decrease in temporal adverbials cooccurring with *ir* + *-ndo*. Overall, their frequency drops between OldSp and MexPop, from 32% to 22% (z = 2.1176, p = .0171). What exactly happened to *ir* + *-ndo* temporal expressions? As shown in Table 22, the proportion of *poco a poco* 'little by little' remains about the same, between 5% and 6%. Most Hispanists recognize that the gradual development meaning of *ir* + *-ndo* has become conventionalized, so that it does not depend on the presence of a lexical expression of gradualness. An example would be *fueron entrando* 'they came in one by one' without explicit *uno a uno* (Lorenzo 1971: 123). Nor does this gradual development meaning depend on the aspectual properties of the predicate, for example, *iba queriéndolo* 'gradually came to love him' or 'loved him more and more' where *querer* cannot be said to inherently express a process like *crecer* 'grow' does (Roca Pons 1958: 64).

The big drop lies in temporal adverbials related to inceptive and continuative uses: from a 7% average of *desque* and other "since" adverbials in OldSp to 2% in MexPop, and from 6% to 1% of *hasta* 'until'. Even if continuative uses have been largely taken over by more specific *seguir* + *-ndo*, as we suggested in Section 3.4.1, *ir(se)* + *-ndo* still has inceptive uses. What has changed is the cooccurrence of explicit expressions of inceptiveness.

In present-day Spanish, expressions such as *ya* 'already' (Roca Pons 1958: 64) or inherently inceptive predicates such as *anochecer* 'get dark' (Spaulding 1926: 245) often reinforce inceptive meaning. But lexical expressions of inceptiveness are not required in *ir* + *-ndo*. Strong evidence for absorption and conventionalization of inceptive meaning are cases where stative predicates take on a "state commences" meaning, as in

(55) *el hombre va teniendo conciencia paulatinamente...*
'man gains (literally: goes having) awareness gradually...'

where *tener* 'have' means *obtener* 'acquire' (Hamplová 1968: 220; cf. Solé 1990: 63; Torres Cacoullos 1999a: 49). The use of Present tense *ir + -ndo* to express surprise, often in a *y que + ir + -ndo* construction, as in...*y que voy viendo al policía y me dio mucho miedo* '...and just then I see the policeman and I got scared (literally: I go seeing)' (UNAM 1976: 199) may also be related to inceptive meaning (Arjona 1991: 128; Luna 1980: 207; Montes 1962; Squartini 1998: 100–2). The expression *ir llegando*, common at least in Mexican Spanish, may be considered a proximative (Heine 1994b) in the sense of "just arriving" or "about to arrive" (Arjona 1991: 133; Lope Blanch 1953: 87; Luna 1980: 209). The following New Mexico example illustrates:

(56) *Y le dije a la- a la señora, "yo voy a chutear el tecolote, y lo voy a matare". Y saqué el rifle, un veintidós, por la puerta, todo lo que pude así. Y por la luna lo estaba cuidando. [...] Y le tiré y le quebré un ala. Y salió volando, se fue volando, y lo cuidé, **hasta que ya iba llegando a la casita**.* (NMmon, NMCSS #245)
'And I said to the lady, "I'm going to shoot the owl, and I'm going to kill it.". And I took out the rifle, a twenty-two, through the door, as far out as I could, like this. And I was watching it by the moon. And I shot it and broke a wing. And it took off flying, it went flying, and I watched it, **until it was just about to reach the little house** (literally: went arriving).'

Here *iba llegando* seems to express something like "was at the point of arriving", or a proximative "about to" meaning.

Frequent occurrence in certain contexts may result in absorption of contextual meanings by a grammaticizing construction (cf. Schwenter 1994). Remember that inceptive uses are prominent in the earliest available texts, beginning with the *Poema de mio Cid*. It is likely that inceptive meaning has been absorbed by *ir(se) + -ndo* from frequently cooccurring inceptive expressions over a period of time in early Old Spanish. The decrease in *ir + -ndo* temporal adverbials suggests that, as locative meaning fades, it may become less necessary to specify the temporal component by means of temporal adverbials.

On the other hand, the average occurrence of temporal expressions with *estar + -ndo* remains virtually unchanged between OldSp and MexPop (Section 3.3). What does change is the distribution of temporal adverbial types. As shown in Table 21, frequentative (e.g. *diario* 'daily') and "now" adverbials

Evidence for semantic reduction   111

(e.g. *ahora* 'now') cooccur with a little over 10% of all *estar* + *-ndo* tokens in MexPop, 16% if we include cases of *ya*. In contrast, these add up to less than 2% in the Old Spanish corpus. The scarcity of these adverbial types in Old Spanish suggests that frequentative and habitual uses of *estar* + *-ndo* are fairly recent, at least more recent than *ir* + *-ndo* inceptive, continuative, and gradual development uses. It is not surprising, then, that lexical expressions consistent with habitual meaning cooccur with these newer uses of *estar* + *-ndo*, in contrast with the decline of inceptive-related adverbials in the case of older *ir* + *-ndo* uses.[7]

It appears that as older uses become conventionalized there is less dependence on contextual elements. We saw that temporal adverbials indicating inceptive-continuative and gradual development meaning were highly associated with *ir* + *-ndo* from the earliest Old Spanish texts. Over time their use declines, suggesting that these meanings have largely been absorbed by the construction. On the other hand, newer uses rely more on context. We saw that habitual and frequentative uses of *estar* + *-ndo*, which are more recent, are expressed with cooccurring frequentative adverbials and "now" expressions in present-day Spanish.

3.8 Summary

The distribution of locatives and temporal adverbials in Old Spanish *-ndo* constructions accords with the meaning of the source constructions, in support of retention in grammaticization. Cooccurring most frequently with *estar* + *-ndo* are *en* 'in' + LOC, *aquí* 'here'- *allí* 'there', *con* 'with' + PERSON and locating adverbials (for example, a *cuando* 'when' clause). These are consistent with location in a specific place. In contrast, *ir* + *-ndo* locatives and temporals agree with directional motion: *a* 'to' + LOC, *de* 'from' + LOC, and *por* 'along' + LOC, on the one hand, and *desque* 'since' and *hasta que* 'until' clauses and *poco a poco* 'little by little', on the other. Finally, *por* + LOCs (multiple locations) in *andar* + *-ndo* is consistent with non-directional motion or "going around".

The data presented in this chapter show that metaphor is not required in the evolution from locative to aspectual meaning: there is no significant increase in cooccurring temporal expressions over time, contrary to what might be predicted by a space > time metaphor account of the semantic evolution of *-ndo* constructions. The differences between OldSp and MexPop in the frequencies of temporal adverbials are not significant for either *estar + -ndo* or *andar + -ndo*. For *ir + -ndo*, the difference is statistically significant, but in the opposite direction, that is, the frequency of cooccurring temporal adverbials decreases. These results and the many examples presented above show that there has been a temporal (aspectual) dimension to *-ndo* constructions from the beginning. That is, locative and motion meaning coexist with aspectual meaning in Old Spanish *-ndo* constructions.

At the same time, the decrease in cooccurring locatives and the qualitative change from more specific locatives to less specific deictic expressions *aquí, allí,* and *ai* provide evidence that the mechanism of semantic change is best described as loss of specific locative and motion features of meaning. In addition, the decrease in temporal adverbials related to inceptive uses with *ir + -ndo* suggests that as spatial meaning is lost, contextual elements are less needed to specify the remaining temporal meaning component.

As we will see in the next chapter, both token and type frequency play an important role in this process of semantic reduction. The spatial component is reduced as *estar, ir, andar* are used in high token frequency combinations with particular main verbs not typically associated with location or physical movement. In addition, these main verbs belong to semantic classes with a large number of types participating in the *-ndo* construction, which leads to the development of a more abstract schema lacking specific features of meaning (Bybee forthcoming; Bybee and Thompson 1997).

Notes

1. The difference in the average of locatives between OldSp and MexPop for *estar + -ndo* may be more significant than shown in Table 19. In 6 of 34 cases of cooccurring *aquí, allí,* there was also another more specific locative (three cases of *con* + PERSON, two of *en* + LOCATION, and one "other", *arriba* 'up, above'). There were three such cases in the Old Spanish corpus (one in PMC, two in EE1). These were counted separately, so a more accurate comparison between OldSp and MexPop totals would be 49/165 = 30% versus 66/338 = 19% (χ^2 = 6.537209, p = .0106).

2. The one Old Spanish case that might be taken as a frequentative is reproduced below, but the meaning here seems to be 'each time' or 'on every occasion on which' rather than 'frequently'.

> % **Cada q<ue>** v<uest>ro no<n>bre yo le esto dez'jendo
> oteame & sospira & esta comedjendo

Evidence for semantic reduction 113

> *abyua mas el ojo / & esta toda bulliendo*
> *paresc'e q<ue> convusco no<n> se estaria dormjendo* (LBA 47v, 811)
> '**Every time** I mention (literally: I am saying) your name to her,
> she looks at me and sighs and meditates
> her eyes begin to scintillate, she's all a-boil and snapping.
> With you, 'tis very clear, methinks, she'll ne'er be caught a-napping'
> (Willis 1972: 218, for first and second line;
> Singleton 1975: 77, for third and fourth line)

3. Temporal expressions with singular *todo*, like *siempre*, pair up with *estar* + *-ndo* to indicate a subjective speaker attitude (Section 3.3). This is not necessarily the case with plural *todos* expressions, for example, *todos los días* (cf. Yllera 1980: 23).

4. The less frequent occurrence of *después* + *ir* + *-ndo* in MexPop compared with OldSp may be attributed, at least in part, to discourse-type (genre) differences: narration of sequences of actions, as in the *Estoria de España*, would probably favor *después* more than conversation.

5. Dowty (1979: 325 ff.) distinguishes between "main tense" adverbials, which indicate reference time and have scope over aspect, and "aspectual" adverbials which occur within the scope of aspect and Aktionsart (cf. Bhat 1999: 60–1). Locating adverbials such as *ayer* 'yesterday' would be "main tense" adverbials, while durative adverbials, such as *un rato* 'for a while' would be "aspectual". The distinction is not always neat. In example (44), *una vez* 'once' indicates both reference time (past tense) and a one-time occurrence (perfective aspect).

6. I counted cases of two locatives in NMmon and NMbil under the category of the more specific one. There were 8 cases of *aquí* or *ahí, en* (counted under *en*) and one of *en, con* in NMbil and one each of *ahí, afuera* and *aquí, con* in NMmon. Adding these cases to the *aquí* count, as done for MexPop (see note 1), does not make the difference between MexPop and NMbil statistically significant (Table 24).

7. It would be interesting to count the proportion of frequentative or habitual uses of *estar* + *-ndo* with and without an explicit item such as *ahora* or *diario*, to see which contexts (main verbs) do not require the cooccurrence of such items for a habitual reading. As we will see in Chapter 5, high frequency, general activity verbs such as *trabajar* 'work', *estudiar* 'study, go to school', *tomar* 'drink' seem to favor habitual uses.

Chapter 4

Frequency effects and layering in the domain of progressive aspect

The shifting semantic territory of -*ndo* constructions

4.1 The changing distribution of -*ndo* auxiliaries

There are two major quantitative differences between Old Spanish (12th–15th c.) and present-day varieties in the frequency and distribution of -*ndo* constructions. First, as we saw in Chapter 2 (Section 2.5), the overall token or text frequency of -*ndo* constructions increases dramatically, doubling at the very least. A second quantitative difference is the reversal in the ordering of the auxiliaries by relative frequency, with *ir* 'go' yielding first place to *estar* 'be (located)'. Given the undisputed preponderance of *estar* + -*ndo* in present-day spoken Spanish, it may seem surprising that less than one hundred years ago Keniston (1936: 171) stated that the commonest auxiliary with the gerund was *ir*.

In Chapter 2 we saw that formal reductive change — as indexed by parallel gerunds, intervening open class material, and clitic climbing — is linked to increases in construction frequency, which we defined as a combined measure of the token frequency of auxiliary-plus-gerund sequences and the proportion of gerunds in such sequences. In this chapter we consider frequency effects in shifts in the semantic territory of -*ndo* constructions, as they emerge as conventionalized expressions of aspectual and non-aspectual meaning.

We begin with an overview of changes in the distribution of -*ndo* auxiliaries. The relative frequency of an auxiliary is the proportion of all -*ndo* constructions with that auxiliary, that is, the frequency of that auxiliary relative to all others. Table 26 shows relative frequencies in Old Spanish texts and compares the Old Spanish corpus as a whole with data for 16th and early

20th c. prose from Keniston (1937a, 1937b). Table 27 shows the relative frequencies of the auxiliaries in present-day data: the written Essays corpus (see Section 1.5.2.2) and oral corpora, popular Mexico City (1.5.2.1), New Mexico monolingual (1.5.3.1) and bilingual (1.5.3.2), as well as educated Madrid (Esgueva and Cantarero 1981, figures from Olbertz 1998).

Table 26. Relative frequencies of -ndo auxiliaries in Old Spanish texts

	ESTAR		IR		ANDAR		Other**		Total
	N	%	N	%	N	%	N	%	N
PMC (1140/1207)	11(9)*	22	63	70	2	2	5	6	90
Apolonio (c.1250)	2(2)	11	26	72	5	14	1	3	36
EE1 (1270–1284)	32(7)	17	114	49	69	29	13	5	235
LBA (1330/1343)	22	29	22	29	18	24	14	18	76
Luc (1335)	24	41	18	31	10	17	6	10	58
Corb (1438)	29	56	12	23	5	10	6	11	52
C01 (1499)	31	45	19	27	8	12	11	16	69
OldSp total	169	27	274	45	117	19	56	9	616
16th c. prose (Keniston 1937a)	94	38	107	44	31	13	13	5	245
Early 20th (Keniston 1937b)	304	32	379	40	31	3	230	24	944

* Figures in parentheses under *estar* column are for *seer*.
** Other auxiliaries: OldSp *quedar* 5, *salir* 17, *venir* 34; 16th c. prose: *quedar* 5, *salir(se)* 5, *venir(se)* 3; early 20th c. prose: *quedar(se)* 26, *salir* 14, *seguir* 138 (= 15%), *venir* 52.

Table 27. Relative frequencies of -ndo auxiliaries in present-day corpora

	ESTAR		IR		ANDAR		Other*		Total
	N	%	N	%	N	%	N	%	N
Essays	67	24	101	36	3	1	107	38	278
MexPop	340	52	146	23	89	14	73	11	648
NMmon	42	51	14	17	16	19	11	13	83
NMbil	144	82	6	3	18	10	7	4	175
Madrid (Olbertz 1998)	262	76	64	19	1	0	16	5	343

* Other auxiliaries: Essays: *continuar* (15), *quedar(se)* NA, *seguir* 81 (= 29%), *venir* (11); MexPop: *quedarse* 10, *salir* 1, *seguir* 39 (=6%), *venir* 23; NMmon: *quedarse* 3, *salir* 2, *seguir* 1, *venir* 5; NMbil: *quedarse* 4, *seguir* 1, *venir* 2; Madrid: *quedar(se)* 2, *seguir* 12 (=3.5%), *venir* 2.

The most striking fact about the changing distribution of *-ndo* auxiliaries is the rise of *estar* and decline of *ir*. In the Old Spanish corpus as a whole (OldSp), *ir*

+ -*ndo* is first, with close to half of all -*ndo* constructions. *Ir* + -*ndo* begins with a relative frequency of 70% in the *Poema de mio Cid* (PMC) and an overall OldSp average of 45%. This drops sharply to 23% in popular Mexico City and to 19% in Madrid. In contrast, *estar* + -*ndo* begins with a relative frequency of less than 13% in 12th-13th c. texts (PMC, *Apolonio*, EE1) and an overall OldSp average of 27%. This about doubles to 52% in MexPop and nearly triples to 76% in Madrid. This reversal in ordering suggests that when the earliest Old Spanish texts were produced *ir* + -*ndo* was more grammaticized, but that over time *estar* + -*ndo* catches up and even outstrips it. We noted the asymmetry in the pace of change for these two auxiliaries with respect to intervening material (Section 2.3) and clitic climbing (Section 2.4.1). Further ahead we will see the same pattern with respect to indices of semantic bleaching (Section 4.5).

In addition to quantitative shifts in distribution, some players have exited while others have entered. One auxiliary has dropped from use entirely, *seer*.[1] In the Old Spanish corpus, there was a total of only 18 tokens, limited to the earliest texts (Table 26). According to Yllera (1980: 50), *seer* + -*ndo* disappears from prose by the 14th century. Old Spanish *seer* 'be (seated)', results from the fusion of the paradigms of Latin *esse* 'be' and *sede:re* 'be seated' (Lloyd 1993: 477). *Seer comiendo*, with four of nine *seer* + -*ndo* tokens in the *Estoria de España* (160r32, 166v32, 194r32, 194r38), may well mean 'be **seated** eating', but otherwise the construction seems to have locative rather than postural meaning. This is especially clear with cooccurring locatives, as in:

(1) *El sedie **en valenc'ia** curiando & guardando* (PMC 1566)
 'he remained **in Valencia** to guard and protect it'

(2) *A**la puerta** dela eclegia sediellos sp<er>ando* (PMC 2239).
 'was waiting for them **at the door**'

In the *Poema de mio Cid*, in addition to *catando* 'watching' (2, 2059, 2439, 3123), main verbs used with both *seer* and *estar* are *(a)guardando* 'watching (over)' (1058, 1566) and *esperando* 'waiting' (1746, 2239). Other *seer* main verbs that appear with *estar* in later texts are *allabandose* 'boasting' (2824), *castigando* 'advising' (3553), *consejandose* 'taking counsel together' (122), *plorando* 'crying' (18), *sanctiguandose* 'crossing himself' (1840), *sonrrisando* 'smiling' (2532). In the EE1, in addition to *comiendo*, main verbs are *catando* 'watching' (19r37), *arando* 'plowing' (61v22), *disputando* 'debating' (117r33), *fablando* 'talking'(194r21), *yantando* 'eating' (78v47). Both

Spaulding (1926: 240) and Yllera (1980: 48–9) observe that Old Spanish uses of *seer* + *-ndo* were similar if not identical to those of *estar* + *-ndo*. The following set of examples illustrates overlapping contexts.

(3) *seer catando*

E quando Cipion oyo aquellas palauras [...] ouo tan grand sanna que souo una grand piec'a catando a Annibal y ell otro a el. (EE1–19r37)
'And when Cipion heard those words [...] he was so outraged that **he remained** (sat there) for a long while **looking** at Annibal and the other at him.'

(4) *estar catando*

e quando cesar la uio estudo la cata<n>do gra<n>d piec'a cuydando. (EE1–5v15)
'and when Cesar saw her **he remained** (stood there) **looking** at her a long while, thinking.'

At least two new *-ndo* auxiliaries have appeared, *quedar(se)* 'remain' and *seguir* 'follow, continue'. *Seguir* + *-ndo* does not appear at all in the earliest Old Spanish texts, and becomes common only in the 18th c. (Spaulding 1926: 262; Yllera 1980: 82). In the last chapter we related the rise of *seguir* + *-ndo* to the decline in continuative uses of *ir* + *-ndo* (Section 3.4.1). In present-day Spanish, the relative frequency of *seguir* + *-ndo* is highest in written, formal varieties, as indicated by figures for Keniston's (1937b) corpus of early 20th century prose, with 15% (Table 26) and for the Essays corpus, with 29% (Table 27). As for *quedar(se)* + *-ndo*, we will see shortly that the early "remain looking at" use of *estar* (and *seer*)-plus-*catando* shown in the set of examples above has largely been taken over by *quedarse*-plus-*viendo* 'seeing' or *mirando* 'looking'.

In following sections we will classify the main verbs that combine with the different auxiliaries. Changes in the distribution of auxiliaries by main verb types show two important processes in grammaticization, retention and layering, in the domain of progressive aspectual meaning in Spanish. We have already seen evidence for retention of meaning features of the source constructions from cooccurrence patterns with locative and temporal expressions (Chapter 3). Thus, different *-ndo* constructions have different aspectual and non-aspectual uses that follow from the retention of parts of their original

Frequency effects and layering in the domain of progressive aspect 119

meaning. On the other hand, layering (Bybee et al. 1994: 21, 148; Hopper 1991: 22) is manifested synchronically in the availability of different forms for the same function, as newer constructions emerge or expand their uses without necessarily replacing older ones. Semantic generalization (reduction, bleaching) in the same direction results in the availability of *estar*, or *ir*, or *andar* + *-ndo* to express progressive and continuous aspect in Spanish. Partial overlap in the uses of constructions evolving in the same domain contradicts structuralist analyses based on the presence versus absence of binary features (e.g. King 1992). We will see that the appearance of one as opposed to another auxiliary in many cases can only be explained as the routinization of frequent collocations, so that *bucando* 'looking for' is nearly always with *andar*, *creciendo* 'growing' with *ir*, and *hablando* 'talking' with *estar*.

Figure 4 represents a rough map of imperfective aspectual territory. Underlined are meaning labels (see definitions in Bybee et al. 1994: 126–7). Upper case highlights layering in the domain of progressive (and continuous) aspect, as locative (*estar*) and motion (*ir, andar*) constructions generalize in the same direction. Directional motion (*ir*) results in the additional specification of gradual development meaning, and on another path, inceptive and continuative meaning. Nondirectional motion (*andar*) may specify frequentative meaning. In bold are new auxiliaries *quedarse*, for *estar*'s early "remain verb-ing" use, and *seguir*, for *ir*'s continuative use. Also indicated in bold letters are newer gradual development, frequentative, and (experiential) habitual uses of *estar* + *-ndo*.

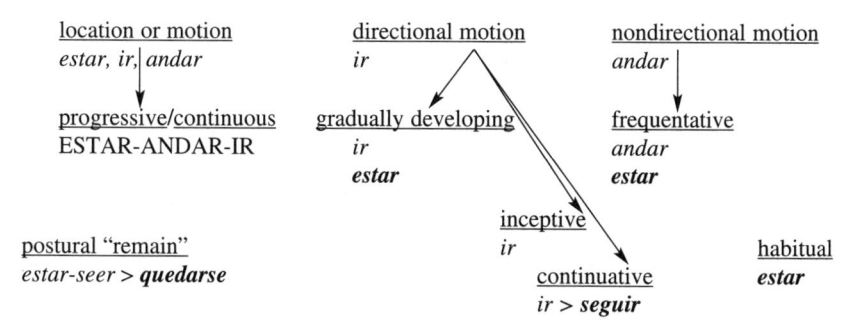

location or motion   directional motion   nondirectional motion
estar, ir, andar   *ir*   *andar*

progressive/continuous   gradually developing   frequentative
ESTAR-ANDAR-IR   *ir*   *andar*
                          estar   ***estar***

                                inceptive
postural "remain"   *ir*   habitual
estar-seer > ***quedarse***   ***estar***
                          continuative
                          ir > ***seguir***

Figure 4. Layering (variation) in the domain of progressive and continuous aspect

The remainder of the chapter is organized as follows. In Section 4.2 we show the importance of both token and type frequency in the evolution of *estar* +

-ndo from a locative to a general expression of progressive meaning. In 4.3 evidence is provided that experiential uses (subject and speaker involvement) derive from frequent occurrence in contexts consistent with the locative origin of the construction rather than from a process of pragmatic strengthening. Section 4.4 investigates the contexts that favor the development of *ir + -ndo* from an harmonic movement expression to a gradual development periphrasis. In Section 4.5 we compare the generalization of *estar* and *ir + -ndo* and adduce support for the role of frequency in constraining the pace of formal and semantic reduction in grammaticizing constructions. Section 4.6 looks at frequentative uses of *andar + -ndo* and variation with *estar + -ndo*. Finally in Section 4.7, a comparison of the distribution of motion-verb auxiliaries in New Mexican and other corpora suggests that a process of specialization of the auxiliaries may be more advanced in bilingual varieties.

4.2 Token and type frequency in semantic generalization: *Estar* + "talking"

In previous sections, increased frequency, formal reduction, and fewer cooccurring locatives were adduced as evidence that *estar + -ndo* has evolved from a locative construction to a periphrastic expression of aspectual meaning. In this section we will look at main verbs to see which semantic class may have favored the emergence of progressive from locative. The results suggest that "talking" and "bodily activity" predicates provide the context in which progressive meaning is conventionalized.

Such verbs refer to uniquely human activities that entail a high degree of involvement by the subject. Crucially, the highest token frequency combinations with *estar* in the Old Spanish corpus are with particular verbs belonging to these classes, *hablando* 'talking' and *llorando* 'crying'. Token frequency leads to bleaching. At the same time, the type frequency of *estar*-plus-talking verb and *estar*-plus-bodily activity verb is also high, that is, these classes have many members participating in the construction. Type frequency also promotes generalization.

4.2.1 *Diachronic ordering of main verbs*

If the original meaning of progressives is 'the subject is located in the midst of an activity' it may be hypothesized that they originate in contexts where the subject is an agent and the activity expressed by the main verb has a characteristic location (Bybee et al. 1994: 135, 292). A nice example would be the following.

(5) *E estando él vañándose, envió nuestro señor Dios un ángel al vaño...* (Luc, Ex. LI, p. 301)
'And while **he was bathing** our Lord God sent an angel to the bath...' (Keller and Keating 1977: 190)

The function of *estar* + *-ndo* here is to give the location of the subject: where he was when the angel arrived. The activity has a characteristic location: bathing in the bathroom. All the elements of meaning listed by Bybee et al. (1994: 136) are present:

(6) a. An agent (he)
    b. is located spatially (in the bathroom)
    c. in the midst of (bathing is ongoing, in progress)
    d. an activity (the bathing)
    e. at reference time (when the angel arrives)

The most frequent examples in the Old Spanish corpus are not exactly of this type, however. Table 28 shows the most frequent *estar* + *-ndo* main verbs, Table 29 the distribution of main verb types by semantic class. Physical activities, such as *arando* 'plowing', *escriviendo* 'writing', *sacodiendo las frutas* 'shaking the fruit off the trees', which may be said to have a characteristic location, add up to only 17, or 10% of all *estar* main verbs (gerunds). This average goes up slightly if we add in some of those classified as bodily activity verbs, such as *bañandose* 'bathing', *comiendo* 'eating', *durmiendo* 'sleeping'. But most bodily activity verbs do not have a characteristic location: *llorando* 'crying', *riendo* 'laughing', *temblando* 'trembling'. Furthermore, the subject of these verbs is closer to an experiencer than an agent. Such verbs add up to 36, or 22%. Even more frequent are those classified as talking verbs, including *hablando* 'talking' and *diziendo* 'saying, telling', which add up to 45, or 27%. Talking cannot really be said to have a characteristic location. These results suggest a refinement of the hypothesis to include an early role for subjectivity in the evolution of *estar* + *-ndo*. The modifications I will propose to the list in (6) are: (a) an agent — **experiencer** and (d) a **human** activity.

Table 28. ESTAR + -NDO: Most frequently occurring main verbs (gerunds)

Gerund tokens/types	PMC	EE1	LBA	Luc	Corb	C01	OldSptotal	MexPop
	20/16	39/24	22/16	24/15	29/23	31/22	165/81	340/162
catando 'watching'	4	4					**8**	
esperando 'waiting'	2		1	3		1	**7**	11
f/hablando 'talking'	1	4	1	3	4	5	**18**	6
llorando 'crying'	1	2		3	1		**7**	2
comiendo 'eating'		5		3			**8**	
f/haziendo* 'doing'		4	1		1		**6**	15
pensando 'thinking'			2		1		**3**	4
dudando 'hesitating'			4				**4**	
durmiendo 'sleeping'			2		1	1	**4**	4
diziendo 'saying'			2		2	2	**6**	**12**
dando vozes 'screaming'				2			**2**	
folgando 'resting'					2		**2**	
mirando ' looking at'				2	1		**3**	3
escuchando 'listening'					3		**3**	
negociando 'negotiating'						2	**2**	
razonando 'reasoning'						2	**2**	
trabajando 'working'						1	**1**	**29**
pagando 'paying'								19
estudiando 'studying'								12
tomando 'drinking'								12
platicando 'chatting'								9
viviendo 'living'								8
jugando 'playing'								7
esperando un hijo 'expecting a child'								5
ayudando 'helping'								4
gustando 'liking'								4
viendo 'seeing'		1					1	4
aguantando 'suffering'								3
bañando(se) 'bathing'				1				3
funcionando 'functioning'								3
soñando 'dreaming'								3
yendo 'going'								3

*Different predicates (*haciendo* + different objects)

Table 29. Estar + -ndo: Semantic classes of main verbs in Old Spanish

	PMC tk/tp	EE1 tk/tp	LBA tk/tp	Luc tk/tp	Corb tk/tp	C01 tk/tp	OldSp %	total tk/tp	
Watching	7/4	5/2		1/1	2/1	1/1	**10**	16/6	=2.7
Waiting	2/1	1/1	2/2	4/2		2/2	**7**	11/2	=5.5
Talking	7/7	6/3	5/4	5/2	9/5	13/7	**27**	45/16	=2.8
Bodily activity	3/3	11/6	4/3	9/5	5/5	4/4	**22**	36/19	=1.9
Physical activity	8/4	3/3	2/2	2/2	2/2		**10**	17/11	=1.5
Mental activity		3/3	7/3	1/1	3/3	1/1	**9**	15/8	=1.9
General activity	4/4	1/1	1/1	5/5	3/2		**8**	14/13	=1.1
Other	1/1	1/1		1/1	3/2	5/3	**7**	11/6	

* Under each column the first is the number of tokens ("tk"), the second the number of different types ("tp") in each class.

Watching: *catando, aguardando* (also: waiting), *curiando & guardando, parando mientes, veyendo, mirando*
Waiting: *esperando, atendiendo*
Talking: *alabando, bendiziendo, castigando, chapullando, chirlando, consejando, contando, dando vozes, diziendo, fablando, loando, llamando, razonando, regañando, rogando, trobando*
Bodily activity: *bañandose, bulliendo, callando, cantando, comiendo, desbauando, deuaneando, durmiendo, p/llorando, refusando, riendo, santiguando, sonrissando, sudando, sufriendo, temblando, torçiendo el rostro, tremiendo, yantando*
Mental activity: *comediendo, concomiendo, cuydando, dudando, marauillando, pensando, remirando, teniendo que*
Physical: *arando, curando caballos, escarbando, escriviendo, faziendo, labrando, leyendo, matando, rezando, sacodiendo, texiendo*
General: *aprendiendo de su arte, asechando, assessagando la tierra, destruyendo, enderecando la prouincia, faziendo bien, hauiniendo el hilo, librando los pleytos, negociando, poniendo su tienda, rebatando, seruiendo, travajando*
Other: 4 location *folgando* (PMC, Luc, Corb); 4 listening *oyendo, escuchando* (Corb, C01); 1 aspectual *perseuerando* (EE1); 2 emotion *adorando, penando* (C01).

Based on the list of most frequent verbs in Table 28 and the distribution of verbs by semantic class in Table 29, the order of appearance of main verbs is the following (cf. Yllera 1980: 30–35):

```
                                              [Not in Old Spanish]
watching
                                thinking          motion
talking   >   physical activity    >                   >
                                general activity  process (change of state)
waiting
```
Figure 5.   Order of appearance of ESTAR + -NDO main verbs

Since watching and waiting verbs, in addition to talking verbs, are the first to appear (see PMC column in Tables 28 and 29), let us first investigate whether either of these might provide the context in which *estar + -ndo* originates as a progressive.

4.2.2 Early postural meaning: "watching" perception verbs

Given that *estar* comes from Latin *stare* 'stand', it could be hypothesized that progressive *estar + -ndo* generalizes from postural meaning. Thus, Olbertz (1998: 301–2) assumes that *estar + -ndo* develops from "positional" uses of *estar* plus a gerund functioning as a predicative adjunct. We already saw evidence for a locative origin in Chapter 3. Here we will see that early positional or postural uses have been taken over by *quedarse + -ndo*, which further detracts from the likelihood of a postural source.

In the earliest text, the *Poema de mio Cid*, the single-most frequent verb with *estar* is *catando*, akin to modern Spanish *mirando*, 'looking, watching', with 20% (4/20) of all *estar + -ndo* tokens (including one token with *seer*). Other "watching" verbs in the PMC are *aguardar* 'watch' (verse 1058), *parar mientes* 'gaze' (2218), *curiar & guardar* 'guard and protect' (1566). As shown in Table 29, watching verbs in the PMC add up to 35% (7/20). It is interesting that Salinas (1963) translates *estar catando* twice with a simple form of *mirar* (2059, 3123), and twice as *quedarse mirando* (2, 2439). This *quedarse* 'remain, stay' sense of *estar*, as in *estar los mandó* (2017) — translated by Salinas (1963) as *que parasen los mandó*, by Such and Hodgkinson (1987) as '(he ordered all his men) to remain behind', and by Hamilton and Perry (1975) as 'to halt' — is related to *estar*'s early postural meaning, 'to stand (still)' (Yllera 1980: 29).

In the 13th c. *Estoria de España*, *estar catando* continues to make up a large proportion of all *estar + -ndo*, with 10% (4/39). Here too the meaning seems to be something along the lines of 'stand and look'. In two cases the phrase *grand piec'a* cooccurs, which implies looking fixedly (EE1 5v15, 19r37; see example (4) above). In another example Nero is standing on top of a tower watching Rome burn (example (3.3)).

Even when there is no explicit expression the context seems most compatible with a "stood there and watched" interpretation, as the following examples illustrate. In the first example the Cid stands and surveys things, since what follows is a list of all he sees. In the second example, people stand along a river and watch someone speaking to them as he goes by: *estar* refers to those standing still watching, *andar* refers to the person going by along the river.

(7) *Delos sos oios tan fuerte mientre lorando*
*Tornaua la cabec'a & **estaua los catando***
Vio puertas abiertas & vc'os sin can<n>ados
Alcandaras uazias sin pielles & sin mantos
E sin falcones & sin adtores mudados (PMC, 2)
'Tears streamed from his eyes as he turned his head and **stood looking** at them. He saw doors left open and gates unlocked, empty pegs without fur tunics or cloaks, perches without falcons or moulted hawks.' (Hamilton and Perry 1975:23)

(8) *E ataron le al cuello una muela de brac'o & echaro<n> lo de la puente en el rio. & ando gra<n>d piec'a sobrel agua fablando con lo[^s] q<ue> lo(^s) **estaua<n> catando**.* (EE1- 111v15)
'And they tied a stone to his neck and threw him from the bridge into the river. And he walked for a long while on the water speaking to those who **were (stood there) watching** him'

The meaning here is not really progressive but postural, the subject is literally standing, as indicated by Hamilton and Perry's (1975) translation of the first example. It is unlikely that this postural "stand and do" use is the origin of *estar + -ndo* progressives. *Catando* disappears from Spanish. Modern *estar viendo* and *estar mirando* most likely derive from a more general *estar + -ndo* schema rather than directly from *estar catando* (see Section 5.5.1 on *estar viendo*).

Instead of giving rise to a progressive construction, the early postural "stand and look" use seems to have been taken over by *quedarse viendo* or *mirando* (cf. Yllera 1980: 30). *Quedar*-plus-gerund is quite rare in Old Spanish, with only five cases in our Old Spanish corpus. The earliest examples found by Spaulding (1926: 249–50) occur in the LBA (mid 14th c., verse 833) and *Calila e Digna* (late 14th c. ms.). The frequency of watching verbs in *quedar(se)*-plus-watching verb was high enough in Spaulding's corpus for him to characterize *quedarse mirando* as a "set phrase". In the Mexico City corpus, there are 10 cases of *quedarse + -ndo:* four *viendo* 'seeing' and one *licando* 'seeing', two *cuidando* 'looking after', and one each *llorando* 'crying', *pensando* 'thinking', *platicando* 'chatting'. In the New Mexico corpora (NMmon and NMbil) there are seven cases: five *mirando* (NMCSS#346, NMbil/Vig, NMbil/Bea) and one each *cuidando* 'watching' (NMCSS#202) and *escuchando* 'listening' (NMbil/Fr).

Present-day *quedarse viendo* or *mirando* seems closest to PMC and EE1 *estar catando* 'stand and look fixedly', as shown in the following MexPop example:

(9) *Y lo vi yo, y lo saludé, y **se me quedó viendo**. Pero no me conoció, y dice mi hermana...* (UNAM 1976: 60).
'And I saw him, and greeted him, and **he just stood there staring at me**. But he didn't recognize me, and my sister says...'

In the following New Mexico examples the speakers use *quedarse mirando* to describe the response to the loss of Spanish, or *mexicano*, in the younger generation. The meaning is evidently 'stand (there) and stare'.

(10) *Si lej habla uno en mexicano, responden en inglés. Lo entienden, pero no lo hablan. [...] Y el "Alan" ej pior. [...] A ese le digo, 'Curre y traime una palita pa' tirar tierra, y **j' queda mirándome** y le- y me dice, "Whachou say?"* (NMmon/NMCSS#346)
'If you talk to them in Mexican, they answer in English. They understand it, but they don't speak it. [...] And "Alan" is the worst. [...] To him I'll say "Run and get me a shovel to throw dirt" and **he just stands there staring** and says to me "Whachou say?" '

(11) *Te pones a hablar mexicano no te entienden. Yo mis hijos, él que vino a hablar, pues le hablo mexicano y él está casado con una gringa, no entiende. Me sale con aaa [...] Y yo **me quedo mirándolo**, digo yo "Pues éste, yo lo crié en mi casa, yo le enseñé en mexicano ende chiquito." A todos. No. El habla todo al revés.* (NMbil/Bea)
'You speak in Mexican and they don't understand you. Me, my sons, the one who came here and talked to you, I talk to him in

Mexican, and he's married with a *gringa,* he doesn't understand. He comes out with aaa [...]. And **I just stare at him**, I say to myself, "I raised this one in my house, I taught him in Mexican since he was little." All my children. No. He says everything backwards.'

The substitution of old *estar catando* by *quedarse viendo* or *quedarse mirando*, and of old continuative uses of *ir + -ndo* by *seguir + -ndo*, is an example of a recurring phenomenon in grammaticization. As older constructions are bleached of particular features of meaning, speakers replace them in particular uses with newer, more specific expressions.

4.2.3 Entrenched locative meaning: "waiting" verbs

Since watching verbs do not provide the context for the development of progressive meaning, what about verbs in the "waiting" class? It turns out that waiting verbs are not likely candidates for favoring the conventionalization of *estar + -ndo* as a progressive either.

Esperando 'waiting' appears in the earliest texts and is among the five most frequent *estar + -ndo* main verbs in the Old Spanish corpus, with seven cases (Table 28). Locative meaning is highly compatible with *estar esperando* and it is likely that in early uses *estar* really meant 'be located there'. Waiting verbs such as *esperando* have a 54% average of cooccurring locatives, nearly twice the overall average (Table 20, Chapter 3). Even in the Mexico City corpus *estar esperando* has a higher average of locatives, at 60%. Of ten MexPop tokens, six have a cooccurring locative (*ai*, p. 121, 401; *allá* p. 207, 209; *allí* p. 331; *ahí* p. 418), which suggests that this phrase is still used frequently with locative meaning.[2] Additional evidence for the persistence of locative meaning is provided by clitic climbing figures in MexPop: CC occurred in only two of five possible cases (not counting one case with two clitics), for an average of 40%, while the overall average for *estar + -ndo* is 89%. In the following examples, the locative component is very prominent, whether with a cooccurring locative, as in the first New Mexican example, or without, as in the second Old Spanish one.

(12) Y mi hijo este **estaba esperándome** ahí en el carro, tú sabes. Me tardé mucho pa salire. (NMbil/Bea)
'And my son **was waiting for me** there in the car, you know. It was a long time before I came out.'

(13) *E los quel* **estavan esperando** *por le matar por mandado del rey, desque vieron que non venía...* (Luc XVIII, p.144)
'And those who **were waiting** to kill him on the king's command, when they saw that he did not come...' (Keller and Keating 1977: 85)

In both examples the subject of the following clause comes to the place where the subject of *estar esperando* is located.

If cooccurring locatives occurred more frequently with waiting verbs, watching verbs such as *catando* had a 25% average of cooccurring locatives, lower than the overall average for *estar + -ndo*, at 30% (Table 20). Thus, the frequency of cooccurring locatives for these two classes deviates from the average in opposite directions. The deviation from the average of cooccurring locatives suggests that neither watching nor waiting verbs provided the context in which progressive meaning is conventionalized. If *estar catando* meant 'stand and watch', *estar esperando* meant 'be located and wait' or 'wait in a particular location'. The former really was postural, the latter locative.

It is important that both these classes of verbs have relatively high token/type ratios (Table 29). The waiting class has only two verbs, *esperando* and *atendiendo* (three if we include some cases of *aguardando*), for a token/type ratio of 5.5. *Esperando* is the most frequent, with seven of 11 tokens in this class. The watching class has a lower token/type ratio, at 2.7, but eight of 16 tokens are of one type, *catando*. The high token frequency of *estar esperando* and *estar catando* corresponds to highly entrenched local schemas in the framework of associative network (Bybee 1985, 1998) or cognitive grammar (Langacker 1987) models of representation. In this framework words, phrases, and constructions are all stored in the lexicon, with a degree of strength of representation or entrenchment based on their frequency of occurrence in actual language use.

These two local schemas had different fates, however. *Estar catando* faded from use and the schema representing the "stand and look" or "remain looking" meaning weakened and eventually disappeared, now replaced by *quedarse viendo* or *mirando*. On the other hand, *estar esperando* continued to be used. The entrenched local schema retains the locative component , but at the same time *estar esperando* is associated with a more general *estar + -ndo* schema in which *estar* is bleached of its locative meaning. Thus, both locative and aspectual uses of *estar esperando* are represented.

4.2.4 Subject involvement: talking and "bodily activity" verbs

If neither watching nor waiting predicates provided the context for the development of a more general *estar* + *-ndo* construction, which classes of verbs did? The distribution of main verbs given in Tables 28 and 29 point to "talking" verbs and those grouped together as "bodily activity" verbs. Talking verbs add up to 27% and bodily activity verbs 22% of all *estar* + *-ndo* tokens.

The single-most frequent verb in construction with *estar* in the Old Spanish corpus is *hablando*, with 18 cases, or 11%. Since the second most frequent verbs have eight tokens, or less than half, we can accept that this result is a true reflection of the high token frequency of *estar hablando* in Old Spanish. We may assume that *estar hablando* originates as a locative, given the relatively high frequency of cooccurring locative expressions. There are seven cases of a *con* word or phrase (Section 3.1.2) and three "other" locatives (*ante el pueblo* 'before the people' EE1–74v32, *o* 'where' EE1–194r21, *detrás* 'in back, in corners' Corb p. 195), for a total of 55% (10/18). Overall, talking verbs have cooccurring locatives in 29% of all cases, which is just about average (Table 20). But even when there is no locative in the same clause, locative meaning is part of early *estar hablando*, as shown in the following example:

(14) % *E cuenta ell estoria q<ue> quando gelo el dixo q<ue>* **estauan amos fablando solos** *q<ue> ningun otro no y estaua.* (EE1 19r37)
'And the story goes that when he told him that **that they were (there) together talking alone**, no one else **was there**.'

That *estaban hablando* means that "they were located spatially in the midst of talking" is demonstrated by the immediately following clause, *ningun otro no y estaua* 'no one else was there' with the locative *y* 'there'. Yet we know that the locative component diminishes over time. How might this bleaching occur?

An implication of being located in the midst of an activity is the involvement of the subject in the activity (Bybee et al. 1994:135; see Section 4.3.3 ahead). Since the involvement of the subject in the activity is already part of the meaning of talking and bodily activities, these kinds of verbs are highly appropriate to the *estar* + *-ndo* construction. Bodily activity verbs include some fairly prosaic activities, such as bathing, eating, and sleeping, but most are manifestations of intense emotions, as with crying, laughing, trembling.

Verbs of this kind make up the second largest class in the Old Spanish data, after talking verbs. *Llorando* 'crying' alone is among the five verbs with the highest number of tokens (Table 28).

Talking and bodily activities occur when the subject is relatively still, in one location, not going someplace, as in *ir* + *-ndo*, or moving around, as in *andar* + *-ndo*. At the same time, talking and most bodily activities are not typically associated with a characteristic location. In addition, in these situations the subject is an affected experiencer at least as much as an active agent. The shift from being located in the midst of an activity to being subjectively involved in an activity, without the specific locative component, is most favored when the activity is a uniquely human activity.

Token frequency is important here. *Estar hablando* makes up over 10% of all *estar*-plus-gerund sequences, *estar diziendo* and *estar llorando* another 4% each. As argued in Bybee (forthcoming), frequency of use is the mechanism that propels bleaching. Repetition leads to dulling of the vigor and original meaning of a linguistic expression, as with habituation in cultural practices (Haiman 1994).

Also important is type frequency. If token frequency is a count of the number of occurrences of a construction in running text, type frequency is a count of the number of different lexical items with which the construction is used, in our case, the number of different main verbs appearing in *estar* + *-ndo*. Unlike watching and waiting verbs, talking and bodily activity verb classes have a large number of members that are used with the construction. In addition to *hablar* and *decir*, talking verbs in the Old Spanish corpus include *alabarse* 'boast', *bendezir* 'bless', *castigar* 'advise', *chirlar* 'chirp', *consejar* 'decide', *contar* 'tell', *dar vozes* 'scream', *loar* 'praise', *llamar* 'call', *razonar* 'reason, explain', *regañar* 'quarrel, scold', *rogar* 'implore', *trobar* 'versify' . Bodily activity verbs include *bañarse* 'bathe', *bullir* 'bustle', *callar* 'be silent', *cantar* 'sing', *comer* 'eat', *desbauar* 'drool', *deuanear* 'rave', *dormir* 'sleep', *p/llorar* 'cry', *refusar* 'balk', *reir* 'laugh', *santiguarse* 'cross oneself', *sonrissar* 'smile', *sudar* 'sweat', *sufrir* 'suffer', *temblar* 'tremble', *torçer el rostro* 'turn one's face', *tremer* 'tremble', *yantar* 'eat'. Type frequency is a measure of the productivity of a grammaticizing construction and propels further generalization (Bybee 1995, 1998). As the resulting *estar* + *-ndo* schema is more general or abstract, specific features of meaning are lost and the construction is more grammaticized. It is locative meaning that is lost, since these main verbs refer to human activities where what is important is the subject's involvement, not location.

Based on these results, we may modify the origin of *estar + -ndo* progressives described in (6) as in Figure 6, using another example:

(15) *¡Vet, amigas, lo que faze este omne! ¡Commo quiera que nos mata, sabet que a grant duelo de nos, e por ende **está llorando**!* (Luc, Ex XIII, p.127)
'Look, friends, at this man: although he is killing us, see how sorry for us he feels. **He is weeping** about it!' (Keller and Keating 1977: 75)

a. An agent-**experiencer** (this man)
b. is located spatially (speaker: look there and see)
c. in the midst of (crying is ongoing, in progress)
d. a **human** activity (crying)
e. at reference time (as speaker points to the man)

Figure 6. Original elements of meaning in ESTAR + -NDO progressives (cf. Bybee et al. 1994: 136)

As shown in Figure 5 (Section 4.2.1), *estar + -ndo* then extends to physical activity verbs in which the subject is more of an external agent such as *curar caballos* 'tend horses', *labrar* 'work', *matar* 'kill'. Locative meaning is further eroded with general activity verbs, which refer to activities made up of several more specific sub-activities that may be realized in different locations, such as *hacer bien* 'do good', *librar pleitos* 'provoke quarrels', *servir* 'serve'. In present-day Spanish, *estar* has extended to motion and process verbs, which used to combine exclusively with *ir*. We can represent the generalization of contexts as in Figure 7.

Subject	Location	Time	Verbs
			catando > Ø
			esperando
human experiencer — agent	*en* + LOCATION	at reference time	talking, bodily activities
	con + PERSON		
	aquí, allí	(*siempre*)	physical activities, mental
agent			
		frequently,	general activities
inanimate subject	*ai*, Ø	(experiential) habitual	
			motion, process

Figure 7. Generalization of ESTAR + -NDO contexts

The class of talking verbs continues to be associated with *estar + -ndo* in present-day varieties (cf. Arjona 1991: 119–20; Fernández 1960: 521; Hamplová 1968: 219; Luna 1980: 204). The relative frequency of *estar hablando* actually shows a decrease between the Old Spanish and Mexico City corpus, from 11% (18/165), to 2% (6/340), but *estar platicando* 'be chatting' is more frequent, with 3% (9/340). The relative frequency of *estar diciendo* remains about the same, with 4% (6) cases in OldSp and 3.5% (12) in MexPop. The most dramatic difference between OldSp and MexPop main verbs in construction with *estar* is the high token frequency of general activity verbs *trabajando* 'working', *pagando* 'making payments', *estudiando* 'attending school' (Table 28). In the following chapter (Section 5.2.2) we relate this to newer experiential habitual uses of the construction.

4.3 Experiential meaning (= subject and speaker involvement): "*Ver*" estar + -ndo

In this section I develop the idea that progressives imply a greater degree of subject involvement and a more overt activity (Bybee et al. 1994: 133ff; Hatcher 1952). The Old Spanish data suggest that these meanings are complementary. That is, subject involvement is complemented by speaker involvement and overtness, specifically, the expression of the speaker's view of the situation as personally witnessed or felt. I will further argue that this evidential-like use derives from the locative origin of *estar + -ndo* and, more generally, that a diachronic approach explains the non-aspectual meanings conveyed by progressives.

4.3.1 *Experiential uses*

Mentions of non-aspectual nuances abound in descriptions of *estar + -ndo*. Connotations of personal involvement (Ozete 1983: 76, Parisi 1992: 56), speaker attitude (Zdenek 1972: 448, Westfall 1995: 289, 297–8) or overtness (Fernández 1960; King and Suñer 1980: 226) may be considered expressions of subjectivity, in the broad sense of expression of self and speaker point of view (Finegan 1995). I group these under the heading "experiential" uses, since they seem to be related in conveying speakers' "experiential interpretation" of a situation (Wright 1995: 168, cf. Lyons 1982).

In a very insightful description, Fernández (1960) focused on the contribution of *estar* to the meaning of the construction. Although *estar* precludes motion, it does imply "being here" at one time "and there" at another. Hence the copular use of *estar* with transitory or changing qualities. This sense of inconstancy contributes to the use of *estar* to express "lo sensible, lo inmediato, lo que puede dejar de ser precisamente porque está siendo ahora y aquí" — 'the palpable, the immediate, that which may cease to be precisely because it is being now and here' (Fernández 1960: 512)The affinity between *estar* + *-ndo* and highly perceptible activities observed by Fernández (1960) is akin to Hatcher's (1952: 269–72) idea of overtness in her description of the English Progressive.

Two striking facts about the distribution of *estar* + *-ndo* support this analysis (Fernández 1960: 511, 513). First, *estar* + *-ndo* subjects are overwhelmingly human. In present-day conversational data, the proportion of inanimate subjects is under 10% (see Table 35 for MexPop and Table 44 for the Chihuahua and New Mexico data; in Luna's (1980) educated Mexico City data, inanimate subjects average 5% (24/482)). Human agents and experiencers are congruent with the idea of active involvement. Second, negative polarity cases are largely limited to exclamatory denials of imputations (cf. Hamplová 1968: 219). Negated *estar* + *-ndo* in MexPop is less than 2%. Three of the six tokens are Imperatives, for example, *No estés chillando* 'Don't be crying' (UNAM 1976: 207). Positive polarity is consistent with overtness.

Subject and speaker involvement show up clearly in *estar*-plus-talking verb. Wright (1995: 160) observes that many of the "verbs of report" occurring with the English Progressive are "richly expressive". We saw that this is the case in Old Spanish with verbs such as *dando voces, loando, rogando* 'screaming, praising, imploring'. Yet even with less graphic verbs, *estar* + "talking" may function more as a commentary than a description (cf. Wright 1995: 161). Fernández (1960: 516) reports that second-person interrogative *¿qué estás diciendo?* is about twice as frequent as *¿qué dices?*, both translatable as 'what are you saying?'. The function of the first is "casi exclusivamente expresiva" — 'nearly exclusively expressive', indicating a higher degree of indignation and vehemence (Fernández 1960: 516).

The complementary ideas of active involvement by the subject and overtness from the point of view of the speaker may also correspond to discourse functions. Imperfect *estaba diciendo* 'I was saying' may have a scene-setting and turn-taking discourse function in announcing an elaboration of what the person was saying to follow. Fernández (1960: 515) looks at the distribution of *decir* and *estar diciendo* in the novel *La colmena* by José Camilo Cela and finds that both cases of *estar diciendo* introduce a change of scene in which the reader catches the intimate sayings of a character. In his analysis of oral narratives, Gonzales (1995: 77) observes that Imperfect *estaba* + *-ndo* "appears to be a restart of the original story opening". For British English, Lawrence (1999) reports increased use of past tense *be* + *-ing* to introduce a quote.

In our Chihuahua data, the two most frequent Imperfect *estar* + *-ndo* combinations are *estaba platicando* 'was chatting' with 16% (16/100) and *estaba diciendo* 'was saying', with 14% (14/100). *Estaba hablando* 'was talking' adds another 3%, so that these talking verbs make up 33% of all Imperfect tokens. In contrast, in the Present tense, these three main verbs add up to only 15% (34/224), less than half their relative frequency in the Imperfect. Another difference between Imperfect and Present *estar* + *-ndo* talking verbs is in person/number. *Estaba diciendo* (first-person-singular Imperfect) has 36% (5/14) of Imperfect *estar diciendo* tokens, but *estoy diciendo* (first person singular Present) has only 27% (4/15) of corresponding Present tokens. This set of observations suggests a scene-setting/turn-taking discourse function where *estaba diciendo* says "now you are going to see/hear about this in detail".

4.3.2 Evidentiality: "see" estar + -ndo

Let us now look at the Old Spanish data and the kind of clauses *estar* + *-ndo* occurs in. Table 30 shows the distribution of *estar* + *-ndo* by clause type. The overall frequency of main clause *estar* + *-ndo* seems low, at 50%, but this result is at least in part an epiphenomenon of the written and overwhelmingly narrative character of the texts. Wright (1995: 164), for example, finds that narrative sections of a 17th century English novel have the lowest proportion of main clause (and Present tense) progressives. Strang (1982: 441–2) reports that *be* + *-ing* occurs mostly in relative and temporal or local subordinate clauses in early 18th c. English narrative, though not in dialogue. Thus, the PMC, which was written to be transmitted orally to a wide audience (Deyermond 1971: 45), has the highest proportion of main clause *estar* + *-ndo*, at 85% (17/20). The *Celestina*, which has the highest proportion of dialogue, has the second highest proportion of main clauses, at 61% (19/31).

Table 30. ESTAR + -NDO: Distribution by clause type in Old Spanish

	PMC N	EE1 N	LBA N	Luc N	Corb N	C01 N	OldSp N	Total %
Totals	20	39	22	24	29	31	165	
Main clause	17	10	12	8	14	19	83	50%
(Main, preceding **"ver"**				1	2		3)	
"Ver" *que* 'see that'			1	2	2	1	6	3.5%
"Ocurrió" *que* 'it happened that'		3	1	1	1		6	3.5%
"Dijo" *que* 'said that'		1			1		2	
Other *que*		1				1	2	
Infinitive *estar*				2 (vio)	1	2	5 **(2)**	
Object relative		5(1)	2	4(3)	2(1)	1(1)	14 **(6)**	8.5%
Subject relative	2	2		3	3	1	11	7%
Locative *o* 'where'		6					6	3.5%
Gerund *estando*		7	2	4	3	2	18	11%
Manner (*como* 'as though')		1				2	3	
Reason**		1		1			2	
Time		1	2			2	5	
Other subordinate	1	1					2	
"Ver" total	0	1	3	6	5	2	17	10%

* Bold numbers in parentheses are cases of preceding "ver" in object relative clauses.
** Reason: *por razón que, ca* 'because'; Time: *mientre* 'while', *en cuanto* 'as soon as', *entre tanto que* 'while'; Other: *maguer* 'although', *si* 'if'.

Non-main clause contexts for *estar* + *-ndo* include subordinate clauses headed by *que*, with 10% (16/165). Some of these are closer to main than subordinate clauses, being of the type "it happened that", as in this example with *seer*:

(16) % Otrosi **auino** aq<ue>l anno en una yuueria **q<ue>** un yuuero **seye arando** con los bueyes (EE1 61v22)[3]
'**It happened** that year in a field in the land of Rome **that** a tenant farmer **was plowing** with the oxen'

There are also 15% (25 cases) of non-restricted relatives, 11% (18 cases) of a gerund clause (*estando* + *-ndo*), and 10% (16 cases) of clauses headed by a locative (*o* 'where'), time (*mientras* 'while'), manner (*como* 'as') or "reason" (*ca* 'because') word. The high frequency of subordinate and relative clauses may be taken as a manifestation of the use of *estar* + *-ndo* to establish a "temporal frame" around another situation (Jesperson 1931: 178ff.). In the following example, the talking encompasses the arrival of the dragon.

(17) ***Ellos estando assi fablando****. llego el dragon. e tharc<us> quandol uio. ouo muy grand miedo del.* (EE1–7v45)
'**While they were thus talking**, the dragon appeared and when Tharcus saw it he was very frightened.'

However, if we look more closely at the function of *estar + -ndo* in subordinate and relative clauses we have support for the view that progressives contribute more than aspectual meaning, deriving from their locative origin (Bybee et al. 1994: 135). Related to the subject-is-involved-in-the-activity meaning is the quasi-evidential meaning in third person *estar + -ndo*, where the speaker expresses that the situation is personally witnessed or experienced. This use is shown in example (3.7), repeated here in fuller context:

(18) *Las gentes luego profaçan e dizen: "Tal murió agora. ¡Dios le aya el ánima! ¿**Vistes** que muerte sóbita? Aun agora **estava conmigo fablando**; agora se partió de mí; aun agora le vi pasar por aquí sano e alegre, e fabló conmigo, aun agora salió de su casa..."* (Corb. Quarta parte, Cap. I, p. 244)
'People then boast and say: "So and so died just now. May God have his soul! **Did you see** what a sudden death? Even just now **he was with me chatting**; just now he took leave of me; just now I saw him pass by here healthy and happy, and he chatted with me, just now he came out of his house...'

In this example *estar + -ndo* may be said to introduce a highly perceptible activity (cf. Fernández 1960), indicated explicitly by *vistes* 'did you see'. Furthermore, the speaker, although not the agent of *estar + -ndo*, participates as an active and affected witness, as indicated in this example by the use of first person deictics *conmigo, agora, aquí* —'with me, now, here'.

Fully 10% of all *estar + -ndo* tokens occur in a clause subordinated to *ver* 'see': 14 *que* subordinate clauses or object relative clauses, plus three main clauses with preceding *ver* (Table 30). This is quite a striking result. In contrast, *ir + -ndo* and *andar + -ndo* have 2% each of a clause subordinated to *ver*, with only only five (Table 33) and two cases (Table 39), respectively. The "personally witnessed" use seems to develop in the 14th and 15th century, as shown by the higher proportion of such cases in the *Lucanor* and *Corbacho* (see "Ver" total row in Table 30). The proportion drops in the *Celestina*, but this may be attributed to the higher frequency of main clause *estar + -ndo* in the text.

An example of an object relative clause with preceding *ver* from *Lucanor* is given below:

(19) *E acordándose de quando rico era e solía ser, que agora con fambre e con mengua avía de comer los atramizes, que son tan amargos e de tan mal sabor, començó de llorar muy fieramente, pero con la grant fambre començó de comer los atramizes, e en comiéndolos,* **estava llorando e echava** *las cortezas de los atramizes en pos sí. E él estando en este pesar e en esta coita,* **sintió** *que estava otro omne en pos dél e bolbió la cabeça e* **vio** *un omne cabo dél, que* **estava comiendo** *las cortezas de los atramizes que él echava en pos de sí, e era aquél de que vos fablé desuso.* (Luc., Ex. X, p. 114).

'When he remembered how rich he had been and thought about the way his hunger and his need forced him to eat bitter lentils, which are very astringent and of bad flavor, he began to weep abundantly. Nevertheless, because of his great hunger he began to eat the lentils, all the while **weeping** [Imperfect *estar* + *-ndo*] **and throwing** [simple Imperfect] the hulls behind him. And while he was in this anguish and this dismal mood, he **noticed** that someone was behind him. Now he turned his head and **saw** that this person **was eating** the hulls which he was throwing away.' (Keller and Keating 1977: 66).

This example is quite interesting, on several counts. The first *estar* + *-ndo*, *estava llorando* 'was weeping', expresses the narrator's view of the situation as highly overt or perceptible, as though telling the audience "look, it's as though you can see him crying" (cf. Strang 1982: 449). The second activity of the subject, *echava* 'was throwing', is in a simple verb form, since the picture of the man has already been introduced with *estar* + *-ndo* (there may also be an aspectual difference here, *echava* being more iterative). Support for this analysis is provided by the striking fact that in all five cases in the *Lucanor* where *estar* + *-ndo* and a simple verb form are conjoined by *e* 'and', as in this example, it is always *estar* + *-ndo* which occurs first (Luc. p.73, 114, 153, 214, 246). We saw something similar in (18), where the first *hablar conmigo* 'speak with me' is in an *estar* + *-ndo* form, the second in a simple form. Returning to the present example, in the second sentence, *vio* 'saw' indicates that the subject personally sees the third person agent of *estava comiendo* 'was eating'. The use of *sintió* 'perceived, felt', as well as the context of the whole story, contributes to the sense of this subject's being personally affected by what he sees. On the other hand, while *estava comiendo* 'was eating' may be thought of as a frame around *sintió* and *vio*, and thus as a backgrounded situation, it is foregrounded relative to *echava* 'was throwing', which is in the simple Imperfect form.

Preceding or cooccurring *como* 'as, like' may also be used with *estar + -ndo* to introduce a picture, as though the situation were overt and personally witnessed (cf. King and Suñer 1980b). In the following example, *estar + -ndo* expands on the descriptive adjective *abajadas*, making for a more vivid presentation.

(20) *...sus cexas abaxadas* **como** *de persona que* **está comidiendo** *en algund grand pensamiento.* (Corb., Quarta parte, Cap. II, p. 277)
'...her eyebrows lowered **like** a person who **is pondering** some great thought'

In the next two examples, *estar + -ndo* follows a series of simple verb forms. The situations referred to by *estar + -ndo* are more vivid and foregrounded relative to the simple verb forms, serving to highlight what follows, a direct quote. The use of *estar + -ndo* to introduce a direct quote illustrates what I have called a scene-setting discourse function (Section 4.3.1).

(21) *Que verás los espectantes del Papa las bocas abiertas como lobos en febrero fambrientos. ¿Quándo morrán los beneficiados? ¿Quándo oirán tañer campanas por ellos? Luego corren e buscan quién murió, e si es clérigo benefiçiado; e lo peor que quando alguno está mal /e/ al paso de la muerte,* **están los espectantes rogando** *a Dios: "¡O si muriese en este mes..."* (Corb, Quarta parte, Cap. II, p. 281)
'You'll see the expectants surrounding the Pope with their mouths open like hungry wolves in February. How long will the beneficiaries remain? When will they hear bells tolling for them? Then they run and try to find out who died, and if the person is one of the benefiting clerics; and the worst thing is that when someone is ill and a few steps from death, **there are the expectants beseeching** God: "Oh, if only he would die this month..."'

(22) *buélvese fazia él e face como que le rasca la cabeça, e con los dedos fázele señal de cuernos; pásale la mano por la cara como que le falaga, e pónele el pujés al ojo; abráçale, e **está torçiendo** el rostro, **faziendo garavato** del dedo, **diziendo**: "¡A le he, así se vos tuerçe, don falso viejo..."* (Corb, Tercera parte, Cap. IX, p. 227) 'and she turns toward him and pretends to scratch his head, but makes horns with her fingers. She pretends to pat his cheek, but makes a fig in his eye. She puts her arms around him, but **turns** her face away and **crooks** her finger at him, **saying**: "Upon my word, that's the way it bends, you false old villain..."' (Simpson 1959: 194)

If our analysis is right, a better translation for this *Corbacho* excerpt would be something like 'She puts her arms around him, but all the while she **is turning** her face away, **crooking** her finger at him, **saying**:....'.

Speaker involvement or perception may be measured by several lexical and grammatical indices in the *Celestina*, the text that comes closest to the present-day oral data we will be examining in the following chapter. First, of 31 tokens of *estar* + *-ndo*, eight have a first person subject (2r23, 19v23, 28r20, 38r14, 61v4, 73r22, 75v12, 83r21), three a second person subject (3r28, 37v20, 47v28), and another four a first or second person oblique object or possessive (38r3, 38r26, 54r8, 62v13), for a total of 48% (15/31) on a grammatical-person-index of subject involvement (see Section 5.3.1). Second, of 12 non-main clauses, four are preceded by a matrix perception or "imagination" verb, as in *a **ver** con quien esta hablando mi señora* '**see** who my mistress is talking to' (Act X, 62v13) (also *se me figura que* 'I can almost imagine' Act IV, 32r28; *considerasse* 'contemplating' Act VI, 38r14; *no sabemos ... hablando estan* 'we don't know...I hear voices' Act XIV, 82r8). Third, in three of eight cases of third person singular *estar* + *-ndo* (not including those in "stage instruction" sections), there is a cooccurring descriptive adjective, as in *temblando esta el diablo **como azogado*** 'The crazy devil is trembling **as if he had absorbed mercury vapors**' (Act VI, 36r19– translation by Singleton (1958); also, 11v30, 38r26). I return to subjectivity and experiential uses in Chapter 5.

4.3.3 Subjectivity: pragmatic strengthening?

We have argued throughout for the view that the grammaticization of *-ndo* constructions involves semantic bleaching and formal reduction. Are experiential uses of *estar* + *-ndo*, whether from the point of view of a subject — agent or experiencer, who is actively involved in a situation, or from the point of view of a speaker, who personally witnesses and/or subjectively comments on a situation, a case of pragmatic strengthening?

Traugott (1995) defines subjectification in grammaticization as the development of grammatical means to express speaker belief or attitude. In this process, concrete, lexical, and objective meanings increasingly take on abstract, pragmatic, and interpersonal functions. An example is the development of adversative or concessive meaning from temporal uses in English *while*. Subjectification is viewed as a kind of pragmatic strengthening, in which semantic features lost through bleaching are replaced by more speaker-based meanings via inference. Thus, pragmatic meaning is reanalyzed as semantic (Traugott 1995: 49).

The Old Spanish data examined here suggest that experiential uses of *estar* + *-ndo* are directly related to the locative origin of the construction. Experiential uses may become more prominent as locative meaning is lost, but subject and speaker involvement are carryovers from locative meaning. Location is concrete. If an activity is circumscribed in a particular location and also, necessarily, circumscribed in temporal duration, the participation of the subject must be more intense than if the situation extends indefinitely in time, as with habituals. From the point of view of the speaker, if someone is located somewhere doing something, the situation is viewable. The overt activity meaning is shown by the relatively frequent occurrence of *ver* 'see' *estar* + *-ndo* sequences in the Old Spanish data. Figure 8 diagrams the locative origins of speaker involvement; I return to subject involvement and complete the figure in Chapter 5, Section 5.6.

VIEWABLE (overtness, evidentiality, speaker participation)

CIRCUMSCRIBED IN SPACE (location)

Figure 8. Locative bounding and speaker participation (Locative origins, part I)

The relationship between being located and being engaged in a highly overt or perceptible activity is illustrated nicely in the following example, where *estar*

+ *-ndo* occurs in a *que* clause subordinated to *falló*.

(23) *Quando el Mal vino algre por veer el su fijo quel nasçiera, **falló** que **estava llorando**, e preguntó a ssu madre que por qué **llorava**.*
(Luc, Ex. XLIII, p. 254)
'And when Evil came in joy to see his newborn son, he **found** that he **was crying**, and he asked his mother why he **cried**' (cf. Keller and Keating 1977: 159)

The subject of *falló* 'found' may be said to have "found" — implying a location — and, at the same time, to have "seen" — implying a highly perceptible activity. *Estava llorando* 'was crying' expresses both location ("found") and overt activity ("saw"). The second occurrence of the same predicate, this time in a clause subordinated to *preguntó* 'asked', is in the simple form *llorava*. The difference between the first and second crying situation is not so much aspectual: in both cases the action takes place simultaneously with the moment of reference, the subject is in the process of crying. Rather, the first crying situation has a locative and quasi-evidential or subjectively experienced nuance lacking in the second.

The evidential-like, speaker-involvement use of third person *estar* + *-ndo* is not limited to subordinate or relative clauses, nor is it strictly context-dependent. In the next example, the difference between *estar* + *-ndo* and the simple form again is not aspectual.

(24) -Par<meno>. *escucha escucha sempronio **troba<n>do** esta nuestro amo.*
-Se<m><pronio>. *o hi de puta el trobador. el gra<n> Antipater. Sidonio el gran poeta Ouidio. los quales de improuiso seles venian las razones metrificadas ala boca. si si desos es. trobara el diablo. **esta deuaneando** entre suen~os.*
-Ca<listo>. *corac'o<n> bie<n> se te emplea: que penas & viuas triste: pues tan p<re>sto te ve<n>ciste: d<e>l amor de melibea.*
-Par<meno>. *no digo yo q<ue> **troba**.* (CO1 54r8, Act VIII).
'-*Pármeno*. **Listen, listen,** Sempronio! Our **master's composing** songs. He's a troubadour!
-*Sempronio.* "A troubadour"? Well, he's a hell of a troubadour, if you ask *me*. Do you think he's like the great Antipater of Sidon or Ovid, who could talk in verse without effort! Hell, no. He sounds like the devil. **He's just raving** in his sleep.

>   -*Calisto.* [Sings] [...]
>   -*Pármeno.* He is *too* composing a song.' (Singleton 1958: 136).

Both times that *trovar* 'compose songs' occurs it is asserted that the subject is in the process of composing verses, that is, in both cases the situation is progressive. But *trobando está* expresses a perceptible activity, as indicated by the speaker's (Pármeno's) repetition of *escucha* 'listen'. That the speaker is personally affected by the situation is indicated by the use of a first person possessive with the subject, *nuestro amo* 'our master'. When the second speaker (Sempronio) expresses **his** take on the situation, he also uses *estar* + *-ndo*: "he's just raving in his sleep". The first speaker then asserts, *no digo yo que troba*, literally 'no, I say that he composes'. Since now the situation is not experienced but simply reported on, and it is the second occurrence of the same predicate, the simple verb form is used. This is better reflected in Simpson's (1955: 99) rendition of Parmeno's retort: "Didn't I tell you?". (Note that Singleton's translation "He is *too* composing a song" uses a *be* + *-ing* form for the Old Spanish simple form, since in present-day English the progressive is an obligatory category.)

In the previous section we saw that *estar* + *-ndo* extends to more semantic classes of verbs from an early association with talking and bodily activity verbs referring to uniquely human activities. We have also shown that experiential uses occur at least as early as the 14th century. These results suggest that subjectivity or speaker point of view plays a role in the semantic evolution of *estar* + *-ndo*. There is no reason, however, to attribute experiential uses to a process of pragmatic inference and strengthening. Rather, these are closely related to the original locative meaning of the construction.

4.4 Harmony and generalization: Gradual development *ir* + *-ndo*

In this section we will look at main verbs to show how *ir* + *-ndo* starts out with motion verbs as an harmonic expression and evolves into a general expression of gradual development or, in Olbertz's (1998: 483) terms, "gradual (manner) aspect"

4.4.1 Motion verb harmony

The distribution of *ir* + *-ndo* by main verb classes (Table 31) shows that in earlier texts *ir* most frequently combined with another motion verb such as *corriendo* 'running', *descendiendo* 'descending', *huyendo* 'fleeing', *llegando* 'arriving', *subiendo* 'going up' (cf. Yllera 1980: 60). Combinations of *ir* and a motion verb are harmonic expressions in the sense of Lyons (1977, cf. Bybee et al. 1994: 214, 295).

Table 31. IR + -NDO: Semantic classes of main verbs in Old Spanish

	PMC tk/tp	Apol tk/tp	EE1 tk/tp	LBA tk/tp	Luc tk/tp	Corb tk/tp	C01 tk/tp	OldSp N	total %
Motion	26/14	5/5	43/18	1/1	4/4	2/2	1	82	**30%**
General	9/8	3/3	31/19	3/3	3/3	3/3	2/2	54	**20%**
Process	2/2		15/5	3/3	2/1	1	5/3	28	**10%**
Talking	4/3	2/1	3/3	4/2	5/3	1	8/3	27	10%
Mental activity	2/2	9/6	8/7	2/1	2/2		1	24	9%
Bodily (incl. perception)	3/3	4/4	6/6	3/3		5/5	1	22	8%
Physical activity	8/5	1/1	4/3	4/4	1/1		1	19	7%
Emotion	8/5	2/2	2/2	1/1				13	5%
Aspectual ('begin, end')	2/2		2/1		1/1			5	2%

Ir has quite a general directional movement meaning, which has allowed it to grammaticize in other constructions, such as the *ir + a +* Infinitive future. *Ir* has such a general meaning that there are examples of copulative uses in the earliest texts, for example,

(25) *Et estonces priso alli Julio cesar los nietos de ponpeyo el grand. [...] & mando los matar; & fuesse luego a roma. &' **yua muy loc'ano** ademas. por tales tierras [...]. Et los Romanos quando lo sopiero<n>. [...] touiero<n> q<ue> la loc'ania q<ue> el yua toma<n>do ademas. por las bien andanc'as q<ue> auie; q<ue> no<n> podrie recodir a bien ni pora ellos ni pora el.* (EE1–57v82) 'And then Julius Cesar captured the grandsons of Pompey the great. [...] And he gave the order that they be killed, and then went off to Rome. And he paraded with great pride [**went vigorous, proud**] as he traveled through those lands. And when the Romans found this out [...] they considered that the pride that he increasingly displayed because of his lucky ventures could not come to a good end either for them or for him'

Given that the directional motion meaning of *ir* was already bleached, it is not surprising that it would combine with more specific directional motion verbs (cf. Bybee's forthcoming study of English *can*). In this context *ir*'s meaning would be further bleached, and what probably began as a manner adverbial became the main verb (Torres Cacoullos 1999a: 35; see also, Heine 1993: 36 on "manner schemas"). This is shown clearly in cases of *ir* plus *viniendo* 'coming', which literally means the opposite of *ir*.

(26) *E depues **fueron uiniendo** por la mar fasta q<ue> llegaron a espanna a aquel logar o es agora bayona.* (EE1–8v6)
'And then they came [literally: **went coming**] by sea until they reached Spain, at that point where Bayona is today.'

In this example the locative *por la mar* 'by sea' and the time expression *fasta que* 'until' may be interpreted as referring either to *ir* or *venir*, or, most likely, to both. The context is consistent with both the physical motion meaning of *ir* and the "gradual development" meaning of *ir* + *-ndo*.

When *ir* combines with itself it is more patent that its contribution is primarily aspectual. Indeed, as shown in Table 32, *yendo* 'going' is among the five most frequent main verbs in the Old Spanish corpus, with 3% (8/274), of all *ir* + *-ndo*.

(27) *E desi **fuesse yendo** contra Roma.* (EE1–109r37)
'And from there he went (literally: **went going**) against Rome.'

In the next example the subject *el pleito* 'dispute, affair' is inanimate, so that physical motion is precluded and the only possible meaning is a future-projecting gradual development sense.

(28) *E quando vos e los vuestros viéredes a los vuestros contrarios más esforçados, tanto desmayaredes más, e así **irá yendo el pleito** fasta que non vos finque cosa en el mundo;* (Luc., Ex. XII, p.125).
'For the more you and your followers see your enemies exerting themselves, the greater will be your dismay, and thus **will the affair progress** (literally: **will go going**) until you have nothing left in the world;' (Keller and Keating 1977: 73).

The proportion of motion verbs in *ir* + *-ndo* appears to decrease steadily in the Old Spanish corpus, from 40% (26/64) in the *Poema de mio Cid* and 38% (43/114) in the *Estoria de España*, to 17% (2/12) in the *Corbacho* (Table 31).

Nevertheless, *ir + -ndo* is still associated with motion verbs in present-day varieties. The difference in the proportion of *ir + -ndo* tokens with a motion verb between the Old Spanish corpus as a whole, at 30% (82/274), and the Mexico City corpus, at 24% (35/146), is not statistically significant, though the difference between the 12th–13th c. texts PMC, EE1 and MexPop, is (p < 0.05). Notice that the particular collocation *ir yendo* declines, from 3% in OldSp to less than 1% in MexPop, with only one token (Table 32). The decline of *ir yendo* is made up for by the rise of *estar yendo* (Table 28), which we come back to in Chapter 5 (Section 5.4).

Table 32. IR +-NDO: Most frequently occurring main verbs (gerunds)

	PMC N	Apol N	EE1 N	LBA N	Luc N	Corb N	C01 N	OldSp N	OldSp %	MexPop N	MexPop %
creciendo 'growing'	1		10	1	2		1	15	5%	10	7%
llegando 'arriving'	4		4		1			9	3%	3	2%
yendo 'going'		1	6		1			8	3%	1	<1%
diciendo 'telling'	1	2	1	3	2			9	3%	0	0
hablando 'talking'	1					6		7	2.5%	0	0
explicando 'explaining'								0	0	4	3%
haciendo(se) 'becoming'			5			2	3	10	4%	5	3%
entendiendo 'understanding'	3			2	1			6	2%	0	0

4.4.2 Process verbs, telicity

Process verbs are dynamic verbs that describe a change of state (Bybee et al. 1994: 55). Examples from Old Spanish are *al(l)ongando* 'growing long' (PMC 1238, Luc. p. 282, 292) *calentando* 'warming up' (LBA 970), *decayendo* 'decaying' (Corb. p.135), *envegeciendo* (EE1 6v43, 109r94) and *haciéndose vieja* (C01 34v8, 56v14), both translatable as 'getting old'. Process verbs are highly compatible with a gradual development meaning. In the following example, both the main verb *decayendo* 'decaying' and the time expression *de día en día* 'day by day' contribute to the sense of a gradually developing situation; *hasta venir a la muerte* 'until he reaches death' adds a sense of projection toward the future, or gradual development toward some built-in end point.

(29) *e de día en día se va decayendo fasta venir a la muerte* (Corb., Parte I-Cap. XXXVII, p. 135)
'and that gradually day by day he decays until death overtakes him' (Simpson 1959: 87)

Mental activity verbs in *ir* + *-ndo* are also consistent with inceptive and/ or gradual development uses. *Ir* + *-ndo* mental verbs are more telic than *estar* + *-ndo* mental verbs. Telic situations, or Vendler's (1967) "accomplishments", are those that have an inherent end-point (Comrie 1976: 44). Although there are three cases of atelic *pensando* 'thinking', which we saw is associated with *estar* (Section 3.2), these all occur in the earliest texts and have cooccurring items associated with *ir* + *-ndo*, such as a *por* + LOC locative and *assi* 'thus', as in *por todas sus tierras assi lo yuan penssando* 'throughout his lands, everyone considered that...' (PMC 2983; other examples in Apol. 181b, EE1–111v99).

The most frequent *ir* + *-ndo* mental verb is *entendiendo*, with 2% (6/274). A routinized phrase seems to have been first-person-Present *vo entendiendo*, literally, 'I go understanding', meaning "I'm beginning to understand" (Yllera 1980: 66; examples in Apol. 233d, LBA 970d, 1708a). Other telic mental verbs in *ir* + *-ndo* are *adevinar* 'think up, come up with'(Apol. 506d), *conocer* 'get to know' (EE1–46v12), and *recordar* 'recover consciousness, remember' (PMC 2790, C01–26r10).

(30) **Van Recordando** *don eluira & don<n>a sol*
Abrieron los oios & viero<n> afelez munoz (PMC 2790)
'Doña Elvira and doña Sol **began to recover consciousness** and opening their eyes, they saw Féliz Muñoz' (Hamilton and Perry 1975: 169)

ya **me voy recordando** *della vna buena piec'a:* (CO1–26r10, Act IV)
'**I'm beginning to remember** her. A pretty piece of goods!' (Simpson 1955: 48)

The inceptive reading of Present-tense *ir recordando* shown in the English translations may be consistent with gradual development toward a culminating point, as in the paraphrase given by Roca Pons (1958: 67) for *ir viendo* (literally: 'go seeing') or *ir entendiendo* (literally: 'go understanding'): "voy acercándome a una visión o comprensión perfecta" — 'I gradually approach a perfect vision or understanding'. It is interesting that *sabiendo*, a stative verb, occurs in *ir* + *-ndo* (two tokens, both in EE1, 82v41 and 82v46–see example (3.10)), and takes on a dynamic, telic, "finding out" meaning (both examples are in the Preterite, Preterite *supe* often means "find out", cf. Bolinger 1963). Telicity suits *ir* + *-ndo*'s meaning of inceptiveness and/or gradual development toward a goal or end point (see Squartini 1998: 249–78 for an interesting discussion on the link between directional movement and telicity).

4.4.3 "Manner" expressions

We saw earlier that certain kinds of locatives and time adverbials cooccurring with *ir + ndo*, such as *de...en...* 'from...to...' and *poco a poco* 'little by little', may indicate a gradually developing situation (Chapter 3, Sections 3.1.3 and 3.4). "Manner" expression *assi* 'thus' may also indicate gradual development when it refers to a series of situations that occur in tandem. *Assi* cooccurs frequently with *ir + -ndo* in the earlier two-thirds of the corpus, with 15 cases, or an average of 6% (PMC-3, EE1-5, LBA-1, Luc-6). In the following example, *fueron diziendo* 'they went telling' is a gradual process of the word getting out. *Assi* refers to the series of individual actions of telling, first by *el negro*, then by *otro que lo oyó* 'another person who heard it', which together make for a gradual "telling" process.

(31) *Desque el negro esto dixo, otro que lo oyó dixo esso mismo, e assí lo **fueron diziendo** fasta que el rey e todos los otros perdieron el reçelo de conosçer la verdat e entendieron el engaño que los burladores avían fecho.* (Luc, Ex. XXXII, p.216)
'But once the Negro had said this, another person who heard it said the same thing, and **soon everyone was saying** it, until the monarch and everyone else ceased to be afraid of knowing the truth and they understood the deceit which the tricksters had performed.' (Keller and Keating 1977: 133)

Subject pairs such as *el negro...el otro* in the above example are highly compatible with gradual development meaning. An even better example is the following, with three subject pairs:

(32) *Connocieron se **ell hermano all hermano** & **el padre al fijo**. & **cada uno a so parient**. E pues que se **fuero\<n\> co\<n\>nociendo** & uieron quamanno era el debdo entrellos. entendieron q\<ue\>...* (EE1- 46v12)
'**Brother and brother** met each other, **father and son**, and **every one his relative**. And as they **got to know each other** (lit: went knowing) and saw how great was their duty to each other, they

understood that...'.

I return to a discussion of the interaction between noun number and verb aspect in relation to plural objects in *andar* + *-ndo* (Section 4.6.1).

Another contextual element contributing to gradual development meaning is a "manner" clause headed by *(así) como* 'as thus', *cuanto más* 'the more', or *mientras más* 'the more', as in *quanto los mas yuan firiendo tanto mas se afazien a ello* 'the more they wounded, the more they became accustomed to it' (EE1–47r95). As shown in Table 33, this is the most frequent subordinate clause type for *ir* + *-ndo*, with 6% (15/248). It seems that these clauses have more of a temporal-aspectual than a strictly manner-descriptive function, serving to connect two situations that occur in tandem. Since the two situations feed each other, they may both be viewed as gradually developing. The following examples illustrate:

(33) a. *&′ cuemo yua subiendo en edat; **assi** iua creciendo en ell la apostura & la nobleza.* (EE1–84v55)
'and **as** he got older (literally: went rising in age), **thus** his gracefulness and nobleness grew (literally: went growing).'

b. *com<m>o me yua calentando **ansy** me yua sonrriendo* (LBA 970b)
'while I was warming up, I smiled to myself' (Willis 1972: 260)

c. *...un omne paró sus redes a las perdizes; e desque las perdizes fueron caídas en la ret, aquel que las caçava llegó a la ret en que yazían las perdizes; e **assí commo** las iva tomando, matávalas e sacávalas de la red, ...* (Luc, Ex. XIII, p.127)
'...a man put out his net for partridges, and when they had fallen into it, he came up to the net where the partridges lay. And as soon as he caught them, he killed them and took them out of the net.' (Keller and Keating 1977: 75)

The translations in (b) (Willis 1972) and (c) (Keller and Keating 1977) do not quite capture the gradual development meaning added by *ir* + *-ndo* and *como...así* to continuousness. Jauralde's (1988: 309) Spanish translation of the *Libro de Buen Amor* verse seems better: "según iba entrando en calor, así iba sonriendo", or, 'as I got warmer, the more my smile grew'.

In some cases gradual development may be inferred pragmatically. In the next example, the subjects are going down a staircase. Staircases have steps,

Frequency effects and layering in the domain of progressive aspect 149

therefore the descending is a gradual process (compare example (3.41), from Talmy 1991: 493). The locative, too, is of the *por* + LOC type indicating a fairly extensive dimension-path along which a subject moves, which we saw earlier is consistent with a gradually developing *ir* + *-ndo* situation (Section 3.1.3).

(34) *E desque esto ovo dicho, llamó al deán; e entraron entramos por una escalera de piedra muy bien labrada e **fueron descendiendo** por ella muy grand pieça, en guisa que paresçía que estavan tan vaxos que passaba el río de Tajo por çima dellos.* (Luc, Ex. XI, p.118)
'After saying this, he summoned the dean, and they went down an elaborately carved stone staircase, and **descended** (went descending) for such a distance that it seemed as though they were down far enough to be below the river Tagus.' (Keller and Keating 1977: 69)

Table 33. IR + -NDO: Distribution by clause type in Old Spanish

	PMC	EE1	LBA	Luc	Corb	CO1	OldSp N	Total %
Main	56	69	17	9	9	8	168	68%
Ver que, como 'see that, how'	1	3				1(*oir*)	5	2%
"Ocurrió" *que* 'it happened that'		4		1			5	2%
"Mandó" *que* 'ordered that'		2			1		3	
"Creer, decir" *que* 'think, say that'				1	2	3	6	2%
Subjunctive *que*				2		1	3	
Object relative	1	6	2		1	2	12	5%
Subject relative	1	2			1		4	
Desque 'since'		10		1		1	12	5%
Other							16	6%
"Manner"	1	6	2	3		3	15	6%
(*así*) *como, quanto — mientras más*								

* "Ocurrió" *que* includes 2 cases of *de guisa que* (EE1–6v43, 8r7); "Subjunctive" *que* is *en cuidado…que* (Luc p.160), *era bien que* (Luc p.161), *que por los sanctos de dios…* (C01 78v); "Other" includes: 3 Infinitival *ir* (all in EE1), 2 locative *do, o* (PMC, EE1), 6 *yendo* (all in EE1), 4 "reason" *ca, pues que* (2 each in PMC, EE1) and 1 *maguer* (EE1).

4.4.4 Routinization of IR CRECIENDO

The single-most frequent *ir* + *-ndo* main verb in the Old Spanish corpus is the prototypical process verb *crecer* 'grow', with 15 tokens, or 5% (Table 32). *Creciendo* does not occur at all with either *estar* or *andar* in this corpus. In the Mexico City corpus, there is one case of *estar creciendo*, but ten cases of *ir creciendo*, or 7% of all *ir* + *-ndo* tokens in that corpus. *Ir creciendo* occurs so frequently that it has largely become an automatized, routine collocation. It often lacks the more specific gradual-development meaning, illustrated by the use of "steadily" in the English translation of the first example, and simply expresses a continuous process of growing, as in the second example.

(35) *Crecʾi[^e]ndo ua ([^3en]) Riq<ue>za [^3a] myo cʾid el de biuar* (PMC 1200)
'the Cid's riches **were steadily mounting**' (Hamilton and Perry 1975: 87)

(36) *la llaga va crezʾjendo d<e>l dolor no<n> mengua nada* (LBA 597)
'the wound **is growing**, in its pain it does not lessen at all' (Willis 1972: 162)

An indication of the bleaching of *ir creciendo* is the reduplication of the gerund or the entire phrase to specify more of a gradually developing as opposed to simply continuous process, as in the following Mexico City examples (cf. Arjona Iglesias 1990: 127, note 43):

(37) a. *Y bueno...fui creciendo, creciendo. Trabajador, ¿no? Porque, eso sí, ese orgullo tengo de que...que crecí ya que [...] m' incontré competente;* (UNAM 1976: 138)
'And, well...I kept (steadily/little by little) growing (lit: **went growing, growing**). (Until I became a) hard worker, right? Because, yes, I am proud that...I grew up, that [...] I was able to make it'

b. *y fui creciendo, fui creciendo, fui creciendo; grande.* (UNAM 1976: 200)
'and I kept growing (steadily/little by little, until I was) grown up (literally: **went growing, went growing, went growing**)'

Frequency effects and layering in the domain of progressive aspect 151

The skewed distribution of *creciendo*, which is associated with *ir*, and of *hablando, platicando, diciendo*, which are associated with *estar*, clearly reflects distinct sources and grammaticization paths (retention). At the same time, the aspectual meaning of the two constructions may be more or less the same, that is, progressive or continuous (bleaching along parallel paths and layering in the same domain).

Summarizing from above, we have seen that Old Spanish *ir + -ndo* has three sets of uses (cf. Yllera 1980: 70–71; Menéndez Pidal 1964, I: 361–2): (1) with *ya* 'already', *desque* 'since', *hasta que* 'until' as an inceptive and a continuative, the latter use taken over by *seguir + -ndo* (Section 3.4.1); (2) with motion verbs, as an harmonic movement expression; and (3) with process verbs, *por* 'along' locatives, *de..en* 'from...to' expressions, *poco a poco* 'little by little' as a gradual development continuous. Given these multiple uses, the emergence of a general *ir + -ndo* future-projecting gradual development schema may be described as a generalization from three separate constructions in different contexts (cf. Bybee's forthcoming study of *can*; Israel's 1996 study of the *way*-construction). This is diagrammed in Figure 9.

(1) IR(SE) + *ya, desque, hasta que*, etc.   = inceptive and continuative
(2) IR + specific motion verb (e.g. *corriendo*)   = harmonic expression
     ↓   ↓
     IR + general motion verb (e.g. *yendo*)   = gradual development
(3) IR + process (telic) verb (e.g. *creciendo*) +
     poco a poco, de...en... , como...así.., etc.. = gradual development

⇒   IR + -NDO   = future-projecting gradual development toward an end-point

Figure 9. Emergence of gradual development IR + -NDO construction

The resulting general *ir + -ndo* construction is composed of the following slots:

Subject	Location &	Time	Manner	Tense	Verb classes
human agent	*por* + LOC	*ya*	*poco a poco*	Present	motion
| &	*de...en...*	*desde, hasta*	*conforme*, etc.	Preterite	process
inanimate subject	|	|		|	general activ.
	aquí, ai	Ø		etc.	

Figure 10. Slots in IR + -NDO construction (IR + -NDO contexts)

4.5 Frequency constraints on generalization

An unanswered question left from Chapter 2 has to do with the asymmetry between *estar* and *ir* in the pace of formal reductive change. For *ir* + *-ndo*, by the time the earliest available Old Spanish texts were written, overall clitic climbing frequencies were already high and preposed clitic position was the most frequent. In contrast, for *estar* + *-ndo* there was a big jump between the Old Spanish and Mexico City corpora, both in overall CC frequencies and preposed position (Section 2.4.1). This difference in pace, slower for *ir* and faster for *estar*, also showed up in the decrease in the average of intervening open class material (Section 2.3.1). We hypothesized that even though *ir* + *-ndo* was more grammaticized at the time the earliest Old Spanish texts were written, *estar* + *-ndo* catches up and eventually outpaces it.

Based on these results, we would expect the same pattern with respect to indices of semantic reduction (bleaching), that is, smaller changes for *ir* + *-ndo* than *estar* + *-ndo*. How might we measure bleaching? The more productive and general a construction, the fewer cooccurrence restrictions will apply. If we compare cooccurrence with main verb classes, we see that *ir* + *-ndo* adds no new verb classes between the Old Spanish and Mexico City corpora. *Ir* + *-ndo* has a broad distribution already in the *Poema de mio Cid* (Table 31). In contrast, *estar* + *-ndo* shows a clear pattern of gradually spreading from talking and bodily activities to physical activities and, in MexPop, adds motion and process verbs (Tables 28, 29 and Figure 5). Let us now look at tense forms and subjects. It turns out that the generalization of *ir* + *-ndo* is slower than that of *estar* + *-ndo* on both counts: the expansion to more tenses and the increase in inanimate subjects.

First, *ir* + *-ndo* is quite broadly distributed over different tenses even in the earliest texts, as shown in Table 34. The *Poema de mio Cid* already has six, and *Estoria de España* eight, of the nine tenses *ir* + *-ndo* covers by the time of the later Old Spanish texts. Added in MexPop is the Present Perfect, as in *he ido viviendo* 'I have been (literally: gone) living' (UNAM 1976: 197). In contrast, the expansion of *estar* + *-ndo* to different tense forms in Table 34 follows a fairly neat diagonal line, with new forms being added over time. In the 13th c. (*Estoria de España*), *estar* + *-ndo* has Present, Imperfect, and Preterite forms (also gerund forms, as in *estando catandolos* 'while he was (stood there) watching them', which are rare in present-day Spanish). By the 15th c. (*Corbacho* and *Celestina*), Infinitive, Conditional, Future, Subjunctive

(Present and Past), Imperative, and Present Perfect have been added.

Another difference in pace of change shows up in the ratio of Imperfect to Preterite forms. This changes dramatically for *estar + -ndo*, from 63/6 = 10.5 in OldSp, to 59/36 = 1.6 in MexPop. In contrast, the ratio (in favor of the Preterite) remains fairly constant for *ir + -ndo*, with 104/60 = 1.7 in OldSp and 22/11 = 2 in MexPop.

Second, *ir + -ndo* has a relatively high proportion of inanimate subjects to begin with (Table 35). Inanimate subjects, for example, *aquel puerto* 'that port' (EE1–32r87, example (3.36)) average 10% (6/62) in the *Poema de mio Cid* and 9% (22/247) overall in the Old Spanish corpus. The average rises to 26% (38/146) in MexPop. In contrast, *estar + -ndo* has no inanimate subjects at all in 167 OldSp tokens. There are two tokens with a metonymic human

Table 34. ESTAR, IR + -ndo : Tenses

	PMC N	Apol N	EE1 N	LBA N	Luc N	Corb N	C01 N	OldSp N	total %	MexPop N	%
				ESTAR + -NDO							
Present	8	1	5	13	1	17	19	64	**38%**	202	60%
Imperfect	12	1	25	3	17	5	0	63	**38%**	59	17%
Gerund			7	2	4	3	2	18	11%	0	0%
Preterite			2	1	1		2	6	**4%**	36	11%
Infinitive				2		2	2	6	4%	24	7%
Conditional				1			1	2		0	
Future					1	1		2		0	
Present Subjunctive						1		1		8	2%
Imperfect Subjunctive							3	3		0	
Imperative							1	1		3	
Present Perfect							1	1		6	
				IR + -NDO							
Preterite	1	19	68	3	9	1	3	104	**38%**	22	**15%**
Present	39	2	4	6	2	9	13	75	**28%**	93	64%
Imperfect	17	4	29	7	2		1	60	**22%**	11	7%
Infinitive	1		3					4		11	7%
Imperative	1	1	1	3				6		1	
Future	2		1	2	4			9	3%	0	
Gerund			6					6		0	
Imperfect Subjunctive			2		1		1	4		1	
Present Subjunctive					2	1		3		3	
Present Perfect										4	

subject, *Affrica* (EE1–158v89, see example (3.25)) and *su cora'con* 'his heart' (Co1–32r28) and seven with an animal subject, *el asno* 'the ass', *la golondrina* 'the swallow', *el lobo* 'the wolf', *el gallo* 'the rooster' (all in the LBA, 239, 750, 766, 1387), *la(s) corneja(s)* 'the crow(s)' (Luc XXI, p.157), and *dos anadones* 'two ducks' (Corb, Part Three, IX, p. 223). In MexPop there are 18/340 tokens with an inanimate subject, or 5%. For example,

(38) a. *se está poniendo **la cosa** mas dura* (UNAM 1976: 135)
'**things** are getting more difficult'
b. *¿Está funcionando **la grabadora**?* (UNAM 1976: 325).
'Is **the tape recorder** working (running)?'

There are also ten cases of an inanimate subject with a human dative, as in[4]

(39) a. ***me** está pasando algo **a mí*** (UNAM 1976: 75)
'something is happening **to me**'
b. *se **nos** está haciendo tarde* (UNAM 1976: 111)
'it is getting late on/**for us**'

Included are four tokens with *gustar*, as in *Me está gustando (andar a la moda)* 'I'm liking it (dressing in fashion)' (UNAM 1976: 80). If these are added in, the inanimate total goes up to 28, or 8%. True, the average occurrence of inanimate subjects is still lower for *estar* than *ir* + *-ndo*. What is important here is the pace of change: *estar* goes from zero to 5%, *ir* from 9% to 26%.

In short, by the measures of expansion to new verb classes, spread to more tenses, and increase in inanimate subjects, changes between OldSp and MexPop are smaller for *ir* than *estar*. With respect to semantic evolution, *ir* + *-ndo* appears to have traveled less distance along the grammaticization path than *estar* + *-ndo*. Gradual development (*va creciendo* 'is growing') seems closer to the original directional movement meaning of *ir* + *-ndo* than habitual (*está trabajando* 'is working') or frequentative (*está yendo diario* 'is going daily') is to *estar* + *-ndo*'s original locative meaning. Why should *ir* + *-ndo* show a slower rate of change — both in form and in function — than *estar* + *-ndo*?

The answer suggested by the data points to the role of frequency in constraining reductive change in grammaticizing constructions. It is precisely differences in the rate of frequency increases that distinguish *ir* + *-ndo* and *estar* + *-ndo*. Let us look first at token frequency, measured per 10,000 words of text. Table 36 repeats Table 12 (Chapter 2, Section 2.5) and adds figures

Frequency effects and layering in the domain of progressive aspect 155

Table 35. *ESTAR, IR + -NDO: Animacy of subject*

	ESTAR + -NDO									MexPop	
	PMC N	Apol N	EE1 N	LBA N	Luc N	Corb N	C01 N	OldSp total N	%	N	%
Human	20	2	38	18	22	28	30	158	95%	308	91%
Human metonymic			1				1	2		1	
Human dative							0	0		10	3%
Animals				4	2	1		7	4%	1	
Inanimate								**0**	**0**	**18**	**5%**

Non-human: EE1: 158v89; LBA 239, 750, 766, 1387; Luc p.157(2); Corb p.223; C01 (32r28).

	IR + -NDO								MexPop	
	PMC N	EE1 N	LBA N	Luc N	Corb N	C01 N	OldSp total N	%	N	%
Human	49	100	20	13	11	15	208	84%	102	70%
Human metonymic	1	1				3	5	2%	3	2%
Human dative	6	2					8	3%	3	2%
Animals				1	2	1	4		0	
Inanimate	6	11	1	3		1	**22**	**9%**	**38**	**26%**

Non-human: PMC 323, 569, 940–1837–2985–3603 (*va pesando*), 1154–1156–1206 (*sonando van las nuevas*), 1200, 1238, 2276, 2762; EE1–8r7, 24v21, 25r23, 32r87, 45r71, 45v97, 46r66, 62r72, 83r11, 84r28, 84v55, 108v76, 118r22, 135r31; LBA 597, 1292; Luc p.111(2), 125, 152, 160; Corb.p.216; C01–21r23, 39r8, 65v10, 81r7.

from educated capital-city (*habla culta*) data (Clegg and Rodríguez 1993) and educated Madrid data (Olbertz 1998), the written Essays corpus, and finally New Mexico monolingual and bilingual data. Comparing Old Spanish and Mexico City figures, the token frequency of *ir + -ndo* increases from 4.7 to 8.4, a 79% increase. The *habla culta* corpus shows a smaller increase, at 6.5, while the Madrid corpus shows a slight decrease, at 4.3. In contrast, the smallest increase in the token frequency of *estar + -ndo* between OldSp and a present-day oral corpus is 510% for Madrid (from 2.9 to 17.7). Things are somewhat modified in the written data. Keniston's (1937a, 1937b) figures for 16th and early 20th c. prose show only a 64% increase for *estar + -ndo* (from 3.1 to 5.1), compared with a 75% increase for *ir + -ndo* (from 3.6 to 6.3). However, it is clear from figures for the Essays corpus that there are bigger differences between written and oral varieties for *estar* than for *ir*. The increase between Essays and MexPop is 940% (from 1.9 to 19.7) for *estar* but only 210% (from 2.7 to 8.4) for *ir*.

Table 36. Token frequency of -ndo constructions (per 10,000 words)

Corpus	Word count	ESTAR	IR	ANDAR	Other*	Total
OldSp	580,000	2.9	4.7	2.0	0.96	10.6
16th c. prose	300,000	3.1	3.6	1.0	0.43	8.2
Early 20th c.	600,000	5.1	6.3	0.05	2.3 (*seguir*)	16.4
MexPop	172,700	19.7	8.4	5.1	4.2	37.5
Habla culta	1,300,000	23.6	6.5	0.04	2.4 (*seguir*)	33.9
Madrid	148,200	17.7	4.3	0.07	1.47	23.5
Essays	376,300	1.9	2.7	0.08	2.1 (*seguir*)	7.4
NMmon**	34,900	10.6	4.0	4.0	3.15	21.8
NMbil**	49,700	23.5	1.2	3.2	1.2	29.2

*   See list of "other" auxiliaries in Tables 26 and 27. Madrid "other" includes *acabar* (0.13), *quedar(se)* (0.13), *seguir* (0.81), *terminar* (0.27), *venir* (0.13).
** The figures for NMmon and NMbil are based on a smaller corpus of 15 and 11 speakers, respectively, for whom I could calculate a total word count.

Second, as we saw at the beginning of the chapter, the relative frequency of the auxiliaries is reversed. The pattern of increasing relative frequency for *estar* + *-ndo* and decreasing relative frequency for *ir* + *-ndo* over time is fairly uniform across all the data sets in Table 27 (Section 4.1). An exception is the Essays corpus, but even here the gap between *estar* and *ir* has narrowed.

Spanish *-ndo* constructions provide evidence in favor of the hypothesis that frequency increases, rather than being the result or a mere concomitant of semantic generalization, are an active constraining force. That is, one way of looking at the relationship between token frequency and grammaticization is to view semantic bleaching as leading to frequency increases: as morphemes become less lexical and more grammatical, bleaching or loss of specific features of meaning enables them to occur in more contexts (Bybee et al. 1994: 8). However, differences in the pace of reduction in *estar* + *-ndo* and *ir* + *-ndo* suggest that frequency itself may constrain formal and semantic change.

We have seen that on a number of measures *ir* + *-ndo* was more grammaticized than *estar* + *-ndo* at the time of the earliest Old Spanish texts. If frequency increases were a result of semantic bleaching, then *ir* + *-ndo* should have continued to lead the way in token and relative frequency. This is not what happens. True, the token frequency of both *estar* + *-ndo* and *ir* + *-ndo* rises over time, as expected. But, comparing the two constructions, we see that token frequency increases for *ir* + *-ndo* are much smaller (Table 36) and that the frequency of *ir* + *-ndo* relative to other auxiliaries actually declines

(Table 27), as *estar* + *-ndo* has expanded to cover ever more territory in the domain of imperfective aspect. And as the pace of frequency increases has been slower relative to *estar* + *-ndo*, so has the pace of generalization for *ir* + *-ndo* compared with *estar* + *-ndo* been slower — whether the pace of formal reduction, as measured in clitic climbing frequencies or the average occurrence of intervening material, or the pace of semantic reduction, as measured in the number of tenses or the average occurrence of inanimate subjects. Thus, a slower rate of frequency increases corresponds to a slower generalization process — or even the detention of generalization, as the absence of new verb classes for *ir* + *-ndo* may indicate.

This result is not meant to contradict the generally accepted unidirectionality hypothesis in grammaticization (Hopper and Traugott 1993: 94 ff.), since there is no reversal in the process of reductive change. The question here is that of the **pace** of reduction, which, our results suggest, is constrained by the **rate** of frequency increases. Our findings provide additional evidence for the active role frequency of use plays in propelling the changes that occur in grammaticization (Bybee forthcoming; Bybee and Thompson 1997).

Frequency effects may operate through priming. It is likely that frequency increases of *estar* + *-ndo* are related to the expanding use of *estar* in numerous constructions, for example, in copula plus descriptive adjective contexts, where *estar* has extended its uses to the detriment of *ser* (cf. Gutiérrez 1992). One way to test this hypothesis is by looking at priming effects, that is, does prior use of *estar* (in another construction) favor the occurrence of *estar* + *-ndo*? If, as we expect, *estar* + X (X = adjective, past participle, locative, etc.) primes *estar* + *-ndo*, in a network-type model as described in Bybee (1998), *estar* + *-ndo* would be associated with a more general, abstract *estar* + X schema. In such an abstract schema, *estar* is more semantically reduced. Initial evidence for a link between frequency and priming is provided by our findings for clitic climbing in formal texts, where lower construction frequency, in particular, a higher proportion of lone-standing gerunds, corresponds to less clitic climbing (see Chapter 2, Section 2.6).

4.6 Layering and sociolinguistic variation: *Andar buscando*

Andar + *-ndo* is described as conveying non-directional movement, or "movimiento vario" (A. Alonso 1954: 259ff.; cf. Gili Gaya 1964: 115; Hamplová

1968: 221; Keniston 1936: 172; Roca Pons 1954, 1958: 66). *Andar* may be used as a lexical verb meaning 'walk, go', as in:

(40)   **Andidieron** *todol dia q<ue> vagar no<n> se dan*
Viniero<n> essa noche en calatayuh posar (PMC 650)
'**they rode** all day without rest and arrived at Calatayud, where they encamped that night' (Hamilton and Perry 1975: 57).

More frequently, however, it participates in numerous constructions, with a very general, non-directional, "go around" meaning, for example,

(41)   *Andidieron en pleyto...* (PMC 3554)

translated as *Todavía andan de pleitos...* by Bolaño e Isla (1976: 199) or simply as *Tras mucho hablar entre sí...* by Salinas (1963:239) and 'They discussed a grievance' by Such and Hodgkinson (1987). It is with this general 'go around' meaning that *andar* combines with *-ndo*, in a construction that may convey physical movement or aspectual meaning, or both.

4.6.1 Plural objects and parallel gerunds in frequentative meaning

We saw earlier that *andar* + *-ndo* is closely associated with *por* + LOC(ations) and we related multiple locations to frequentative meaning (Section 3.1.4). Most analyses coincide with this designation (e.g. Roca Pons 1958: 65), sometimes under labels such as "iterative" (Keniston 1936: 172; Squartini 1998: 263) or descriptions such as "emphasis on the repeated nature of the action" (De Bruyne 1995: 541). A. Alonso (1954: 266, note 1) describes the difference between *andas diciendo* 'you go around saying' and *estás diciendo* 'you are saying' as one between frequentative and continuous: *andar* has a sense of "conducirse en variados momentos" — 'behavior at diverse moments'. The Old Spanish data show that this frequentative meaning is linked to cooccurrence patterns with plural objects, parallel gerunds, and "general activity" main verbs.

Plural objects are highly congruent with frequentative meaning. In Langacker's (1996: 301) terms, "plurality reflects multiple instances of the event type" (see also Comrie 1976: 45, note 2 and Greenberg 1991 on the relationship between noun number and verb aspect). If a transitive action is distributed over many patients, it must occur repeatedly. Since the agent of the action is simultaneously "going around", it must be repeated on several

Frequency effects and layering in the domain of progressive aspect 159

occasions. The resulting aspect is not iterative, which is repetition on one occasion, but frequentative. The following example illustrates.

(42) *E vos, señor conde Lucanor, si queredes saber quál es el pior omne del mundo e de que más mal puede venir a las gentes, sabet que es el que se muestra por buen crisitano e por omne bueno e leal, e la su entençión es falsa, e **anda asacando falsedades e mentiras** por meter mal entre llas gentes.* (Luc Ex. XLII, p. 251)
'And you, Lord Count Lucanor, if you want to know who is the worst man on earth, and the one who does the most harm to people, you must know that he is the one who pretends to be a good and devout Christian while his life is false, **going about spreading his lies** so as to create discord among people.' (Keller and Keating 1977: 156)

As shown in Table 37, the ratio of plural to singular direct objects of *andar + -ndo* is 1.2 (37/30). If "tierra" objects, such as *toda la tierra* 'all the land', *tierra de Francia* 'land of France', *las Espannas* 'the Spains', which make up 23% of *andar + -ndo* objects in *Estoria de España*, are added in with plural objects, the ratio goes up to 1.8. For the sake of comparison, the ratio of plural to singular nouns in four different language samples in Greenberg (1966: 32) ranges from 0.2 to 0.4. That is, singular is generally the unmarked member in the nominal category of number. But in *andar + -ndo* direct objects, plural is "unmarked".

Table 37. Plural objects in ANDAR + -NDO

	PMC N	Apol. N	EE1 N	LBA N	Luc N	Corb N	C01 N	OldSp N	total %
Plural Direct Object	1		20	6	4	3	3	**37**	**32%**
No D.O. (Intransitive)		2	18	7	3	1	2	33	28%
Singular Direct Object	1	3	15	4	3	1	3	**30**	**26%**
"tierra"			16	1				17	15%

Parallel gerunds, which express multiple activities, or a "pluralidad de manifestaciones" — 'plurality of manifestations' (Alonso and Henríquez Ureña 1969, §156), are also consistent with frequentative meaning. In the following example, the different activities indicated by the three gerunds are all part of a general wooing plan, which is realized by the frequent occurrence of these activities.

(43) *E después andan tras los moçuelos **besándolos, falagándolos, dándoles** joyuelas, dineros e cosillas que a su hedad convienen.* (Corb Quarta parte, Cap. I, p.260)
'And then they follow after the young men **kissing** them, **flattering** them, **giving** them jewels, money, and little things such as correspond to their age.'

Table 38 shows that multiple gerund constructions average 19% (22/117) for *andar + -ndo*, compared to 13% and 12% for *estar* and *ir*, respectively (Chapter 2, Section 2.2).

Table 38. ANDAR + -NDO mulitple gerund constructions

	PMC N	Apol. N	EE1 N	LBA N	Luc N	Corb N	C01 N	OldSp total N	%
Two parallel gerunds	1	1	7	4	2		2	17	
Three or more gerunds			3	1		1		5	
Multiple gerund total	1	1	10	5	2	1	2	22	**19%**

4.6.2 General activity main verbs

Let us now look at *andar + -ndo* main verbs. Frequentative meaning is most likely when *andar* combines with a general activity verb such as *travajando* 'working' (EE1-167r26; Luc p. 250) or *vendiendo* 'selling' (LBA 700, 938). "General activity" verbs are those which refer to an activity composed of more specific sub-activities none of which alone constitutes the general activity. This is the biggest class for *andar + -ndo*, with about 25%. In the following examples, *pedir limosnas* 'beg' is a general activity predicate since it may involve several specific sub-activities: stationing oneself in an appropriate location, extending one's hand or hat, saying something to passers-by. *Andan / ando pidiendo (limosnas)* clearly refer to a frequentative or even habitual situation.

(44) *estos omnes que **andan pidiendo** las limosnas andando en sus romerías* (Luc Ex. I, p.78)
'wanderers who beg alms' (Keller and Keating 1977: 46)

(45) *ca non **ando pidiendo** nin só homne mendigo* (Apol 470d)
'I don't go around pestering nor am I a beggar'

In the second example *andar* + *-ndo* is conjoined with a *ser* copulative, which indicates "essence" (Bolinger 1973). Alvar's (1976, Vol. 2:450) translation "pues no soy pedigüeño ni mendicante" 'I am not a pest nor a beggar' leaves no doubt about a frequentative-habitual interpretation. Nevertheless, in both examples, *andar* + *-ndo* retains a literal "going around" physical motion meaning as well.

Even the communication verbs found in *andar* + *-ndo* are congruent with "going around", for example, *preguntando* 'asking (about)' (EE1–118r26, 147r52; Luc p. 294), *predicando* 'preaching' (EE1–77r89, 193v44), and *pregonando* 'proclaiming' (Luc p. 255). Unlike *hablando* 'talking', which is associated with *estar* and is usually done while one is stationary in one place, these predicates involve motion, though not in a particular direction or to a particular destination, as *ir* would imply.

It is interesting that, of all texts in the Old Spanish corpus, *andar* + *-ndo* has its highest relative frequency in the *Estoria de España*, at 29% (Table 26). The EE1, being a history of heroes and great events, is replete with "destruction" and "conquering" verbs such as *astragando tierra* 'ravishing the land', *destruyendo* 'destroying', *conquiriendo* 'conquering', *guerreando* 'warring'. This class of verbs makes up about a third of *andar* + *-ndo* main verbs in the EE1. Such verbs are highly compatible with the "going around" meaning of *andar*, since conquering involves large expanses and many victims. The "general activity" verb average for *andar* + *-ndo* in the Old Spanish corpus goes up to around 45%, if we include the "conquering" verbs of the EE1.

The association of *andar* with struggle and war continues in present-day varieties, as shown by the following excerpt on the activities of Pancho Villa, a central figure in the Mexican revolution of 1910. The speaker, from the village of Ascención, Chihuahua, was about ninety years old at the time of the recording.

> (46) *Y así fue. E. Cuando la revolución, cuando Villa. [...]* **Andaba andaba pegando** *muy duro. Ves. A todos les* **andaba pegando**. *A los ricos. A los pobres casi no les hacía nada. No a los pobres no les hacía nada. En lo más a los puros ricos [...] que decían ellos querían mandar ellos más que de nos[j]otros. Ese es lo, es lo que* **andaba peleando** *Villa, e, muy cierto.* **Anduvo peleando** *muy duro. Les echó unos fregazos aquel carajo. Sí. [...] Sí. Mucha gente* **andaba**. *Muchos soldados* **andaban** *mucha gente* **andaba** *con él. Sí, sí es cierto. Ahi peleaban en Diaz se iba para allá hasta [ ] hasta*

*Columbus. Sí. Ya cuando ya cuando no hubo nada entonces, entonces el pendejo fue [risas] fue a, a las tiendas a todo le quemó. Y aquí también quemó muchas tiendas. Bendito sea dios. Aquí en la colonia Diaz también quemó muchas tiendas. Sí. A los ricos todos. No, el el **andaba pegando** a al rico, no al pobre, al rico. Sí. Si tenos tiene ahumillados, a los pobres. Ese es lo que **andaba** él **peleando**.* (Chih'97#23A)
'And that's how it was. At the time of the revolution, at the time of Villa. He **was (going around) was (going around) hitting** very hard. He **was (going around) hitting** all of them. The rich. To the poor he really didn't do much. No, he didn't do anything to the poor. Just the rich, the ones who said they wanted to boss around more than us. That's what, that's what Villa **was (going around) fighting**, it's very true. He **was (going around) fighting** very hard. He really gave them some blows, that devil. Yes. Yes. A lot of people **were (going around)**. A lot of soldiers **were (going around)** a lot of people **were (going around)** with him. Yes, yes it's true. There in Diaz they fought, he went there up to up to Columbus [across the United States border]. Yes. Then when then when there was nothing left then the idiot went [laughter] went to the stores, and burned everything. And here too he burned a lot of stores. Yes. Of the rich, all of them. No, he he **was (going around) hitting** the rich man, not the poor, the rich. Yes. If- the rich man has us humiliated, the poor. That's what he **was (going around) fighting**.'

Non-directional motion in *andar* + *-ndo* may also be congruent with progressive or continuous, rather than frequentative, meaning. According to A. Alonso (1954: 268), in *Puse mi atención en una mosca que andaba volando* 'I placed my attention on a fly that was (going around) flying', the speaker is referring not to something occurring frequently but to a singular act of flying (which may be iterative). Progressive or continuous as opposed to frequentative meaning seems most likely with motion and physical activity main verbs. In the Old Spanish corpus, 14% of *andar* + *-ndo* tokens are with a motion verb, for example, *bolando* 'flying' (three cases, all in LBA), *corriendo* 'running' (three in EE1, one each in LBA, Corb), *fuyendo* 'fleeing' (three cases, all in EE1), *siguiendo* 'following, chasing' (one each in EE1, LBA). Even metaphorical motion uses are consistent with *andar*'s "going around" meaning. Thus, while the fixed expressions *subir en edad* 'grow (go up) in age' and *caer en olvido* 'fall in oblivion' occur in *ir* + *-ndo* (e.g. example (3.42)), the expression *desviar de la verdad*, with non-directional *desviar* 'deviate', occurs in *andar* + *-ndo*:

> (47) Mas ell emperador Vale<n>t **andaua desuiando** de la uerdat de la eglesia. & trabaiauasse de la heregia de Arrio. (EE1–142r25)
> 'But the emperor Valent **was** (literally: going around) **wandering** off the course of the church's truth and was becoming interested in the heresy of Arrio.'

Here non-directional motion blends with continuous meaning. Another 10% of the Old Spanish tokens are with physical-bodily activity verbs, for example, *llorando* 'crying' (EE1–26r56), *matando* 'killing' (Corb p.271), *pac'iendo* 'grazing' (LBA 897), *tirando a pájaros* 'shooting birds' (C01–34v6). In the next example, physical motion — activity *trebejando* 'cavorting, playing' is in progress when the ice cracks, and non-directional motion blends with progressive meaning.

> (48) Ebro el Rio q<ue> estaua una uez yelado & un ni<n>no q<ue> auie no<m>bre Trabs. **andaua trebeiando** por somo del yelo. & foradosse el yelo en un logar. & fuesse el ni<n>no afo<n>don (EE1–59v31)[5]
> 'The river Ebro was once frozen and a child whose name was Trabs **was** (going around) **playing** on top of the ice. And at one place the ice cracked into a hole and the child went to the bottom'

On the other hand, *andar +-ndo* seems to lack the evidentiality associated with *estar* + *-ndo* progressives in that it may indicate a general or vague location where the situation is ongoing at the moment of reference. In A. Alonso's (1954: 269) example, *¿Dónde está don Sixto? — Andará pintando por el jardín* 'Where is don Sixto? — He's probably painting around the garden', the idea of non-directional motion lies in the speaker's vague locating of the situation rather than in the agent's physical movement or in the frequentative aspect of the situation. Vague location in *andar* contrasts with specific location in *estar*. Thus, one way *anda pintando* 'goes around painting' may be different from *está pintando* 'is (located) painting' — when both refer to an ongoing moment-of-speech situation — is that personally experienced or witnessed is conveyed with *estar* but not with *andar*. This analysis is supported by the paucity of *andar + -ndo* clauses subordinated to *ver* 'see', with only two cases in the Old Spanish data (object relatives in Apol 121, EE1–82r96), compared with 17 cases, or 10%, for *estar + -ndo* (Table 30). The distribution of *andar + -ndo* clauses is given in Table 39.

Table 39. ANDAR + -NDO: Distribution by clause type in Old Spanish

	N	%
Main	36	31%
"Ocurrió" *que*	3	3%
Object relative	20	17%
Subordinate *que* (*decir, saber, soñar*)	14	12%
Gerund *andando*	13	11%
Infinitive *andar*	8	7%
Subject relative	6	5%
Other subordinate*	15	13%

* Other: *mientre* 3, *ca-porque* 2, *como* 2, *cuando — en cuanto* 3, *donde* 2, *desde que* 1, *aunque* 1, *si* 1.
** *ver* + object relative: two cases only (Apol 121, EE1–82r96)

The most frequent *andar + -ndo* main verb is *buscando*. This predicate is highly compatible with the non-directional movement meaning of *andar*, since one often has to "go around" in order to *buscar* 'look for' something. Other verbs may be said to belong to the same "look for" class. *Demandando*, with two tokens in the earliest texts, the PMC (1292) and *Apolonio* (71c), means 'enquire about, pursue'. *Andar catando*, with three tokens (EE1–43v60, 146v91; Luc p.161), may also have a "looking **for**" rather than just a "(stand) looking **at**" meaning, as *estar catando* does. This is shown in the following example:

(49) ...*quel dixiese que se reçelaba que el toro* **andava catando manera** *para le traer quanto daño pudiesse*,... (Luc Ex. XXII, p. 161)
'to tell the lion that he was afraid the bull **was looking for a way** to harm him,...' (Keller and Keating 1977: 96)

The "looking for" interpretation of *andava catando manera* 'was looking for a way' is supported by the use of the expression *anda buscando maneras* 'goes around (literally) looking for a way' in the same text (Luc p. 160). Likewise, mental verb *guisar* 'prepare, arrange' takes on a "go around looking for" sense with *andar*, as in:

(50) **andaua** *quanto podie* **guisando** *cuemol matasse* (EE1–85r54)
'he **went around looking for a way** to kill him'

Other verbs similarly acquire a "looking for (a way)" sense, for example, *conseiando cuemol lo matassen* 'deciding how they would kill him'(EE1–86r98) or *aparejando oportunidad* 'the devil is back of all of this, preparing my opportunity'(C01 26v10, Act IV), in Singleton's (1958: 73) translation (or simply, 'the devil's about!' in Simpson's (1955: 48)).

In short, *andar* + *-ndo* may specify frequentative meaning, especially with *por* + LOCs (multiple places), plural direct objects, and general activity verbs, or it may be used as a progressive or continuous, especially with motion and physical activity verbs. It often blends physical "going around" with aspectual meaning. In the course of this study we have seen that each auxiliary is more likely to combine with different locatives, time expressions, and main verbs. By way of a summary, let us look at the next example and try to answer the question: why *andar* and not *estar* or *ir*?

(51) *E Tito el fijo deVespasiano q<ue> uio todas las cueuas & las carcauas de aderredor de la uilla llenas de muertos. &* **la sangre q<ue> andaua a dessuso corriendo a todas partes** (EE1–82r96)
'And Tito the son of Vespasiano who saw all the caves and trenches (ditches) around the city full of corpses and **the blood that was running down all over the place** (literally: was going around running)'

Estar is disfavored by the motion verb *corriendo*, while *ir* is disfavored by the multiple location expression *a todas partes* (cf. Squartini 1998: 276–7). Given someone moving in many directions, *andar* + *-ndo* is the most likely auxiliary (and this example is truly exceptional, being the one clear Old Spanish *andar* + *-ndo* token with an inanimate subject).

4.6.3 *A newer construction — negative nuances*

Table 36 (Section 4.5) indicates that *andar* + *-ndo* has a lower token frequency than either *estar* or *ir* + *-ndo*. As we would predict, semantic and formal reduction is less advanced in *andar* + *-ndo*. On the measure of subject animacy, 98% of *andar* + *-ndo* subjects in the Mexico City corpus are humans (the remainder are animals) (Table 40). In the Old Spanish data, subjects are humans (87%), metonymic humans (4.5%), for example, *toda la villa* 'the whole group' (LBA 1240d) and *su alma* 'his soul' (C01–76r17, example (3.46)), or animals (4.5%), such as *el toro* 'bull' (Luc Ex. XXII, p.161). There were only two inanimate subjects in OldSp, *sangre que andaua... corriendo a todas partes* 'blood that was running all over the place' (EE1–82r96, see example (51) above) and *ac'ucar ally anda bolando* 'sugar is poured out by the handfuls there' (LBA-1337; Joset's edition (1990: 581), however, has the Past Participle form *ballonado*).

Table 40. ANDAR + -NDO: Animacy of subject

	PMC N	EE1 N	LBA N	Luc N	Corb N	C01 N	OldSp N	total %	MexPop N	%
Human	2	68	9	9	5	7	100	89%	87	98%
Human metonymic		4				1	5	4.5%	0	
Animals			4	1			5	4.5%	2	2%
Inanimate		1	1				2	2%	0	0

Non-human: EE1- 82r96; LBA 210, 211, 413, 835, 897, 1085, 1240, 1292, 1337; Luc p.161; C01–76r17.

On measures of formal reduction, *andar* + *-ndo* is also less advanced, as indicated by the proportion of cases with intervening open class items. In the *Estoria de España*, cases with intervening open class items average 48%, compared to 36% for *estar* + *-ndo* and 24% for *ir* + *-ndo* (Section 2.3). The average goes up to 53% if cases of more than two intervening items are included in the *andar* + *-ndo* total. These measures indicate that *andar* + *-ndo* is a newer construction. The greater degree of retention of locative-movement meaning is indicated by the higher average of cooccurring locatives, at 37%, compared to 30% for *estar* and 28% for *ir* + *-ndo* (Section 3.1.4).

The retention hypothesis predicts that newer constructions make a richer semantic contribution than older ones. Keniston (1936: 172) calls *andar* "the most affective" of the auxiliaries. Connotations of solicitude, busyness, or anxiety in the agent of *andar* + *-ndo* have been observed by several scholars (Cuervo 1994 [1886]; Keniston 1936: 172; Roca Pons 1954, 1968: 65). Another nuance is negative attitude in the speaker toward a repeated situation (Hamplová 1968: 222) or one that represents pointless activity (Butt and Benjamin 1994: 303), as in *andan diciendo* 'they go around saying' in reference to a false rumor (Yllera 1980: 77). It is interesting that the idea of negative attitude in the speaker appears to be linked to that of busyness or anxiety in the agent (*andar* + *-ndo*), while active involvement by the agent-experiencer is linked to personally witnessed or felt by the speaker (*estar* + *-ndo*).

Both frequentative aspect and connotations of negative attitude in *andar* + *-ndo* arise from the original non-directional motion meaning of the construction. Going around in space and time while doing something is frequentative and, in certain contexts, may not be a good thing. For example, with a negative polarity Imperative and a lexical expression of negativity (*palabras malas* 'swearwords'), *andar diciendo* obviously conveys disapprobation, as in the following New Mexico example:

(52) *Le digo "No no vas a **andar diciendo** tú esos, esas palabras"*. (NMbil/Vig)
'I tell him, "don't **go around saying** those words"'
(in the previous clause referred to as *palabras malas*)

One index of negative attitude is the occurrence of *andar* + *-ndo* in a construction of the form *qué* (or *cómo*) + *ir* + *a* + *andar* + *-ndo*, as shown below:

(53) *qué* (or *cómo*) + *ir* + *a* + *andar* + *-ndo*
'what (or 'how') + go + to + go around + gerund'
= negation or rejection of situation construction

This is used to deny a situation or express rejection of a course of action:

(54) *"Ah, que son mentiras, **qué va a andar apareciendo** aquí una [ ]"* (Chih97#12MamEd)
'Oh, it's all lies, how would a [ghost] be appearing here?'

(55) ***qué me voy a andar casando** con ese* (UNAM 1976: 57)
'I'm going to go (around) marrying that guy — for what?'

This negative attitude use of *andar* shows up in the distribution of tense forms, shown in Table 41. If we compare the results with those for *estar, ir* (Table 34, Section 4.5 above), we see that in the Mexico City corpus *andar* occurs more frequently in Infinitive (22%) and Present Subjunctive (6%) form than the others.

Table 41. ANDAR + -NDO: Tenses

	PMC N	Apol N	EE1 N	LBA N	Luc N	Corb N	C01 N	OldSp N	Total %	MexPop N	%
Imperfect	1	3	38	3	5		1	51	44%	22	25%
Present	1	2	3	12	4	3	3	28	24%	32	34%
Preterite			9		1			10	8%	6	7%
Gerund			13					13	11%	1	
Infinitive			5	2		1	1	9	8%	20	**22%**
Present Subjunctive							2	2		5	**6%**
Other								4		3	

Other: Imperfect Subjunctive (EE1, Luc, C01 and one in MexPop); Future (one in LBA), Imperative, Present Perfect (one each in MexPop)

4.6.4 Routines and sociolinguistic factors in variation

Andar buscando alone makes up 13% (15/117) of all *andar + -ndo* tokens in the Old Spanish corpus, quite a substantial proportion. The association between *andar* and *buscando* continues into present-day varieties, with 9% (8/89) of all *andar + -ndo* tokens in the Mexico City corpus. Looking at it from the point of view of *buscando*, 66% (8/12) tokens in MexPop are with *andar*. *Andar buscando* is so frequent that it "is really a set phrase" (Spaulding 1926: 259), or a case of "lexical specialization" (Squartini 1998: 261).

This collocation reflects both retention and layering in grammaticization. *Buscar* pairs up with *andar*, rather than *estar* or *ir*, because both may involve non-directional motion (retention). At the same time, *andar buscando* may be used to indicate a continuous situation of looking, without particular physical motion or affective connotations (bleaching and layering). If all occurrences of *andar buscando* retained physical motion and/or negative meaning, then we would expect to find a fair number of tokens of *buscar* with another auxiliary, for precisely those occasions in which no such connotations were intended (unless, of course, "looking for" inherently involves physical motion and some degree of anxiety!). There were only two tokens of *ir buscando* in MexPop (UNAM 1976: 109 (*cómo*); 398 (*la mira de*)) and two of *estar buscando* (UNAM 1976: 302 (*buscándole*); 354 (intransitive)). Together these make up only 33% (4/12) of all *buscando* tokens, while *estar* and *ir* combined make up 75% of all auxiliaries in this corpus.

Thus, *estar hablando*, *ir creciendo*, and *andar buscando* seem to be well-established routines, each making up a relatively high proportion of the corresponding *-ndo* construction. Linguists are often tempted to pinpoint meaning differences when different forms are used. But the distribution of different forms may sometimes be just the residue of older patterns of use that were once meaningful (cf. Poplack's 1992 findings on French subjunctive use with *falloir*).

Beside the routinization of frequent cooccurrence patterns, another set of factors contributing to the choice of progressive auxiliary is sociolinguistic. The relative frequencies in Table 27 (Section 4.1) indicate that, in addition to diachronic changes, there are dialect and social or register differences in the distribution of *-ndo* auxiliaries. We saw earlier that *seguir* 'follow, continue' is a newer auxiliary (Sections 3.4.1 and 4.1). It is also appears to be associated with educated, written varieties. *Seguir* has a relative frequency of 6% in MexPop, but 29% — close to one-third — in the Essays corpus. Indeed, *seguir* + *-ndo* is even more frequent than *estar* + *-ndo* in this corpus. On the other hand, *andar* 'go around' is more frequent in popular/oral than in educated/written varieties and more frequent in Mexico City than in Madrid. In educated Madrid oral data there was only one token from a total of 343 *-ndo* constructions (Olbertz 1998: 549), in educated Mexico City oral data there were 24 from a total of 868, or 3% (Luna 1980: 211), but in popular Mexico City data the relative frequency of *andar* + *-ndo* reaches 89/648, or 14% (Table 27; also, Arjona 1991: 124).

Spaulding's (1926: 259) comment that "*andar* often seems to be merely a lively, and colloquial, substitute for *estar*" is interesting in light of the skewed distribution of *andar* + *-ndo*. Luna (1980: 206) finds that *andar* + *-ndo* could be substituted, with loss of "expressive nuances", by *estar* + *-ndo*, but not by *ir* or *venir* + *-ndo* in educated Mexico City data. Based on popular Mexico City data, Arjona (1991: 124–5) concludes that there is a preference for *andar* where *estar* might be used in that variety. Arjona's (1991: 125) hypothesizes that "a los hablantes cultos el uso frecuente de *andar* + gerundio les parece poco elegante, al tiempo que a los informantes de habla popular les resulta sumamente expresivo" — 'the frequent use of *andar* + gerund seems not elegant to educated speakers, while it turns out to be highly expressive for popular speech informants'. Comments such as these hint at the possibility that *andar* and *estar* + *-ndo*, at least to some extent, are variants of a single linguistic variable in the sociolinguistic sense, in other words, that they covary with social/register factors (Silva-Corvalán 1997a: 121).

Initial support for the social stratification of *estar* – *andar* + *-ndo* is the distribution of *estar/andar* according level of education in the Chihuahua data. Of 22 speakers (counting only those who contributed at least 5 tokens), 6 had a university education. Two of these were teachers in secondary schools, one taught in a post-secondary institution, one was a lawyer and another a writer. All of them live in the urban city of Chihuahua, the state capital. The results are shown in Table 42. University-educated speakers show a relative frequency of under 10% for *andar*. This compares to 27%, nearly three times greater, for speakers with a primary school or at most secondary school education.

Table 42. *Relative frequency of ESTAR and ANDAR by speaker level of education*

	ESTAR N	%	ANDAR N	%	Total N
University level	158	91%	15	9%	173
Non-university level	198	73%	73	27%	271
Totals	356	80%	88	20%	444

Chi-square = 20.32413, p = .0000.

4.7 Specialization in New Mexican Spanish

Studies of Spanish in the United States have noted the increased frequency of *estar* with respect to other *-ndo* auxiliaries (e.g. Silva-Corvalán 1994: 46). In this section I propose that the increased relative frequency of *estar* + *-ndo* in varieties of Spanish in contact with English may be understood as a process of specialization, in the framework of diachronic changes in the distribution of *-ndo* auxiliaries, rather than as a process of simplification resulting from language contact.

Specialization in language change is the process in which one form in an emerging group of constructions is increasingly used to the detriment of other forms. The end result may be obligatorification (Lehmann 1995: 139), when the choice among forms narrows to the point where one becomes obligatory Hopper's (1991: 26) example is that of French negation, where the choice is narrowed from several nouns in Old French to four by the 16th century — *pas* 'step, pace', *point* 'dot, point', *mie* 'crumb', *gote* 'drop' — and then to two by the modern period, until *pas* became a general negator.

Is specialization underway with *-ndo* auxiliaries? The best answer seems to be yes (cf. Squartini 1998: 208), but it is a slow process, and there is no indication that *estar* will annihilate other *-ndo* auxiliaries any time soon. One reason for the slowness of specialization so far is that the process has had to go through a reversal of the earlier favoring of *ir*. As shown in Tables 26 and 27 at the beginning of this chapter, the relative frequency of *estar* increases from 27% in the Old Spanish corpus to 52% in the popular Mexico City corpus, as the relative frequency of *ir* decreases from 45% to 22.5% in the same corpora. That is, there is a switch in the predominant form. Even the figures for the Madrid corpus, with a 76% relative frequency for *estar* and 19% for *ir*, seem to simply reverse the ratio in the earliest OldSp text, the *Poema de mio Cid*, with 22% for *estar* and 70% for *ir* (the proportion of *estar* + *-ndo* in Madrid is not significantly different from the proportion of *ir* + *-ndo* in the PMC). A second reason for the slowness of specialization is the addition of new auxiliaries, such as *quedar(se)* and *seguir*. Indeed the proportion of "other" auxiliaries remains about the same, at 9% in OldSp and 11% in MexPop. In short, the diachronic trend is toward specialization in favor of *estar*, but layering (several auxiliaries still available) rather than obligatorification (*estar* beats out other auxiliaries) best describes the present state of affairs.

Let us now look at the New Mexico corpora to see if the process is more advanced. We will begin with the near monolingual group. The distribution of auxiliaries in NMmon mostly follows MexPop patterns. As shown in Table 27, *estar* has a relative frequency of 51%, *ir* 17%, *andar* 19%, and "other" 13%; corresponding figures for MexPop are 52%, 23%, 14%, and 11% (none of the differences are statistically significant). In this corpus *ir* occurs with process verb *crecer* 'grow'; with directional motion verbs, such as *llegar* 'arrive', *subir* 'go up', *volar* 'fly'; with physical activities, for example, *barrechar* 'prepare land for planting'; and with general activities, for example, *sacar ganancia* 'make profits'. *Andar* occurs with *buscar* and general activity verb *trabajar* 'work', as well as with a variety of physical activity and physical motion verbs, for example *arrear* 'herd', *cargar* 'carry', *huir* 'flee', *limpiar* 'clean'. "Other" auxiliaries are *quedarse* (three tokens, all with *mirando*), *salir* (2), *seguir* (1), and *venir* (5).

What are the uses of *venir* 'come'-plus-gerund? Of five *venir* + *-ndo* tokens in NMmon, one may be read as combining physical motion with "retrospective" meaning (Coseriu 1996[1976]:107, Dietrich 1983: 210; Solé 1990: 68). This use seems to correspond to an English Past Perfect Progressive, for example,

(56) - *El llegó cansa'o, pero pero me trujo.*
      |
      - *Porque vino arreando todo el-*
      - *Porque andaba arreando, él **venía arreando**. Ya 'staba muy cansa'o. Pero me trujo.* (NMmon/NMCSS#217)
      '- He arrived tired, but he got me there.
      - Because he had been driving fast the whole-
      - Because he was driving fast, **he had been driving fast** (literally: **was coming driving fast**). By then he was very tired. But he got me there.'

Two other *venir* examples seem to literally mean "coming while verb-ing", as in:

(57) *Y había veces que venía no más temblando como el caballo cuando los usaba uno* (NMCSS#219)
'And there were times when I would arrive just trembling, like a horse when you've worked them'

The remaining two or 40% were the expression *viene siendo*, more or less equivalent to 'that is' or 'which is', for example,

(58) *¿Un sitio viene siendo qué? ¿Un taxi?* (Chih'97#18A)
'A *sitio* is what? A taxi?'

This fixed phrase also makes up 13% (3/23) of all *venir* + *-ndo* tokens in MexPop and 70% (!) (26/37) in the Chihuahua data.

One difference with MexPop is the continued use of *salir* 'go out'-plus-gerund in NMmon, with 2% (2/83). While there was only one token (of 648) in MexPop, the relative frequency of this combination is 3% (17/616) in the Old Spanish corpus. The persistence of *salir* + *-ndo* provides one more piece of evidence for the continuation of older patterns in New Mexican Spanish. Additional evidence for archaism in this variety was the higher proportion of parallel gerunds and overall lower construction frequency (Section 2.7).

Let us now look at the distribution of auxiliaries in the bilingual New Mexico group. With respect to the relative frequency of *andar*, NMbil (10%) is not significantly different from MexPop (14%) and NMmon (19%) (at p < .01).[6] In this corpus *andar* is used with motion verbs (*correr* 'run'), talking verbs (*decir* 'say), physical activity verbs (*juntar trastes* 'bus (dishes)', *llorar* 'cry', *manejar trocas* 'drive trucks'), but mostly with general activity verbs, with over half of all tokens (10/18), for example, *hacer males* 'do bad things', *pelear* 'fight', *trabajar* 'work'. There were three tokens of *andar penando* all in versions of the story of the *Llorona*, who (literally) goes around mourning and lamenting the loss of her children. There does not seem to be any loss, then, of this shared feature of New Mexican and popular Mexican Spanish.

Estar + *-ndo* has a relative frequency of 82%, with 144 of 175 *-ndo* constructions. The NMbil *estar* proportion is not significantly different from the Madrid proportion, at 76% (262/343). Thus, by itself the relative frequency figure does not reveal much. What is different — from all other data sets included in Table 27 — is the very low proportion of *ir* + *-ndo*. The ratio of *estar* to *ir* is 24-to-one (144/6)! This compares with 2.3-to-one in MexPop (340/146). In his study of compound verbs in Indo-Aryan languages, Hook (1991) shows that differences among languages in the token frequency of these forms are accompanied by a narrowing of the possible "quasi-auxiliary" verbs. Moreover, he finds that concomitant with specialization of the would-be auxiliaries is expansion of the semantic classes of the "main" verbs. This measure turns out to be more revealing in our case.

In the bilingual group, *estar* + *-ndo* is used with directional motion verbs and process verbs that in the Old Spanish corpus occurred with *ir* + *-ndo*. Motion verbs occurring with *estar* are *ir* 'go' (2), *venir* 'come' (4), *volver* 'return', *caminar* 'walk', *entrar* 'enter' (one token each), adding up 6% (9/144). The average occurrence of these kinds of verbs with *estar* in the Mexico City corpus is lower, at 2% (7/340). I return to *estar*-plus-motion verb in the following chapter (Section 5.4). Process verbs occurring with *estar* in NMbil are *crecer* 'grow', *cambiar* (intransitive) 'change', and *hacerse vieja* 'grow old', adding up to 8% (12/144). Again, the proportion of *estar* -plus-process verb is lower in MexPop, with 3% (11/340). *Crecer* occurred 10 times with *ir* and only once with *estar* in MexPop (UNAM 1976: 72; see Section 4.4.4). In NMbil the ratio is reversed, at only one token with *ir* and seven with *estar*. Examples are:

(59) **Está creciendo** mucho pa cuando nosotros nos mudamos para acá. (NMbil/Edw)
'It (Albuquerque) **is growing** a lot compared to when we moved here'

(60) ...porque siempre hablo de mi familia y y y de lo que pasó **cuando estaba creciendo** yo. (NMbil/ Nin)

'because I always talk about my family and the things that happened **when I was growing up**'

The increased frequency of *estar creciendo* in the bilingual group is at least in part a case of lexico-syntactic permeability as discussed in Silva-Corvalán (1994: 166, 172–84). English uses 'grow (up)' where Spanish uses a copular construction. For example, 'when I grow up' would be *cuando sea grande* 'when I am big'. Transfer of this expression would show up in *cuando estaba creciendo*, as the corresponding form to monolingual *cuando estaba* (or *era*) *chico*. Indeed, most occurrences of *estar creciendo* in the bilingual group are *cuando* + first person Imperfects, as in the example above. *Cuando estaba(mos) creciendo* makes up 71% (5/7) of all *estar creciendo* tokens in NMbil.

In short, *estar* + *-ndo* has expanded to motion and process verbs to a greater extent in NMbil than in MexPop. On this measure, then, the process of specialization seems to be more advanced is this variety than in popular Mexico City Spanish. The study of other corpora with a skewed distribution of auxiliaries, like the educated Madrid corpus in which *andar* + *-ndo* is virtually absent, may indicate to what extent *estar* has taken over main verbs associated in OldSp with *ir* or *andar* in other present-day varieties.

The shrinking of *ir* + *-ndo* is a diachronic process, as shown by the steadily declining figures in Table 26. Differences between present-day corpora shown in Table 27 suggest that the process is slowest in written, especially formal, registers. This seems to be the case not just in Mexican Spanish, as indicated by the figures for the Essays corpus — where *ir* is more frequent than *estar*, but in other dialects as well. For example, the frequencies of *-ndo* constructions in Peninsular Spanish provided in Olbertz (1998: 549) show a 4.1-to-one ratio for *estar* over *ir* in the oral Madrid corpus (262/64), but a 2.1-to-one ratio in a corpus of literary texts (132/63) (it is interesting that in journalistic texts the ratio is highest, at 7.7-to-one (93/12)). Register, then, is an important factor in the degree to which the specialization process has advanced.

Register considerations explain, at least in part, the decline of *ir* + *-ndo* in NMbil compared with the continuing use of *andar* + *-ndo*. The higher frequency of *ir* is associated with written texts, while *andar* is associated with oral, especially popular, Mexican Spanish (Section 4.6.4). Given the absence of written models and standardization pressures in New Mexican Spanish (see Chapter 1, Section 1.4.3), we expect that specialization would show up in the shrinking of more learned *ir* rather than of dialect feature *andar*.

If the distribution of auxiliaries in NMbil were the straightforward result of simplification (as defined in Silva-Corvalán 1994: 3) brought on by language contact, *estar* should be replacing **all** the motion verb auxiliaries. Although preliminary analysis in Silva-Corvalán (1994: 46) suggests that this may be happening among bilinguals in Los Angeles, the more detailed findings provided here indicate a more complex process, in which diachronic and register variation must be taken into account. Describing the process as specialization, rather than simplification, situates it in the framework of diachronic — and related register — developments. We found register to be an important factor in evaluating the effects of language contact on the overall token frequency of *-ndo* constructions (Sections 2.6–2.7). Register turns out to be important in the distribution of auxiliaries as well.

4.8 Summary

In summary, frequency of use propels and constrains changes in grammaticization. Token and type frequency of "talking" and "bodily activity" predicates play an important role in the development of *estar + -ndo* as a progressive. Frequent occurrence in clauses subordinated to *ver* 'see', which is consistent with the locative origin of the construction, contributes to evidential uses; overtness from the perspective of the speaker complements active involvement from the perspective of the agent-experiencer. On the other hand, the pace of semantic and formal reduction in *ir + -ndo* is constrained by the smaller frequency increases of this construction compared with *estar + -ndo*.

Frequent collocations (cooccurrence patterns with locatives, temporal expressions, and main verb types, such as *estar hablando*, *ir creciendo* and *andar buscando*) and specific features of meaning (such as gradual development for *ir + -ndo* and frequentative for *andar + -ndo*) follow from the original uses of the source constructions. At the same time, semantic reduction (generalization) results in partial overlap of uses and layering in the domain of progressive aspect.

Besides persisting meaning differences and routines, contributing factors to variation in *-ndo* auxiliaries are dialect and register differences. In this framework, changes in the distribution of *estar + -ndo* main verbs in bilingual varieties are part of a process of specialization rather than the result of simplification brought about by language contact.

Notes

1. Other verbs combining with a gerund in Old Spanish that disappeared are *yazer* 'lie' and *fincar* 'remain' (Yllera 1980: 50–52, 53–54).
2. There are a total of 15 cases of *estar esperando* in MexPop. Five mean 'be pregnant' (UNAM 1976: 64, 180, 263, 265, 265). Four of the remaining 10 have no locative (UNAM 1976: 111, 283, 443, 444).
3. Thanks to David Pharies for deciphering *yuueria* and *yuuero* (example (16) from *Estoria de España*) as *jubería* and *jubero*.
4. It is likely that generalization to inanimate subjects procedes gradually through an intermediate stage where a human, though no longer the agent, is directly affected or involved. Of 12 *ir* + *-ndo* inanimate subjects in the PMC, six are in constructions with a human benefactive (dative). Five are the expression **les** *va pesando* 'it grieves **them**'. Another example is *Yal creçe la barba e vale allongando* (verse 1238) 'His beard grows long (**on him**)'. From inanimate subjects with human benefactives, the construction may have generalized to apply to situations where there is still a human element, though not as an argument of the verb, as in *Sonando van **sus** nuevas* '**His** fame spreads' (verse 1156), and from there on to an implied human element, as in ***las** nuevas de mio Çid, sabet, sonando van* 'the Cid's fame spreads far and wide' (verse 1154), finally losing the requirement for a human element altogether.
5. Example (48) is interesting because it is a translation from Latin. The larger excerpt reads:

    Trabs puer astricto glacie du<m> ludit in ebro.Frigore concretas pondere rupit aquas. Dumq<ue> impartes rapido traere<n>tur ab amne. P<er>cussit tenerum lubrica testa capud. Orba q<uod> jnne<n>tum mat<er> du<m> cond<er>et urna. Hoc reperi flammis cet<er>a dixit aquis.
    Q<ue> quiere dezir. q<ue> Ebro el Rio q<ue> estaua una uez yelado & un ni<n>no q<ue> auie no<m>bre Trabs. andaua trebeiando por somo del yelo. & foradosse el yelo en un logar. & fuesse el ni<n>no afo<n>don. pero trauossele la cabec'a en aq<ue>l forado.&' uoluieron le las aguas el cuerpo tanto a cada parte. q<ue> se le corto la cabec'a. [%] &' acabo de muchos dias. uino su madre a coger agua en una orc'a muy grand. & cogio y en uuelta dell agua la cabec'a de su fijo. & connosciola & dixo.(EE1–59v)

6. The difference between NMmon and NMbil in the relative frequency of *andar* is significant at $\chi^2 = 3.977984$, p = .0461.

Chapter 5

From progressive to experiential habitual

In the last three chapters we have seen diachronic evidence for the conventionalization of the *estar* + *-ndo* construction as an expression of progressive aspect. Grammaticization of the construction involves emergence as a fused unit with formal reduction (Chapter 2) and loss of locative features of meaning with semantic reduction (Chapter 3). In the last chapter we saw evidence for the initiation of a process of specialization, as *estar* is increasingly used to the detriment of motion verb *-ndo* auxiliaries, particularly *ir*. Underlying these changes are two kinds of frequency increases: construction frequency, a measure combining token frequency and the proportion of gerund tokens in the construction (Section 2.5), and relative frequency, a measure of the frequency of *estar* relative to other auxiliaries (Section 4.1). In this chapter we focus on present-day uses of *estar* + *-ndo*, drawing on data from Chihuahua (Chih'97, see 1.5.2.3) and New Mexico (NMmon – NMbil, see 1.5.3).

There are two consequences of diachronic frequency increases for present-day variation in *estar* + *-ndo*. One is change with respect to simple Present and Imperfect verb forms, as these are increasingly restricted to non-progressive uses. This change is important in evaluating the effects of language contact, since the increased frequency of *estar* + *-ndo* in bilingual varieties has been assessed on the premise that simple forms are available to express progressive aspect in Spanish. A second consequence is variation in the uses of *estar* + *-ndo* itself. In this chapter I show that the next step in the evolution of the construction is extension to experiential habitual uses. It is important that these newer uses have a subjective meaning component, in that they express the speaker's point of view of the situation as new and noteworthy. We will see that this pragmatic constraint on habitual uses of *estar* + *-ndo* is maintained among New Mexico bilinguals.

In Section 5.1, I consider evidence for a change in the grammatical status of *estar* + *-ndo* toward becoming an obligatory progressive and compare token frequencies in bilingual and monolingual varieties. In Sections 5.2 and 5.3, I discuss the extension of *estar + -ndo* to experiential habitual uses and relate these to deixis. Sections 5.4 and 5.5 zero in on uses with motion verbs and stative predicates. Finally in Section 5.6, I propose that it is subjectivity rather than just transitoriness in *estar + -ndo* and return to the idea that temporal bounding and subject/speaker involvement follow from locative circumscription.

5.1 Change in progress in the grammatical status of *estar + -ndo*

5.1.1 Definitions of ESTAR + -NDO

We may group definitions of *estar + -ndo* into three sets, based on the features of durativity, limited duration, and actualization. The meaning label most commonly applied to *estar + -ndo* is "durative". Since the earliest treatment of Spanish verbal periphrastic constructions by Cuervo, in note 72 to Bello's grammar (Dietrich 1983: 117), the trend in most reference grammars has been to assume overlap in meaning between simple and corresponding *estar + -ndo* forms, with the additional nuance of enhanced durativity. For example, Gili Gaya (1964: 113, §97) asserted that "Entre *escribo* y *estoy escribiendo* no hay más diferencia que la impresión duradera que produce la segunda" 'Between *escribo* (I write) and *estoy escribiendo* (I am writing) there is no difference other than the impression of durativity conveyed by the latter'. It is interesting that not even a difference of degree was acknowledged less than three hundred years ago in the *Diccionario de Autoridades*: "*estar leyendo, estar escribiendo* vale lo mismo que *leer* y *escribir*" '*estar leyendo, estar escrbiendo* (to be reading, to be writing) is equivalent to *leer* and *escribir*' (to read, to write)' (RAE 1732:629). Durative is the label for *estar + -ndo* in grammars by Alcina y Blecua (1975: 781), Criado de Val (1966: 140, §136, 137), RAE (1931: 412, §456; 1973: 448, §3.12.5), R. Seco (1966: 172), M. Seco (1989: 221, §14.5.2).

Other scholars have stressed the greater preciseness or specificity of *estar + -ndo* as an expression of limited, rather than enhanced, duration. Lorenzo (1971: 121, 132) held that there are cases where *estoy comiendo* 'I am eating' and *como* 'I eat' are not interchangeable because of the advances of *como* into both future and past territory (cf. Butt and Benjamin 1994: 231; Solé and Solé 1977: 41, 47–9). Stockwell et al.'s (1965: 141–44, 156–60) term "modification for explicit duration" reflects an analogous view. In their example, *gastaba su dinero*, the simple Imperfect could be interpreted as "used to spend" (though they hasten to add, it is not limited to habitual meaning), while *estaba gastando* "focuses attention on a single occasion of money spending" (Stockwell et al. 1965: 158).

It has been claimed that temporal adverbials can neutralize the opposition between *estar* + *-ndo* and corresponding simple forms. Thus, according to Rallides (1966: 108–110), if a friend calls on the phone and asks what you are doing you can either use either the *estar* + *-ndo* or the simple Present, provided you add *ahora* 'now', for example, *Escribo cartas ahora* 'I write letters now' or *Estoy escribiendo cartas* 'I am writing letters'. Similarly, a cooccurring *cuando* 'when' clause is said to neutralize the opposition between Imperfect forms, for example, *Cuando llegaste, llovía/estaba lloviendo* 'when you arrived, it rained/it was raining'. Nevertheless, elsewhere Rallides (1971: 44) pointed out that, with *llovía*, "the rain [...] could still be going on when I say it" (cf. Bello 1973: 221, §629), but *estaba lloviendo* would not be used if the rain was continuing at speech time, indicating a limited duration. In his response to Rallides (1966), Douglass (1967: 100–1) built on Bull's (1965) distinction between cyclic and non-cyclic events and qualified the difference between *estar* + *-ndo* and simple Present and Imperfect forms as one of restriction of the duration of time around a reference point for a non-cyclic event, such as *canto* 'I sing', or possibly a series for a cyclic event, such as *salgo* 'I leave'.

A third set of treatments of *estar* + *-ndo* has emphasized a feature of actualization. Working in the Prague structuralist framework, Hamplová (1967: 217) proposed moment-of-speech currentness ("actualización") and dynamic ongoingness ("expresión dinámica") as the two distinctive features of *estoy escribiendo*. Quesada (1995: 27–8) also identified [actual] together with [progressive] as defining features of *estar* + *-ndo*. In a similar vein, from data from the *Norma Culta* project (cf. Lope Blanch 1986), Parisi (1992: 61–2) argued that differences between *estar* + *-ndo* and simple Present and Imperfect forms derive from a distinction between "iterative" (read: habitual) versus "actual" duratives. Related to actualization is King and Suñer's (1980b; cf. King 1992: 84–99) feature [overt]. These scholars proposed that the single invariant meaning yielding the appropriate contrast between *estar* + *-ndo* and a corresponding simple form in a given context is overtness, "*as if* [the activity] *were actually* taking place and being viewed by the speaker" (emphasis in original).

Several studies have focused on past tense forms. Based on judgements and semantic tests within the framework of situation and viewpoint aspect developed by Smith (1991), Westfall (1995: 358) proposed that Imperfect *estaba + -ndo* is distinguished by dynamism from the simple Imperfect, since it generally does not occur with statives nor accept a habitual interpretation. Likewise, in his analysis of oral narratives (Labov 1972b; Labov and Waletzky 1967) and expositions of past situations (Silva-Corvalán 1991: 265), Gonzales (1995) showed that *estaba + -ndo* background situations are simultaneous with foregrounded narrative events, while simple Imperfects are mostly "habitually repeated" (cf. Quesada 1995: 26, note 18). Preterite *estar + -ndo* is extensively discussed in Squartini 1998: 35–70; other mentions are Comrie (1976: 22–3); Fernández (1960: 514); Hamplová (1968: 218); Moliner (1966: 1393); Rallides (1966: 111); and Westfall (1995: 299–305). I do not take up the Preterite here, except to note the diachronic decrease in the ratio of Imperfect to Preterite forms (Section 4.5).

5.1.2 Obligatoriness

In the evolution of lexical into grammatical material some constructions become obligatory. A relevant example is that of the English Present Progressive. According to Strang (1982: 429), its use was unsystematic up to the 17th century, but after 1700 it was grammatically required. Thus, in present-day English it is obligatory that ongoing dynamic situations be expressed by the Present tense *be + -ing* construction. For example (from Bybee 1994: 239),

(1) I drink decaf.
(= habitual choice of coffee)

Right now I am drinking a cup of decaf.
(= action simultaneous with moment of speech)

*Right now I drink a cup of decaf.

As Bybee (1994) argues, a consequence of the development of the Present Progressive as an obligatory expression of progressive aspect is restriction of the simple Present to habitual and generic uses. Cross-linguistically, when a morpheme takes over progressive territory the erstwhile general present form is left with a default present habitual meaning (Bybee et al. 1994: 151). The question is, what is happening in Spanish?

Reference grammars of Spanish generally include a statement to the effect that the simple Present may be used to express progressive meaning (e.g. De Bruyne 1995: 437; cf. Bull 1965: 164, Solé and Solé 1977: 42, Stockwell et al. 1965: 289). The assumption that the simple Present is available to express progressive meaning is very widespread (e.g. Comrie 1976: 33, 112) and forms the basis for the thesis of Spanish-English grammatical convergence with respect to the use of *estar* + *-ndo* in contact situations. The claim is that bilinguals make less use of the option to use the simple Present than monolinguals to refer to progressive situations (Klein 1980). However, no study I know of so far has used the test suggested by Poplack (1993: 276), that is, to count and compare the proportion of *estar* + *-ndo* and simple Present forms with progressive as opposed to habitual uses.

The question of obligatoriness has taken different forms in treatments of *estar* + *-ndo* over the years. A common frame of reference is inquiry into the nature of the "opposition" between *estoy cantando* and *canto*, as in the exchange between Rallides (1966) and Douglass (1967) in the pages of *Hispania*. Another way the question materializes is in evaluations of the form's status in the verb system. For example, Alarcos (1980: 84) determined that *estar* + *-ndo* is not on the same structural level as *haber* + Past Participle, while King (1992: 85) argued for including the set of Progressive forms within the Spanish verb system. The question is often phrased in terms of whether two sets of forms are in "free variation". Thus, Marchand (1955: 50–51) asserted that Spanish speakers, unlike their English counterparts, have a choice between "two variants" to answer the question "what are you doing at this moment?". Underlying such deliberations on free variation, integration into the conjugational paradigm, and opposition with simple verb forms is the question of obligatoriness.

It is not surprising that teleological arguments about structural gaps or needs are not helpful in appraising the evolution of *estar* + *-ndo*, since the reasoning can go either way. For example, Marchand (1955: 51) reasoned that, since Spanish already has an imperfective, there is not much room for *estar* + *-ndo*, in contrast with English *be* + *-ing*. On the other hand, Keniston (1936: 165) found that, because the simple tenses are so broad, there is a need for expressions of particular aspects. As Lehman (1985: 314) observes, structural explanations of change inevitably encounter the question: "if a given linguistic system functions today, why can it not function in the same way tomorrow?"

5.1.3 Restriction of the simple present to stative and habitual

The distribution of simple Present forms in the educated Mexico City oral data (Lope Blanch 1971) analyzed by Moreno de Alba (1978) indicates that, at least with dynamic situations, the simple Present is rarely — if at all — used with progressive meaning. Table 43 summarizes Moreno de Alba's (1978: 18–41) classification of the uses of the simple Present based on 8355 tokens. The six largest groupings are *actual momentáneo* 'current punctual', *actual durativo* 'current durative', *habitual* 'habitual', *intemporal* 'atemporal', *con valor futuro* 'with future meaning', and *con valor de pretérito* 'with Preterite meaning'.

Table 43. Uses of simple Present (Moreno de Alba 1978: 18–41)

	N	%
Actual momentáneo 'current punctual'	684	8.1%
Actual durativo 'current durative' = non-progressive continuous (statives)	4065	48.6%
Habitual = habitual	1631	19.5%
Intemporal 'atemporal' = gnomic situations	1098	13.1%
Futuro = future	599	7.1%
Pretérito = past	226	2.7%
Casos especiales 'special cases'	52	0.6%
TOTAL	8355	

Presente actual momentáneo or moment-of-speech uses make up only 8.1% of all simple Present tokens. But even most of this low percentage is not really progressive. This grouping is composed overwhelmingly of expressions with verbs of speech, as in *Yo te aseguro que...* 'I assure you that...' (220/684 = 32%) and mental verbs, as with *Yo creo que..., me parece que...* 'I think that...' (211/684 = 31%). Such main clause predicates seem to function more as performatives or epistemic phrases (cf. Thompson and Mulak 1991).

Presente actual durativo or durative best corresponds to Comrie's (1976: 25) non-progressive continuous. Most cases are with stative predicates. Indeed, 32% (1298/4065) of all tokens in this category are with *ser* 'be' alone. Adding in tokens of *tener* 'have', *estar* 'be (located)', *hay* 'there is/are', *saber* 'know', *llamarse* 'be called', *conocer* 'know', *existir* 'exist', and other "verbos de modo de acción imperfectivo – durativo" 'verbs of imperfective – durative Aktionsart' for which figures are provided (Moreno de Alba 1978: 24–25), gives us a stative predicate total of 83% (3382/4065) in this category. The figure is undoubtedly higher, since Moreno de Alba's (1978: 25) "other verbs" includes statives *vivir* 'live', *gustar* 'like', *necesitar* 'need'. Overall, the "presente actual durativo" grouping constitutes close to half (48.6%) of all simple Present tokens.

Other simple Present uses in Moreno de Alba's data are habitual, as in *En la mañana estudia, en la tarde trabaja* 'in the morning she studies, in the evening she works', for about 20% of all simple Present tokens; gnomic, that is, describing generic situations, as in *El bien de uno es el bien de todos* 'the benefit of one is the benefit of all', for another 13% (*ser* 'be' again makes up close to half of the tokens (485/1098) in this grouping); future, including the periphrastic *ir a* + Infinitive future, conditional *si* 'if' clauses, and expected future uses, as in *Cumple 76 años en agosto* 'he is 76 years old in August', for 7%; and past, including narrative time, for example, *Eso pasó el año pasado y por poco me ponen en pijama de madera* 'this happened last year and they nearly put me in a wooden pajama (I nearly died)', for 3%.

The increasing restriction of the simple Present to non-progressive imperfective uses is evidence that *estar* + *-ndo* is becoming an obligatory expression of progressive aspect in the present. The obligatoriness of *está* + *-ndo* as a present progressive morpheme is affirmed by Blansitt (1975: 5–6), who makes the unequivocal statement that the simple Present cannot generally be used to express progressive meaning with dynamic verbs ("verbs of action"), especially in declarative-affirmative sentences. He stars as ungrammatical an example parallel to English **Right now I drink a cup of decaf*:

(2) **(Él) come en este momento*
'He eats at this moment'

Quesada (1995: 27) provides evidence from an oral corpus from San José, Costa Rica that simple Present *como* 'I eat' is not a possible answer to *¿qué haces?* or *¿qué estás haciendo?* 'what are you doing?'. In a count of all present progressive contexts, this scholar found that *está* + *-ndo* occurred in 88.12% (282/320) (Quesada 1995: 23).

The changing status of *estar* + *-ndo* is slowly making its way to reference grammars. Kattán-Ibarra and Pountain (1997: 416) affirm that the "tendency" in present-day Spanish is to use *está* + *-ndo* for moment-of-speech progressives. Although the authors state that the simple Present may be used with durative predicates such as 'speak', 'play', 'sleep', two of three of their examples are questions. It is actually quite difficult to find satisfactory examples of declarative-affirmative Present forms with progressive meaning among those provided in reference grammars. Solé and Solé's (1967: 43) examples are an expression of modality (ability), *el niño camina ya* which really means 'the child **can** walk', and a question, *¿A quién buscas?* 'Who are you looking for?'.

It is not surprising that progressive uses of the simple Present survive in questions since these are more conservative environments. Progressive use of the simple Present is strongest in the formulaic *¿qué haces?* 'what are you doing?' A pattern we note in the Chihuahua data is the use of a simple Present form in a question, replied to with an *estar* + *-ndo* form (sometimes elliptical) in the answer.

(3)   R: *¿Tú qué haces?*
      CJ: *Viendo uno de los cuentos de ese señor que te decía.*
           (Chih'97#2B)
      'R: What are you doing? [literally: what do you do?]
      CJ: [I'm] looking at one of the stories of that man I told you about'

Beside the strength of formulas, the subjectively-experienced meaning component of *estar* + *-ndo* (Section 4.3) may also account in part for the use of the simple Present in questions. In a section entitled "Subjetividad y aspecto" 'subjectivity and aspect', Roca Pons (1958: 30) illustrates the difference between *llueve* 'it rains' and *está lloviendo* 'it is raining' thus: the latter is said to be uttered "después de observar la calle" 'after observing the street'. Butt and Benjamin's (1994: 232) discussion of essentially the same example supports the view that this subjective difference is related to whether the speaker directly experiences the situation:

> It seems that a continuous action must be **perceived** to be in progress: Peninsular informants said *está lloviendo* on seeing rain through a window, and thought that *llueve* might sound poetic or archaic. But most said *asómate a ver si llueve* 'look out and see if it's raining', or *¿llueve o no llueve?* 'is it raining or not?', the reason apparently being that someone who asks whether it is raining has obviously not perceived rain actually falling (Butt and Benjamin 1994: 232, my underlining).

5.1.4 Token frequency increases

The creation of obligatory categories is reflected in a rise in frequency, since an obligatory expression comes to be used in both redundant and non-redundant contexts (Bybee et al. 1994: 8; Bybee and Dahl 1989). In the case of

English *be* + *-ing*, some estimates put the rate of increase at a doubling every century since 1500 (Dennis 1940; see also Visser 1973, §1864). We have already shown a diachronic process of frequency increases for *-ndo* constructions (Chapter 2, Section 2.5). In the absence of any synchronic empirical data comparing the proportion of simple and *estar* + *-ndo* forms used with progressive meaning in monolingual and bilingual varieties, one way to evaluate the claim that *estar* + *-ndo* is used more frequently in bilingual varieties is to compare token frequencies.

Table 44 shows the average occurrence of *estar* + *-ndo* per 10,000 words of running text in eight corpora (cf. Table 36, Chapter 4).

Table 44. Token frequencies of ESTAR + -NDO (per 10,000 words)

Corpus*	Word count	Estar + -ndo tokens (N)	Token frequency
Early 20th c. prose	600,000	304	5.1
1965–90 novels	1,300,000	1318	10.1
Essays	376,300	67	1.9
Madrid	148,200	262	17.7
Habla culta	1,300,000	3068	23.6
MexPop	172,700	340	19.7
Chihuahua	152,000	356	23.4
NMbil	49,700	117	23.5

* See Table 12 and Table 15 (Chapter 2) on word and token counts.

A comparison of token frequencies suggests a change in progress in the grammatical status of *estar* + *-ndo*. The figures for the first two rows indicate that the rate of token frequency increases has accelerated. In roughly half a century, the text frequency of *estar* + *-ndo* in literary texts has nearly doubled, increasing from an average occurrence of 5.1 per 10,000 words in Keniston's (1937b) corpus of early 20th c. (1900–1933) prose texts, to 10.1 in Clegg and Rodríguez's (1993) corpus of novels published approximately between 1965 and 1990. In comparison, it took four centuries for *estar* + *-ndo* text frequency to get from 3.1 in Keniston's (1937a) corpus of 16th c. prose to 5.1 in his early 20th c. corpus, less than a twofold increase (see *estar* column in Table 12, Chapter 2). Even allowing for differences in the kinds of prose surveyed, the increase between Early 20th c. prose and 1965–90 novels is consistent with our findings on diachronic frequency increases and points to an acceleration of the change in progress.

Is the change near "consummation" or, in other words, is there a frequency threshold for obligatoriness? I am not aware of cross-linguistic frequency data but a comparison with English gives some indications. In her study of *be + -ing*, Strang (1982: 432), takes a rate of about 30 tokens per 10,000 words as "representing the maturity of the construction", a stage reached "by the mid-nineteenth century". From Table 44 we see that in oral corpora *estar + -ndo* has a frequency of about 20, so it seems to be getting close. Figures from Nehls (1988) put the token frequency of *be + -ing* at 1.6 in Chaucer, 4 in Shakespeare, 25 in Jane Austen's *Pride and Prejudice* and 83.7 for a corpus of plays written around 1960.[1] If modern plays reflect spoken varieties, the latter figure (83.7) indicates that *be + -ing* is still about four times more frequent than *estar + -ndo*, based on the oral data figures in Table 44, in the range between 17.7 and 23.6. Of course, the comparison is not fair, since other *-ndo* constructions are used as progressives in Spanish; if these are included the figures go up in the range of 29.2 to 37.5 (see Table 15, Section 2.6). Another complication is that the corpus of English plays might have more dialogue or rapid exchanges than the Spanish data we are comparing. The data we have for journalism show a smaller difference between Spanish and English. Mair and Hundt (1995: 118) report mid-30s to low 40s for four corpora of newspaper texts, two from 1961 and two from 1991/2. Olbertz (1998: 549) shows 19.2 (93 tokens in 48,559 words) for Peninsular Spanish 1990 journalistic texts, or about half the English frequency. On the other hand, the results of Dahl's (1985: 90) questionnaire data put English and Spanish at about the same frequency, with an average of 39 and 37, respectively (in questionnaire responses). From all this, we can say that Spanish *estar + -ndo* is still probably less frequent than English *be + -ing*.

The results in Table 44 also confirm that there are tremendous register differences in the token frequency of *estar + -ndo*. Academic prose as sampled in the Essays corpus has the lowest token frequency, at approximately 2 occurrences per 10,000 words. In oral data, both educated (Madrid and Habla culta) and popular (MexPop, Chihuahua, NMbil) token frequency is around 20 occurrences per 10,000 words. This is about ten times greater (!) than in formal academic prose (Essays) and two times greater than in literary prose (1965–90 novels). Differences between written and oral modes and between formal and informal varieties in the token frequency of *estar + -ndo* support our hypothesis of a change in progress since written language is generally more conservative (cf. Silva-Corvalán 1994: 130).

Correlations between register and linguistic variables have formed a productive line of research in recent years (e.g. Biber and Finegan 1994). In Spanish, stylistic and genre effects on variation have been found in phonology (Cameron 1996; Medina-Rivera 1996), verb morphology (Silva-Corvalán 1991, 1992), relative-clause syntax (Gervasi 1997), and direct quotation strategies (Cameron 1998). Several scholars mention that *-ndo* constructions are characteristic of oral, especially, "colloquial" or "popular" varieties (Dietrich 1983: 483; Lenz 1925: 417; M. Seco 1989: 221; Spaulding 1926: 256). With respect to past tense forms, Westfall 1995: 379, 384) states that *estaba + -ndo* is used for backgrounding in oral narrative where a simple Imperfect would be used in a literary text (cf. Kattán-Ibarra and Pountain 1997: 439). Appraisals such as these confirm that register is an important factor in the token frequency of *estar + -ndo* (see Section 2.6 and 2.7).

Register differences are relevant in evaluating changes in bilingual with respect to monolingual varieties, since the former are less subject to normative pressure (Section 1.4.3). As shown in Table 44, the token frequency of *estar + -ndo* in the bilingual New Mexico group is 23 tokens per 10,000 words. This is about double the figure for literary data (1965–90 novels). However, if we compare oral data, we find that the NMbil figure is only slightly greater than figures for educated Madrid (18) and popular Mexico City (20), and identical to figures for Chihuahua (23.4) and educated capital city or *habla culta* Spanish (23.6). In sum, a comparison of token frequencies fails to provide support for changes in bilingual with respect to monolingual varieties.

To summarize, increasing restriction of the simple Present to non-progressive uses and increases in the token frequency of *estar + -ndo* support the hypothesis that a change in the grammatical status of *estar + -ndo* is in progress. Thus, "loss" of the option to express present progressive with the simple Present is a process that appears to be underway in oral varieties of Spanish, both bilingual and monolingual.

Future studies can contribute to what we know about the creation of obligatory progressive categories by investigating some of the questions brought up by the case of *estar + -ndo*: Does the change affect one group of verbs before it affects others (for example, telic before atelic)?[2] Does it occur in certain types of clausal environments (for example, main declarative clauses) before others (for example, subordinate clauses and questions)? Is the change more advanced in the present than in past tenses?

5.2 Experiential habitual uses

Grammaticization not only produces changes in the relations among different morphemes, it is relentless in the production of variation in a single form. At the same time as Present-tense *estar* + *-ndo* is pushing the simple Present out of progressive territory, it is itself making incursions into habitual territory. This will be the subject of the next two sections.

5.2.1 From progressive to experiential habitual

A widely held assumption, especially in grammars for English speakers, is that Present *estar* + *-ndo* is restricted to situations that are actually ongoing at the moment of speech (cf. Bybee et al. 1994: 136; King and Suñer 1980b: 223, note7). Nevertheless, instances of "iterative" or "frequentative" uses are cited by several scholars (e.g. Gómez Torrego 1988: 147; Markič 1990: 184; Quesada 1995: 13–15).

Studies of spoken Mexico City Spanish confirm that the purported restriction to progressive uses simply does not hold. Moreno de Alba (1978: 39), applying the groupings used for all Present forms (Table 43), divides his 222 tokens of Present *estar* + *-ndo* into three groups, *actual momentáneo* 'current punctual' (10%), *actual extenso* 'current extended' (62%), and *habitual* 'habitual' (28%), as shown in Table 45. *Actual momentáneo* are dynamic situations coinciding with the moment of speech, as in *la música que **están oyendo** en este momento* 'the music **they are listening** to at his moment'. *Actual extenso* are dynamic or stative situations which began in the past and continue uninterruptedly into the present, including the moment of speech, for example, *necesidades de la época que **están viviendo*** 'necessities of the time **they are living**'. *Habitual* are repeated, mostly dynamic, situations, as in *Salgo de aquí a las seis y media de la mañana y **me estoy trabajando** hasta las doce* 'I leave here at six thirty in the morning and I work (literally: **I am working**) until twelve'.

Table 45. Uses of ESTAR + -NDO Present (Moreno de Alba 1978: 39)

	N	%
Actual momentáneo 'current punctual' = progressive	22	10%
Actual extenso 'current extended' = continuous	138	62%
Habitual	62	28%
TOTAL	222	

From progressive to experiential habitual 189

Moreno de Alba's (1978: 39) three groups roughly correspond to progressive, continuous, and habitual, respectively, in Comrie's (1976) terms. In this data, then, moment-of-speech progressives make up the lowest proportion of Present *estar* + *-ndo*. Similarly, Luna (1980: 202–4) finds that only 9% (43/482) of Present *estar* + *-ndo* refer to a (dynamic) situation strictly taking place simultaneously with the moment of speech, while Arjona (1991: 119) finds 8% (20/244) such cases. In both studies "talking" verbs such as *hablando* 'talking', *platicando* 'chatting', *diciendo* 'saying' make up more than half of all tokens in this grouping.

Although the groupings and meaning labels used in these studies are not always clear, it is evident that Present *está* + *-ndo* is not limited to present progressive meaning. From a crosslinguistic perspective, Bybee et al. (1994: 140–8) discuss the generalization of erstwhile progressives to habitual contexts and use with stative predicates. For example, the Turkish suffix *-yor* has habitual uses in the spoken language although it is restricted to progressive meaning in written texts; the Progressive form in Scots Gaelic has become an Imperfective, as in *tha e a' seinn* 'he is singing, he sings' (Comrie 1976: 100); other cases of erstwhile progressives assuming present tense or general imperfective functions are cited in Dahl (1985: 93) and Heine (1994: 280).

I propose that the next major step in the generalization of *estar* + *-ndo*, following locative and progressive, is extension to what I call experiential habitual. The major steps in the bleaching process can be diagrammed as follows:

(a) subject is **located spatially** in action simultaneous with moment of reference
 ↓
(b) subject is Ø in action **simultaneous with moment of reference**
 ↓
(c) subject is   in action   Ø

Figure 11. Steps in bleaching of ESTAR + -NDO

This diachronic path of evolution is reflected in present-day variation, as shown in Figure 12.

```
LOCATIVE
 (examples 4)         >
    PROGRESSIVE
     (examples 5)        >
        EXPERIENTIAL HABITUAL
         (examples 6)
```

Figure 12. Synchronic variation in the uses of ESTAR + -NDO

The following Chihuahua examples illustrate:

(4) a. - *¿Dónde está la niña?*
- *Viendo la tele ¿no?* (Chih'97#1A)
'Where is the child?
Watching TV, isn't she?'

b. - *¿Ahí está Martina?*
- *Está planchando.* (Chih'97#23A)
'Is Martina there?
She's ironing'

(5) a. *nos estamos tomando un refresquito, si gusta una- [] una soda o algo.* (Chih'97#2A)
'we're having a drink, would you like a soda or something?'
b. *No no no no. Estoy diciendo la verdad.* (Chih'97#3A)
'No no no no. I'm telling the truth'

(6) a. *Que ahorita nos están pagando 580 a la s[h]emana. Nos pagaban 493, ahora de hace- Pues apenas teníamos dos semanas que nos subieron a 580. Ahí trabajamos 58 horas por semana. Para ganar los 580.* (Chih'97#VIA)
'Now they are paying us 580 a week. They were paying 493, since- Well it was only two weeks ago that they raised it to 580. We work there 58 hours a week. To make the 580.'
b. *...se fue a Tijuana. El pelado ahorita está ganando entre quinze o veinte mil pesos. Quinze o veinte millones de los antiguos.* (Chih'97#13A)
'...he went to Tijuana. The guy right now is earning between fifteen or twenty thousand. Fifteen or twenty million of the old ones [Mexican pesos].'

In (4) the actions have a characteristic location and the subject can be located, in front of the TV in the first example, at the ironing board in the second. In (5) the locative meaning component has been lost, leaving a temporal meaning of ongoingness at speech time. In (6) the actions are no longer single situations but ones that are repeated on different occasions, at regular pay periods.

We can group analyses of present habitual uses of *estar* + *-ndo* into two main sets, one based on durativity and the other on transitoriness.

The first set of analyses subsume habitual uses under a special reading of durativity. A clear exposition consistent I think with this approach is provided in a typological study of Romance periphrases by Squartini (1998). Unlike Spanish, the Italian Progressive is restricted to situations viewed as ongoing at reference time. Squartini (1998: 74–5) explains the difference as a manifestation of different stages in a grammaticization process, which he outlines as follows:

(7)   LOCATIVITY > DURATIVITY > IMPERFECTIVE PROGRESSIVITY > ?
        [+ ACTIONALITY]   >   [–ACTIONALITY]
        [– ASPECT]   >   [+ ASPECT]

"Actionality" roughly corresponds to Smith's (1991) "situation aspect" (as opposed to "viewpoint aspect") or to Vendler's (1967) predicate classes (Squartini 1998: 4–7). In stage 2 the Progressive is restricted to durative atelic situations (actional restrictions) but is compatible with both perfective and imperfective morphology (no aspectual restriction). In stage 3 the form evolves into a marker of imperfective aspect with fewer actional restrictions. In this analysis, *estar + -ndo*

> is at a stage that encompasses both durativity and imperfective progressivity: in Spanish [as in Italian] the periphrasis occurs as an imperfective form referring to an on-going situation, but this is not its only possible function, since it still has a durative perfective value (Squartini 1998: 75).

It is this ability to denote pure durativity without insisting on a particular reference time that allows *estar + -ndo* to indicate repeated situations, each occurrence of which is durative but not viewed as ongoing at reference time (Squartini 1998: 76–7).[3] This, for example, is the case in:

(8)   *yo salgo de aquí a las seis y media de la mañana y me **estoy trabajando** hasta las doce, la una de la mañana*
      'I leave here at six thirty in the morning and I work (literally: **I am working**) until twelve, one in the morning'

Particular understandings of durativity also underlie analyses of *siempre* 'always' + *estar + -ndo* that explain this combination as presenting a regularly repeated situation as durative. Parisi's (1992) account of *está + -ndo* habitual uses is based on a distinction between two kinds of durative, "actual" versus "iterative". Thus, examples like

(9) *ella **está siempre hablando** en esos términos*
'**she is always speaking** in those terms',

express actual duration in that "the 'speaking' ... [is] understood as ... continuous, i.e., emphasizing that the succession is unbroken" (Parisi 1992: 61–2). Squartini (1998: 81), following Yllera (1980: 25), presents essentially the same view: "the situation is such a constant habit that it is presented as uninterrupted". This is similar to Brinton's (1988: 41) formulation, "the effect ... is to portray the habit, which is not continuous *as if* continuous".

Rather than explaining habitual cases as special manifestations of durativity, another set of approaches emphasizes the transitory character of these habituals. Many Hispanists have observed a nuance of transitory or unexpected situation in *estar* + *-ndo* (e.g. Butt and Benjamin 1994: 233; Lope Blanch 1962; King 1992: 126; Zdenek 1972). The English Progressive, too, may have a transitory habitual use. Blansitt (1975: 3), following Chafe (1970), distinguishes "non-generic" or moment-of-speech progressive and "generic" progressive, which is used in a restricted habitual sense, as when someone has been ill, and *"now he is eating"*. Akin to Blansitt's "generic" progressive is Bull's (1965: 164) proposal, in line with his analysis of *estar* versus *ser*, that *está* + *-ndo* expresses a deviation from the norm encoded in the simple Present. In Bulls examples, *llora mucho* 'she cries a lot' is the normal pattern, while *está llorando mucho* 'she is crying a lot', indicates that something is wrong; similarly, *¿qué haces?* 'what are you doing', would be directed to a child playing a new game, while *¿qué estás haciendo?* 'what are you doing', to a child setting fire to his grandmother's skirt (cf. Kattán-Ibarra and Pountain 1997: 416–7). It is this second approach that I will build on here.

I am calling "experiential habitual " a situation that is habitual in the sense of Comrie (1977: 27–8), that is, one which is characteristic of a whole period, but which is further specified to be new or noteworthy from the point of view of the speaker. The main refinement proposed here is that experiential habitual may or may not refer to a transitory — temporally delimited — situation. Experiential habitual crucially specifies a subjective meaning component, which is related to the use of *estar* + *-ndo* to express personal involvement in the situation (see Chapter 4, Section 4.3). Thus, *estar* + *-ndo* has clear affective connotations in example (8), *me estoy trabajando hasta las doce* 'I am working until twelve'. In (6), *ahorita nos están pagando* 'now they are paying us' and *ahorita está ganando* 'now he is earning', *estar* + *-ndo* expresses a perceived recent and contrastive situation.

From progressive to experiential habitual 193

In the following section (5.3), I provide evidence for subjectivity from cooccurring deictic elements such as *ahorita* 'now'. First, though, I mention two measures of the extension of *estar* + *-ndo* into habitual territory, cooccurrence with frequentative adverbials and general activity main verbs.

5.2.2 Indices of habituality: frequentative adverbials and general activity main verbs

An evident measure of compatibility with habitual meaning is cooccurrence with frequentative adverbials. We have already seen that this represents a change from Old Spanish (Chapter 3, Section 3.3). As shown in Table 46, the average cooccurrence of frequentative adverbials with Present *estar* + *-ndo* in the Chihuahua data is 3% (7/224). Of course, most of the time — 71% (158/224) — there is no cooccurring temporal adverbial. If we subtract the number of tokens without a temporal adverbial, we see that frequentative adverbials make up about 11% (7/66) of all Present-tense *estar* + *-ndo* temporal expressions. Frequentative adverbials in the data are *a veces* 'sometimes', *muchas veces* 'many times', *cada cinco minutos* 'every five minutes', *constantemente* 'constantly', *diari(o)* 'daily', *mes por mes* 'every month' and *siempre* 'always'. In the New Mexico monolingual and bilingual groups combined there was one token each of *a veces* 'sometimes', *siempre* 'always' and *todo el día* 'all day', for an average of 3% (3/98), or about 8% (3/39) if we subtract tokens without any temporal adverbial. These percentages are virtually identical to the ones for the Chihuahua data.[4]

Table 46. Frequentative adverbials in Present-tense ESTAR + -NDO

	% all tokens	% tokens with temporal adverbial
Chihuahua (Chih'97)	3% (7/224)	11% (7/66)
New Mexico (NMmon & NMbil)	3% (3/98)	8% (3/39)

In the following example with cooccurring *por mes* 'monthly' the speaker is talking about the high cost of electricity needed to pump water from the wells:

(10) *Y nos cuesta mucho, mucho. Ahorita aproximadamente pagamos nosotros por los... [] **por mes estamos pagando** por cada pozo se paga aproximadamente entre cinco y seis mil pesos. O sea hablamos de pesos de los viejos, seis millones.* (Chih'97#21B)
'And it costs us a lot, a lot. Right now we pay approximately for

the... **every month we are paying** for every well, you pay approximately between five and six thousand pesos. Or in terms of the old pesos, six million'

In this example, paying 5–6,000 pesos a month is a customary situation, repeated monthly over a period of time, hence habitual. At the same time it is a new situation, prices have gone up, as indicated by *ahorita* 'right now'. Indications of subjectivity are repetition of the adjective *mucho* 'a lot' (speaker point of view) and the first person plural dative in *nos cuesta* 'it costs us' (personal involvement). The subject of the *estar* + *-ndo* construction is a first person plural, *estamos pagando*. In contrast, immediately afterwards the speaker uses the simple Present in an "impersonal *se*" construction, *se paga* 'one pays, you pay'.

Another measure of the degree to which *estar* + *-ndo* has extended to habitual uses is the frequency of "general activity" main verbs. General activity main verbs refer to an activity that is made up of specific sub-activities, so that there is no one specific activity one can point to as constituting the general activity (see Section 4.6.2). It is striking that the single-most frequent *estar* + *-ndo* main verb in three of four corpora for which figures are available is *trabajando* 'working'. In the next set of examples, "working in Delicias" or "working in the bank" are general activities composed of specific sub-activities such as counting money, talking with a customer, printing a statement. In neither case is the job in progress at the moment of speech.

(11) *Todos estamos aquí nada más que mi papá y mi mamá* **están trabajando** *en Delicias, tenemos una casa allá. Y* **están trabajando** *allá ahorita andan, pues andan en qué. En el ajo creo.* (Chih'97#1B)
'We're all here, only my father and mother **are working** in Delicias, we have a house there. And **they are working** there, now they are in, in what? In (picking) garlic I think'

(12) *Ya está grande, ahora* **está trabajando** *ella en el banco. En Belén.* (NMbil/Bea)
'She's already grown up, now **she is working** in the bank. In Belen'

Estar trabajando makes up 9.7% (16/165) of all *estar* + *-ndo* tokens in Parisi's (1992) *habla culta* sample; 8.5% (29/340) in MexPop; and 8.9% (20/225) in New Mexico (including all groups).[5] Only in the Chihuahua corpus does *trabajando* not hold first place, but even here this verb comes third, after *deciendo* 'saying' and *platicando* 'chatting', with 5.6% (20/356). Other general activity main verbs are *estudiando* 'studying, attending school', fourth most frequent in Parisi's (1992) data and in MexPop, and *pagando* 'paying', second most frequent in MexPop and ninth in Chihuahua. These predicates could be grouped with *trabajando* in an "occupations — income/expenses" class. That speakers use *estar* + *-ndo* instead of a simple form when talking about these things may well be a reflection of the lack of economic stability in modern times. The label "experiential habitual" represents this nuanced kind of habitualness.

5.3 Subjectivity and deixis in *estar* + *-ndo*

How can we operationalize the notion of subjectivity or experiential uses with respect to *estar* + *-ndo*? In Chapter 4 we briefly looked at polarity and subject animacy as a way to quantify overtness and active involvement (Section 4.3.1). We return here to subject animacy and also consider two structural variables related to deixis and the category known as shifters (Jakobson 1971). We will look at what I am calling a "grammatical-person-index" of speaker involvement, which includes first and second person subjects and first person object pronouns (cf. Benveniste 1971: 161–187). Then we will look at the cooccurrence of deictic adverbials of time and place. Throughout we will be comparing Chihuahua and New Mexico data, to see if there is loss of the experiential meaning component in bilinguals, since a major hypothesis in Spanish-English contact studies is that foreign influence may be manifested in the weakening of discourse-pragmatic constraints (Silva-Corvalán 1994).

5.3.1 Subject animacy

Estar + *-ndo* begins with human agents or experiencers and gradually generalizes to inanimate subjects, probably through an intermediate stage where a human, though no longer the grammatical subject, is an affected participant, as in constructions with a human dative, for example, *me está pasando algo **a mí*** 'something is happening **to me**' (Chapter 4, Figure 6 and Table 35). In a situation of contact with English, either a convergence hypothesis or an acceleration-of-change hypothesis would predict that inanimate subjects are more frequent than in monolingual varieties (Chapter 1, Section 1.4.1). In a convergence hypothesis there will be more inanimate subjects as Spanish achieves greater similarity with English (assuming inanimate subjects are more frequent in the English Progressive than in the Spanish *estar + -ndo* construction). In an acceleration hypothesis, the internal or native process of generalization to inanimate subjects will be sped up in a contact situation.

Table 47 shows the distribution of *estar + -ndo* subject types by animacy. The average occurrence of human subjects ranges from 86% in the Chihuahua group (Chih'97) to 93% in the New Mexico monolingual group (NMmon). In between these extremes are the bilingual group (NMbil), at 90% and the Mexico City corpus (MexPop), at 91% (Table 35, Chapter 4). The differences in the proportion of tokens with a human subject are not significant statistically at p < .01, an appropriate level of significance given the small sample sizes.[6] Thus, contact with English has not resulted in increased use of inanimate subjects.

Table 47. Animacy of subject in ESTAR + -NDO (Chihuahua and New Mexico)

	Chih'97 N	%	NMmon N	%	NMbil N	%
Humans	306	**86%**	39	**93%**	130	**90.3%**
Objects	14	4%	1	2.4%	3	2.1%
Situations	13	3.6%	1	2.4%	5	3.5%
Machines	10	3%	1	2.4%	2	1.4%
Organizations	7	2%			4	2.7%
Weather	5	1.4%				
Animals	1					
Total	356	100	42	100.2	144	100

* Differences among groups in the proportion of human subjects are not significant at p < 0.01 (see note 6).

English influence might not show up quantitatively as a difference in inanimate subject frequencies, but qualitatively as a difference in inanimate subject types. Neither on this measure, however, do we find a difference between the corpora. In Chihuahua, inanimate subjects fall into five classes (numbers of tokens are given in parentheses):
1. Physical objects, such as *agua* 'water', *chile* 'chili', *ejido* 'land', *gas* 'gas', *papel* 'paper', *pozo* 'well', *terreno* 'land';
2. "Situations", such as *cosas* 'things'(2), *esto* 'this' or *eso* 'that', *la situación* 'the situation'(4), *lo que* 'that which' (2);

3. Machines, most frequently, *la grabadora* 'tape player' (5) and *la impresora* 'printer' (3);
4. Organizations, institutions, cities, or states, for example, *bancos* 'banks', *Chihuahua* (the state of Chihuahua), *fábricas* 'factories', *gobierno* 'government', *partido* 'political party', *sindicato* 'trade union';
5. Weather expressions, for example, *está haciendo mucho calor* 'it's very hot' (literally: it is doing much heat).

The distribution of inanimate subjects in the New Mexico corpus is virtually identical. Inanimate subjects are:
1. Physical or cultural objects (*cultura* 'culture', *idioma* 'language'), for example, *pa hacer el atole, [] ponen [] agua o leche, hasta que está hirviendo* 'to make *atole*, they put water or milk, until **it** is boiling' (NMmon/Mar).
2. "Situations", as in, *las nuevas son las que me gustan mucho mejor [ ] para sabere, que está pasando* 'What I like best (to listen to) is the news, so I can know **what** is happening' (NMmon/NMCSS#214).
3. Cities, as in, *Está creciendo mucho pa cuando nosotros nos mudamos para acá* 'It (**Albuquerque**) is growing a lot compared to when we moved here' (NMbil/Edw).
4. Machines. The most common machine subject is "tape recorder", with five tokens in Chih'97 and two in the New Mexico corpus. This is not surprising, since recording was in progress throughout the data collection.

(13) a. *Ahí está grabando.* (Chih'97/10A)
'It is recording'
b. *¿Está corriendo o no?* (NMmon/NMCSS#245)
'Is it running (recording)?

A measure of speaker involvement when the grammatical subject is inanimate is the occurrence of a first person object pronoun. In the Chihuahua data we have *nos* 'us', *me* 'me', or *a uno* 'one'. In some cases the main verb is a "reflexive", for example, *interesarse* 'to interest (one)' or *afectarse* 'to affect (one)' (cf. Silva-Corvalán 1994: 122–3). In others the pronoun clitic can be considered an accusative object, as in the first example below, or a dative-benefactive (Givón 1984: 114), as in the second example.

(14) *...es que nadien se ha propuesto a hacer un sindicato aquí. Por eso yo digo que si se propusiera alguien, lográbamos unirnos y lo hacíamos, verdad, ¿por qué no? Porque sí hace mucha falta, el sindicato porque, **es el que lo está defendiendo**.* (Chih'97/VIA)
'It's that nobody has tried to form a union here. That's why I say that if someone took the initiative, we would be able to unite and we would form it, right, why not. Because it is really needed, the union, because **it is what is defending one**'

(15) *Y luego no sé ahora yo creo que iban a cambiar de proveedores porque **no nos estaba llegando siempre el material**. No sé de dónde lo van a mandar ahora.* (Chih'97/1B)
'I don't know, I think they were going to change suppliers because **the material wasn't always arriving to us**. I'm not sure from where they'll send it now'

The average occurrence of first person object pronoun clitics with inanimate subjects is 18% (9/50) in the Chihuahua data. There was only one such case (of 14 inanimate subjects) in the New Mexico bilingual group, with *olvidarse* 'forget' (*Ves, se me está olvidando el español* 'You see, I'm forgetting Spanish' (NMbil/Vig)). It is possible that a larger sample would reveal a difference between the corpora, but as we will see right away, the average occurrence of first person object pronoun clitics overall, for all third person subjects (human and inanimate combined), is about the same in Chih'97 and NMbil.

5.3.2 Grammatical person

Let us look now at subject person and number. As shown in Table 48, first person singular *estar* + *-ndo* subjects average 18% in the Chihuahua corpus, 38% in the New Mexico monolingual group and 17% in the bilingual group. The exceptionally high average in NMmon may be attributed at least in part to the difference between interview and conversational data (see Chapter 2, Section 2.7). As we would expect, there is a higher proportion of second person subjects in the conversational data, both Chih'97 and NMbil, than in the NMmon interview data (there was only one second person form in the NMmon corpus, and that in the plural!). Differences narrow if we calculate what I call the grammatical-person-index of speaker involvement, that is, if

From progressive to experiential habitual 199

we total first and second person subjects, singular and plural: differences between 45% (19/42) in NMmon, 37% (53/144) in NMbil, and 38% (136/356) in Chih'97 are not statistically significant (p = .6093).

Table 48. *Person and number in ESTAR + -NDO (Chihuahua and New Mexico)*

	Chih'97 N	Chih'97 %	NMmon N	NMmon %	NMbil N	NMbil %
1s	64	**18%**	16	**38%**	24	**17%**
2s	27	**8%**	0	0	4	**3%**
3s	131	37%	13	31%	52	36%
1p	39	11%	2	5%	16	11%
2p	6	2%	1	2%	9	6%
3p	77	22%	9	21%	37	26%
Ger/Inf	12	3%	1	2%	2	1%
Total	356		42		144	

2s includes cases of non-specific *tú* or *usted* (in Chih'97, 5 = 1.4%); 3s includes cases of impersonal constructions, e.g. *ya se está levantando cebolla* (in Chih'97, 8 = 2.2%) as well as cases where the subject is *uno* (8 = 2.2%); 3p includes cases of impersonal constructions, e.g. *ya están dando permisos por seis meses* (in Chih'97, 11 = 3.1%)

Another measure of speaker involvement with third-person singular subjects is the occurrence of first person object pronouns *me* (singular) and *nos* (plural), for example,

(16) *Les dije "Van a tener que aprender a hacer tortillas ustedes porque ya me están fregando" les dije []*. Tita don't make em as good as I do, hers turn to crackers right away. (NMbil/Joe)
'I told them "You're going to have to learn to make tortillas yourselves because **you are already wasting me**" I told them. Tita ...'

Table 49 summarizes. In the Chihuahua data, 13% (26/200) third-person *estar* + *-ndo* tokens (subtracting cases where the subject was *uno* 'one'), had first person object pronouns *me* (singular) or *nos* (plural).[7] In New Mexico bilingual data, the average is 10% (9/89), which is not significantly different from the Chih'97 average (p = .4873). If we define the grammatical-person-index of speaker involvement to include first person pronoun objects in addition to first and second person subjects, we get 46% for Chih'97 (162/356), 48% in NMmon (20/42), and 43% in NMbil (62/144), that is, close to half the tokens in all three data sets. In sum, we do not find a change in the New Mexico data with respect to either subject animacy or grammatical person.

Table 49. First person object pronouns with third person subjects in ESTAR + -NDO

	Total 3s & 3p*	me N	%	nos N	%	Total me-nos N	%
Chih'97	200	13	6.5%	13	6.5%	26	13%
NMbil	89	8	9%	1	1%	9	10%

* 3s total does not include subject *uno*.

5.3.2 Deictic time and place adverbials

Parisi (1992: 53–6) observed that Present *estar* + *-ndo* cooccurs with "temporal restrictors" (*esta mañana* 'this morning', *ahora mismo* 'right now', *en este momento* 'at this moment') and "locative restrictors" (*allí, allá, ahí* 'there', *aquí, acá* 'here'), although she did not report any quantitative results. Let us look in our data, first at deictic time adverbials. Included in this class are *ahora, ahorita* 'now, now-diminutive', *ya* 'now, already', and temporal expressions with a proximal demonstrative, as in *este momento* 'this moment'. I counted tokens in which the adverbial could either be said to be a pre-clausal modifier or a VP modifier, as opposed to being a modifier of some other element in the clause (cf. Koike 1996: 270); in most cases the adverbial immediately precedes or follows *estar* + *-ndo*.

Table 50 shows figures for deictic temporal adverbials cooccurring with Present-tense *estar* + *-ndo* in the Chihuahua and New Mexico bilingual data.[8] Deictic temporals cooccur with 23% (52/224) of all Present-tense tokens in Chih'97 and 25% (20/79) in NMbil. Subtracting tokens with no temporal adverbial, the proportion of deictics is 79% (52/66) in Chih'97 and 67% (20/30) in NMbil (the difference between the proportions is not statistically significant, p = .2036). In other words, deictics make up between two-thirds and three-quarters of Present-tense temporal adverbials, quite an impressive proportion.

Table 50. Deictic temporal adverbials cooccurring with Present-tense ESTAR + -NDO

	Chih'97 N	%	NMbil N	%
Ahora, ahorita 'now, now-diminutive'	19	8.5%	10	12.6%
Ya 'now, already'	19	8.5%	5	6.3%
Ya, ahora combination	6		2	
Demonstrative *este* 'this'	3		1	
Other*	5		2	
Total deictic temporal adverbials	**52**	**23%**	**20**	**25%**
Other temporal adverbials	14		10	
No temporal adverbial	158		49	
Total Present-tense	224		79	

* Other deictic temporal adverbials: *actualmente, apenas, hace* + time, *hasta ahorita, hoy en día*.

Ahora/ita alone cooccurs with about 10% of all Present-tense *estar* + *-ndo* tokens (the difference between Chih'97 8.5% and NMbil 12.6% is not statistically significant, p = .2780). This is quite a substantial proportion.[9] In its own grammaticization, *ahora* has been evolving from a temporal to a discourse deictic and an epistemic marker, with a "light adversative" function (Silva-Corvalán 1997b). In our data the *ahora* + Present-tense *estar* + *-ndo* string may express a contrast with a past situation. In the following example, the idea of change is reinforced lexically with *cambio* 'change' and *diferente* 'different'.

(17) **ahorita estamos viviendo** una, un cambio de generación diferente (Chih'97#13B)
'**right now we are living** a, a change of different generations'

The habitual — progressive distinction is neutralized in stative *vivir* 'live' (cf. Bybee 1994: 238). In the next example, however, *está tocando el piano* 'she is playing the piano' is clearly a habitual situation.

(18) [talking about a "telenovela" character]
Y como va creciendo con el con la historia, está más viva y más viva. [ ] Y **ahora está tocando hasta el piano** (NMbil/Marg)
'And as she gradually matures as the story goes on, she is more and more bright. And **now she is even playing the piano**.'

The idea of change is reinforced here by *hasta* 'even'. In both examples, from the speakers' point of view, the habitual situations are new and noteworthy.

Cooccurring *ya* 'already; now; soon' also has both temporal and discourse functions. In a study of Mexican narratives, Koike (1996) analyzes *ya* as a discourse marker of emotional emphasis. The next example is from the same speaker as the previous one, a comment about the same "telenovela" character. Emotional emphasis or the expression of speaker point of view is evident from use of the evaluative adjective *pobre* 'poor (girl)'.

(19) *Pero esta esta pobre muchacha digo tan joven y **ya le están pintando el cabello**, para que quizás que que tome la parte* (NMbil/Marg)
'But this poor girl, really, so young and **already they are dyeing her hair**, maybe so that she can play the part'

That *ya* is associated with subjective evaluations is supported by De Jonge's (1993: 75) finding that *ya* favors *estar* over *ser* in age expressions in educated Mexico City Spanish. As this scholar observes, in an example such as,

(20) *...pero se me hace que ella **ya está grande** para determinados papeles*
'but it seems to me that **she is already old** for certain parts'

the speaker is not just stating that the actress is old, but is expressing her view that she is too old for certain parts (De Jonge 1993: 74).

Ya cooccurs at essentially the same levels in the Chihuahua and the New Mexico bilingual data, with 8.5% (19/224) and 6.3% (5/79) of all Present-tense tokens, respectively (again, the difference is not statistically significant, p = .5424). Studies of other regions may reveal whether the frequency of *ya* in this context is a Mexican macro-dialect feature or one shared in Spanish-language conversational data; Koike (1996, notes 5 and 9) indicates that there may be important dialect variation in the uses of *ya* in narrative discourse.

Let us now look at deictic adverbials of place (Table 51). These are *aquí* 'here', *ahí, allí, allá* 'there', and combinations of 'here' or 'there' with an *en* + LOC(ation) phrase, as in *la idioma especialmente aquí en el* ninety two *aquí en los Estados Unidos se está perdiendo* 'the language especially here in ninety two **here in the United States** is being lost' (NMbil/NMCSS#21).

Table 51. *Deictic locative adverbials cooccurring with Present-tense ESTAR + -NDO*

	Chih'97 N	%	NMbil N	%
Aquí 'here'	9		5*	
Ahi, allí, allá 'there'	15		4*	
Other**	3		1	
Total deictic locative adverbials	27	12%	10	12.6%
Other locative adverbials	13		9	
No locative adverbial	184		60	
Total Present tense	224		79	

* Includes combinations of *aquí* or *allí* with an *en* + LOC adverbial.
** Other deictic locative adverbials: *de aquí, pa allá*

The spatial and temporal circumstances of the speaker are bound together, so that the distinction between adverbials of space and adverbials of time is blurred with deictics. The next example with *aquí* 'here' is very similar to example (17), repeated here as (22), with *ahorita* 'now' from the same speaker.

(21) *...se me afigura a mí que **aquí se está viviendo** como que un realismo mágico* (Chih'97#13A)
'it seems to me that **here one is living** a kind of magical realism'

(22) ***ahorita estamos viviendo** una, un cambio de generación diferente* (Chih'97#13B)
'**right now we are living** a, a change of different generations'

In both examples the predicate is the same, *estar viviendo* 'be living'. Besides the deictic adverbials *aquí* (example 21) and *ahorita* (example 22) themselves, other indices of speaker involvement are the first person plural subject in example (22) and matrix clause *se me afigura* 'it seems to me' reinforced by tonic first person object pronoun *a mí* in example (21).

Thus, both "locative" *aquí* and "temporal" *ahorita* express a unified notion of 'here and now', so that a locative versus temporal distinction is not obviously relevant with deictics. However, locative deictics are less frequent than temporal ones. They occur about half as often, averaging around 12% in both corpora (Table 51), compared with about 24% for temporal deictics (Table 50). This result is congruent with the diachronic trend toward fewer cooccurring locatives, as we saw in Chapter 3.

In summary: Cooccurrence facts — first and second person subjects and deictic time and place adverbials — provide evidence for experiential uses of *está* + *-ndo*. These uses encode what Lyons (1995: 337) calls locutionary subjectivity in that they are expressions of the speaker's point of view.

5.4 Generalization to motion verbs

Counter-examples to purported restrictions on uses of *estar* + *-ndo* with motion verbs and stative predicates have been cited as evidence of English interference, for example in Spanish varieties spoken in Puerto Rico (Ramos-Pellicia 1998) and Texas (Chaston 1991). In the next two sections we will see that newer uses with motion verbs and statives are related to experiential meaning.

5.4.1 *Estar yendo*

The combination of *estar* with the gerund of motion verbs *ir* 'go' and *venir* 'come' is considered incorrect or impossible in some reference grammars (M. Alonso 1964: 428; cf. Solé and Solé 1977: 45). All the same, several scholars register examples from "real" data (e.g. Arjona 1991: 124 and Luna 1980: 203 for oral Mexico City data; Hamplová 1968: 219 for written Latin American data).

There are clear aspectual or temporal differences between *voy* 'I go' and *estoy yendo* 'I am going'. The simple form has present habitual, present progressive, or future meaning, as shown in the following set of examples (adapted from Blansitt 1975: 5).

(23) a. *Voy al centro cada tres días*   = present habitual
'I go downtown every three days'
b. *Voy al centro*   = present progressive
'I'm going downtown' (i.e. on my way now)
c. *Voy al centro mañana*   = future
'I'm going downtown tomorrow'

On the other hand, *estoy yendo* indicates an experiential habitual situation, which may include a transitory change from the norm in the sense of Bull (1965; cf. examples in Butt and Benjamin 1994: 232–3). Blansitt (1975: 5) calls *estoy yendo* a "generic progressive":

> d. *Estoy yendo al centro cada tres días.* = experiential habitual
> 'I'm going downtown every three days (now).'

English influence might be manifested in changes in the meaning and/or frequency of *estar yendo*. We come back to frequencies of *estar*-plus-motion verb in Section 5.4.3. Let us first look at uses of Present-tense *estar yendo*. Either present progressive uses, as in the English translation of (b), or futurate uses, as in (c), would be innovative with respect to monolingual Spanish. There were no such examples in the New Mexico data. That is, we do not find something like "*estoy yendo al centro*" in answer to the question 'Where are you going?' (present progressive), nor with temporal adverbials like *mañana* (future).[10]

What we find is the use of Present-tense *estar yendo* to indicate experiential habitualness. In the following example, the situation represents a change, a situation that is new and newsworthy from the point of view of the speaker, who is talking about her granddaughter.

> (24) ahora [ ] ya **está yendo** al catequismo para la primera comunión (NMbil/Edwin)
> 'now she **is going** to catechism (classes) for the first communion'

The cooccurrence of *ahora* 'now' and *ya* 'already' supports an experiential interpretation. That the meaning of Present-tense *estar yendo* is better described as habitual rather than continuous or progressive — in terms of Comrie's (1976: 25) classification of aspectual oppositions — is illustrated by the following Chihuahua example.

> (25) L: ¿Y como está Laura?
> M: ¿Tirada, no?
> CJ: No, ya camina muy bien. Sí. Lo que pasa es que **está yendo** a las terapias **diarias**. Y claro ni toma el niño ni nada por el estilo pero- Ya ya ya tiene mejor movimiento y todo. (Chih'97#11A)
> 'And how is Laura?'
> 'Flat on her back right?'
> 'No, she already walks very well. Yes. It's that she **is going** to **daily** therapy. And of course she doesn't pick up the baby or anything like that but- She already has much better movement and all that.'

'Going to therapeutic treatments' is a customarily repeated situation. Cooccurring *diarias* 'daily' further specifies that it is frequent (cf. Bybee et al. 1994: 127). At the same time, the situation is transitory, in that it represents a new stage in the recovery. The speaker is giving an update on her friend's progress. That the situation is new and noteworthy shows up in the linguistic context with *ya*, in *ya camina* 'she already walks' and *ya tiene mejor movimiento* 'she already moves better'. It is interesting that the other two examples of *estar yendo* in the Chihuahua data also involve going to a medical practitioner (*...porque me llevaron a rehabilitación a Juárez. Estuve yendo a fisitría* (#22A) 'because they took me to rehabilitation in Juarez. I was going to physical therapy'; *...de aquí de México [ ] está yendo mucha gente [ ] con los oculistas [] a Cuba* (#12A) 'from here Mexico a lot of people are going to oculists in Cuba').

In the New Mexico data there were five cases of *estar yendo*. In the monolingual group one speaker used Preterite *estar yendo* to indicate duration over a delimited period of time in the past, in accordance with what is taken to be standard usage: *Ahora estuve yendo a Laughlin pero- estuve yendo **como tres años** a Las Vegas, y me aburrí, y ahora voy a Laughlin* 'Now I was going to Laughlin but- I was going **for three years** to Las Vegas, and I got bored and now I go to Laughlin' (NMCSS#214). In the bilingual group, there was one case of Present *estar yendo* (example (24) above) and one in the Imperfect, from the same speaker:

(26) *yo nunca trabajé hasta que no entró mi hija, su mamá de ella que **estaba yendo a la universidad** que, que había una católica. Y luego ella me, necesitaban en la cafetería, su su patrón — trabajaba entre medio de clases allí en la cafetería. Y y me dijo "Mamá," dijo "se cuite- una mujer se salió del trabajo"...* (NMbil/Edw)[11]

'I never worked until my daughter started [going to school], her mother who **was going to the university**, there was a Catholic one. So she, they needed in the cafeteria, her boss — she worked between classes there in the cafeteria. And she told me "Mom", she said, "a woman quit-left work"'

The use of simple Imperfect *trabajaba* indicates that the speaker has not lost imperfective bound morphology with dynamic verbs, a trend noted in Silva-Corvalán (1994: 47) in her study of Spanish in Los Angeles. But does *estaba yendo* 'was going' indicate loss of the lexical meaning of *iba* (the simple

Imperfect of *ir*)? Silva-Corvalán (1994: 46) finds that *iba* is used exclusively as an auxiliary in the *ir a* + Infinitive construction among many bilinguals. Is the use of *estaba yendo* here "strained" — in Chaston's (1991) terms — in that it neither serves to clarify nor emphasize ongoingness? Or, alternatively, does *estaba yendo* express an experiential habitual situation in the past? It is hard to make a definitive case, whether for loss of the simple Imperfect *iba* or retention of pragmatic nuances. In favor of the latter interpretation is the phrase *entró mi hija*, which indicates that going to school was a change.

The analysis is complicated by the likelihood that the higher frequency of *estar yendo* in the New Mexico data is at least in part the result of lexical permeability, as described in Silva-Corvalán (1994: 172–84). Spanish '**attend** school' corresponds to English '**go** to school'. It is interesting that Chaston's (1991: 308) *estar yendo* example also involves 'going to school'. Similarly, we saw that the higher frequency of *estar creciendo* as opposed to *ir creciendo* is largely because of the English expression 'grow up' for Spanish 'be old' (see Chapter 4, Section 4.7).

On the other hand, it is likely that *iba* has indeed been lost as the past habitual of 'go' among transitional bilingual speakers (see Chapter 1, Section 1.5.3.3). In the following example, *estábamos yendo* means past habitual 'we would go', without any additional pragmatic connotations. The same example illustrates deterioration of the Preterite — Imperfect contrast in the use of *hicimos conciertos* 'we gave (Preterite) concerts' in a past habitual context.

(27) *Yo luego cuando comencé el grado, o el libro diez, comencé con el a Mariachi Tigre. En el* Taos High School. *Y con eso me divertí muncho, porque. Hicimos conciertos,* **estábamos** *[pause]* **yendo a lugares.** *Por ejemplo vinimos a Albuquerque...* (NMTB/Melis)
'And then when I began grade, or book ten, I began with the Mariachi Tigre. At Taos High School. And with this I had a lot of fun, because. We gave concerts, we **were going to places** [i.e. 'would go']. For example, we came to Albuquerque.'

The use of *estábamos yendo* for *íbamos* does not seem to be the direct result of transfer, since the corresponding English form "we were going" is a past continuous, not a past habitual. The English translation in this example would be 'went', 'would go', or 'used to go'. Rather, this example suggests loss of Imperfect morphology and weakening of pragmatic constraints on *estar yendo*, in agreement with Silva-Corvalán's (1994) findings.

In summary, experiential habitual uses demarcate *estar yendo* from *ir* in both the Chihuahua and the New Mexico data. The blurring of the distinction occurs in the transitional bilingual group. Thus, our data suggest that loss of constraints on the use of *estar yendo* as an experiential habitual involves language attrition (in transitional bilinguals) rather than direct English interference (in bilinguals).

5.4.2 General motion and experiential habitual

Another group of motion verbs with experiential habitual uses in construction with *estar* are those with a general 'coming' or 'returning' meaning. In the next set of examples, *están volviendo* 'they are returning' refers to the recent coming back into favor of old things. Both examples have a cooccurring *ahor(it)a*. The first example is from Chihuahua, the second, with a code-switch to English, is from the bilingual New Mexico group.

(28) a. *Los yoyos, que ya **están volviendo ahorita** nuevamente.* (Chih'97/#13)
'Yoyos, which **are now coming back** again'
b. *muchas cosas que **están ahora volviendo** uh to the benefit of of even health, you know, I uh went to a uhm a doctor yesterday that that that cures with herbs and-* (NMbil/Dorot)
'many things that **are now coming back**...'

It is striking that the only two *estar volviendo* cases in the corpus occur in such similar contexts.

The similarity between the New Mexico and Chihuahua contexts of use also shows up in the next set of examples, this time of *están viniendo* 'they are coming'. In both cases the speakers are referring to the recent arrival of newcomers. The similarity is all the more remarkable because of the very small number of *estar viniendo* tokens, only one in Chih'97 and four in NMbil.

(29) a. *Como hace como unos tres años. Esos de Oaxaca, como unos tres años [] que **están viniendo**.* (Chih'97/#17Sab)
'It's been about three years. Those people from Oaxaca, [it's been] about three years that they **are coming**'

b. *Y ahora que ya ya toda- ves esto de, esto que* **están viniendo** *mucha gente [ ] de otros estados.* (NMbil/Edw)
'And now that all- you see all this that, that a lot of people from other states **are coming**'

The first speaker is commenting on the arrival of laborers from the southern Mexican state of Oaxaca to work picking crops in Ascención, Chihuahua. The second speaker is commenting on people from other states moving to New Mexico. Both situations represent a change, as indicated by *hace tres años* 'it's been three years' in (a) and *ahora que* 'now that' in (b). Both situations may be unwelcome, as indicated by the use of distal demonstrative *esos* to refer the arrivals in (a) and by the use of *esto de...*, roughly translatable as 'this thing of (a lot of people arriving)', in (b).

One measure of experiential habitual use is the cooccurrence of *ya* or *ahora*. 33% (6/18) of *estar*-plus-motion verb tokens in the Chihuahua data had a cooccurring *ya*, including cases with *ahor(it)a*. In contrast, there was only one case of *ya* in nine *andar*-plus-motion verb tokens and no cases with *ir* (of 17 tokens).[12] In the New Mexico bilingual group, 30% (3/10) of *estar*-plus-motion verb tokens have a combination of *ya* and/or *ahora*. Other "now" adverbials in NMbil are an *hace años* phrase 'it's been x years...' and *hoy en día* 'nowadays'. On this measure then, there is no indication of loss of an experiential meaning component among bilinguals.

It is important, though, that even without a cooccurring temporal deictic *estar*-plus-motion verb conveys connotations of newsworthiness. In the following example the speaker is talking about the price of gas used for farm machinery, which is — metaphorically — going up:

(30) **Constantemente está subiendo**, *digo, mensualmente, y ahora creo que tuvo dos alzas en este mes* (Chih'97#21B)
'**It is constantly going up**, monthly, and now I think it went up twice this month'.

In this example *ahora* does not cooccur (as we have defined cooccurrence, that is, in the same clause), though it is close by. The rate of price increases is clearly a change viewed negatively by the speaker.

Our discussion of experiential habitual in *estar*-plus-motion verb so far has been limited to the present tense. What about experiential past habitual uses? Westfall (1995: 321, 329) states that Imperfect *estaba + -ndo* is incompatible with frequency adverbials such as *todos los días* 'every day', *generalmente* 'generally', *frecuentamente* 'frequently'. However, she concedes, it may be used "nonstandardly" to indicate a past habitual situation that no longer holds, for example (from Westfall 1995: 385),

(31) **Antes estaba corriendo** *todos los días pero ya no*
'**Before I was running** every day but not any more'

In the following example from our data, with motion verb *caminando* 'walking', the speaker is talking about physical therapy to help her walk (this is the person who was going to daily therapy in example (25)).

(32) *Pero hubo dos veces que me jaló muchisisisisímo, que grité terriblemente. Creo que fue cuando más avancé. De hecho caminaba, ya sí* **estaba caminando** *así-* (Chih'97#9A)
'But there were two times that she yanked me a whole lot, that I screamed terribly. I think that that was when I made the most progress. In fact I was walking, yes indeed **I was walking** like this'

Estaba caminando 'I was walking' here is not past progressive, that is, the 'walking' was not in progress at some past reference point. But neither is it clearly past habitual. It could be viewed as continuous as opposed to customarily repeated, in the sense of a single stative situation of 'being able to walk'. At the same time, an experiential component is indicated by *así* 'like this', as the speaker demonstrates how she walked in that period (overtness), which represented a new development in her recovery (personal involvement).

It is important that not all motion verbs yield habitual uses. While with general motion verbs *ir* 'go', *venir* 'come' and *volver* 'return', *estar* + *-ndo* has habitual meaning, with lexically rich motion verbs the meaning is more progressive or continuous. In the next example, the speaker is talking about an accident she witnessed. Imperfect *nos estábamos acercando* 'we were approaching' is in progress at reference time, when she stopped (fuller context for this example appears in example (4), Chapter 1).

(33) *Y nos fuimos acercando a la troca que estaba completamente destrozada del frente en el poste.[ ] Y entonces* **nos estábamos acercando** *y yo me detuve.* (Chih'97/#11A)
'And we gradually approached the pickup which was completely destroyed in the front at the post. [ ] And **we were approaching** and I stopped'

Acercarse 'approach' specifies a kind of motion, while *ir, venir,* and *volver* are quite general, indicating only a direction of motion. It is interesting that we find this interaction between generality of lexical meaning and the aspectual meaning of the construction. Goldberg (2000) finds similar lexical semantic influences in the omission of patient arguments of causative verbs in English. These findings point to a relationship between the richness of lexical meaning of verbs and the grammatical constructions they appear in.

How then might we account for habitual — stative uses of *estar corriendo* and *estar caminando,* since these are specific kinds of motion? *Correr* 'run' (example (31)) as well as *caminar* 'walk' (32) are different from *acercarse* 'approach' in that they may be specific states in Vendler's (1967: 108) sense. One can be a "runner" or a "walker", that is, one can say "I run" or "I walk" as a habitual form of exercise, but one cannot "approach" as a general customary practice.

The distinct behavior of general as opposed to specific motion verbs in construction with *estar* is important in evaluating the results of language contact: are habitual uses limited to general motion verbs in bilingual varieties, as they appear to be in monolingual Spanish, or do such uses extend to any kind of motion verb? The following example from a New Mexico bilingual speaker seems to be a clear case of habitual use with *caminar*:

> (34)   *...ya llevo onze años que que voy de Albuquerque hasta Santa Fe día a día. [ ] Onze años hace. Que* **estoy caminando** *patrás y pa delante. Ciento cinquenta millas al día. Salgo de mi casa a- quinze para las seis y regreso patrás pa mi casa en la tarde a quinze para las seis...* (NMbil/Marg)
> 'It has now been eleven years that I go from Albuquerque to Santa Fe every day. Eleven years. That I have been walking (literally: **I am walking**) back and forth. One hundred fifty miles a day. I leave my house at- quarter to six and return back to my house in the evening at quarter to six...'

Caminar here does not literally mean 'walk' but has a more general physical motion meaning. *Caminar* fits nicely in the context because it underscores the tediousness of the drive, to and from Santa Fe, one hundred and fifty miles, day in and out, for eleven years. Nevertheless, present habitual use of *estar caminando* may represent a change with respect to monolingual data, where non-progressive uses with *caminar* appear to be limited to specific state or stative-continuous interpretations, as in examples (31) and (32). Alternatively, this might be a case of loss of the Present Perfect Progressive, as in *he estado caminando*, although Silva-Corvalán's (1994: 29–33) has shown that the Present Perfect is retained into the lower stages of the bilingual continuum. The innovation does not seem to be the result of direct transfer, since the English translation is not a Present Progressive but either a Present 'I walk (go)' or a Present Perfect Progressive 'I have been walking (going)'. Rather, the possible extension of habitual uses to specific motion verbs is related to the increased frequency of *estar*-plus-motion verb in the bilingual group. We look at this in the next section.

5.4.3 Frequencies of ESTAR-plus-motion verb

The use of *estar* + *-ndo* with motion verbs in present-day Spanish represents a change from Old Spanish (Chapter 4, Section 4.2.2). In both the New Mexico and Chihuahua data, *estar* occurs with *caminando* 'walking', *corriendo* 'running', *yendo* 'going', *pasando* 'passing', *viniendo* 'coming', *volviendo* 'returning'. However, there is a quantitative difference. Table 52 shows the distribution of motion verb gerunds by auxiliary.

Table 52. Distribution of motion verb gerunds (main verbs) by auxiliary

	ESTAR N	%	IR N	%	ANDAR N	%	TOTAL N
MexPop	7	12%	32	56%	18	32%	57
Chih'97	18	37%	17	35%	14	28%	49
NMmon	6	43%	3	21%	5	36%	14
NMbil	9	64%	1	7%	4	29%	14

Estar has 64% of all motion-verb gerunds in the bilingual New Mexico group, much more than either the monolingual New Mexico (43%) or the Chihuahua group (37%). It is not so much *andar* that has suffered. The proportion held by *andar* ranges between 28% and 36% across corpora. Rather, in NMbil *estar* has "stolen" motion verbs from *ir*, which is left with 7%. This is about three times less than NMmon (21%), five times less than Chih'97 (35%), and eight times less than MexPop (56%).

It is tempting to view the decreasing proportion of *ir*-plus-motion verb shown in Table 52 as following a geographic route from the interior of Mexico toward the United States. In the absence of data from other regional and, especially, social and stylistic varieties, it is difficult to determine whether this geographic route reflects contact with English or distance from the educated, standard variety. As we argued in the last chapter (Section 4.7), diachronic and register differences in the distribution of auxiliaries and the continued vitality of *andar* in NMbil are evidence that the decline of *ir* + *-ndo* among New Mexico bilinguals is part of a process of specialization rather than an instance of contact-induced simplification.

Whether the increased relative frequency of *estar* + *-ndo* is a manifestation of specialization in the framework of grammaticization or of simplification in the framework of language contact, we would expect further semantic generalization as a result. Preliminary evidence for possible further generalization in the bilingual group is provided in example (34) above, *onze años hace / que estoy caminando* 'it's been eleven years / that I am walking'. The potential change here is extension of present experiential habitual uses from general motion verbs such as *ir* to more specific verbs such as *caminar*. It apparently begins with verbs like *caminar* which may have a specific state, as well as a dynamic activity, interpretation. It is important, though, that this change — if more data confirms it — would represent an extension of a well-established use in monolingual varieties and would be occurring in tandem with the increased frequency of *estar*-plus-motion verb.

In summary, we have shown that Present-tense *estar* combines with the gerund of general-motion verbs, most frequently *ir*, *venir* and *volver*, to indicate an experiential habitual situation. We did not find innovative present progressive or futurate uses for these combinations, either in the Chihuahua or the New Mexico bilingual data. However, *estar*-plus-motion verb has a higher relative frequency in the bilingual data, with a corresponding decline of *ir*-plus-motion verb. The next step in the generalization process may be extension of present habitual uses to specific-motion verbs.

5.5 Generalization to statives

5.5.1 *Frequencies of ESTAR-plus-stative*

The relevance of the state versus dynamic situation distinction for Spanish has been questioned by King and Suñer (1980a), who present numerous examples of *estar* + *-ndo* with main verbs classified elsewhere as statives. However, while *estar*-plus-stative combinations need not be starred as ungrammatical, there are frequency restrictions on their use (cf. Givón 1979: 22–43). Acquisition data also point to restrictions, since *estar* + *-ndo* appears in child language only with dynamic verbs (Jacobson 1986: 105–7). In addition, the state — dynamic situation dichotomy for Spanish is upheld in uses of the Future to express possibility or probability in the present. The suppositional Future is restricted with dynamic verbs, for example, *estará trabajando hoy* vs. **trabajará hoy* 'she may be working today' (Silva-Corvalán 1995: 103, note 17).

Comrie (1976: 50) defines a state as a situation that continues without change unless something happens to change it. Numerous stativity tests have been proposed for English (cf. Binnick 1991, Chapter 6). For present purposes I adopted the following rough test from Shirai (1994: 72): If the verb does not have a habitual interpretation in the simple Present, it is a state. Statives in the Chihuahua data are *afectar* 'affect', *aprobar* 'approve', *colindar* 'be adjacent', *desear* 'desire', *entender* 'understand', *faltar / hacer falta* 'lack' (5), *interesar* 'interest' (2), *ocupar* 'ocupy', *prestarse* 'lend itself to', *sentir(se)* 'feel' (2). In the New Mexico bilingual data, there are examples with *querer* 'want' and *tener* 'have' (2).

In the Chihuahua corpus *estar*-plus-stative combinations make up about 7% (26/356) of all *estar* + *-ndo* tokens; in the New Mexico bilingual group about 5% (6/117). For journalistic data, Olbertz (1998: 330) reports 3% (3/93). Some "statives" evidently occur more often than others. *Viviendo* 'living', which I return to below, is the most frequent. On the other hand, there were no examples in our data of proscribed *estar siendo* 'be being', which is widely considerred an anglicism.[13] Similarly, Luna (1980: 203, note 425) reports only one token (of 482 *estar* + *-ndo*) in her educated Mexico City data. *Estar siendo* may be more common in written language (cf. Ramos 1972). In the Chihuahua data, *siendo* 'being' is associated with *venir* 'come', with 93% (26/28) of *siendo* tokens and *seguir*, with the remaining 7% (see Chapter 4, Section 4.7).

Ver 'see' is often included among statives (King and Suñer 1980a: 186). *Viendo* is actually among the ten most frequent main verbs in Present-tense *estar* + *-ndo* in the Chihuahua corpus, at 3% (7/224). In Parisi's (1992) and Luna's (1980) data, where separate counts by tense are not provided, *estar viendo* averages 3% (5/165) and 5% (22/482), respectively. Lenz (1925: 463, §301) had suggested that *estoy viendo* 'I am seeing' may be more akin to Preterite *vi* in the sense of *descubrí* 'I discovered', while simple Present *veo* is closer to

Imperfect *veía*. Entry-into-the-state or "state commences" (cf. Bybee 1994: 238; Bybee et al. 1994: 318) is attributed to *estar*-plus-stative by King and Suñer (1980a: 192; cf. King 1992: 93) in examples like *En su viaje estaba conociendo a mucha gente interesante* 'On his trip he was meeting a lot of interesting people', where *conocer* 'know' is translated 'meet' (but see Bolinger (1963) on the *conocer, saber, tener*, etc. class of verbs). There were no clear-cut examples of entry-into-the-state in our data.

The first example below might be compatible with such an entry-into-the-state interpretation.

(35) *"Me **estás viendo** mis cohibiciones?" "Pos sí, sí veo que le pones ganas sude y sude y remándole pero le remas para la fregada, no sabes."* (Chih'97#15B)
' "**Are you seeing** my problem?" "Well yes, yes I see that you are making an effort sweating and rowing but you row terribly, you don't know how".'

But more often the meaning of *está viendo* is ongoing situation, as in the following set of examples.

(36) a. *¿Ya **estás viendo** la tele?* (Chih'97#1B)
'Are you watching the TV already?'
b. *Dije "Te voy a levantar de donde **estás viendo**..."* (NMbil/Edwin)
'I said, "I'm going to get you up from where you are watching [TV]..."'

(37) a. *Allí **está** adentro **viendo** la tele* (Chih'97#1B)
'He is there inside watching the TV'
b. ***está cuidando** televisión.[ ] Ai en el cuarto allá del otro lado.* (NMbil/Vig)
'He is watching TV. There in the room there on the other side'

Again, the coincidence between the Chihuahua and New Mexico contexts of use is striking. In (36) the speakers scold the person watching TV. In (37) they give the person's location. A difference is that New Mexican speakers may use *cuidar* for *ver* (and omit the definite article with *televisión*).

With *ir*, on the other hand, *viendo* has an inceptive meaning, along the lines of 'just then I see (suddenly, unexpectedly)', in the formula *que* + Present-tense *ir* + *viendo* (see Section 3.7). An example of this construction is in the following description of an accident:

(38) *Ese día [] hasta gritaba yo, "Ay, vayan a ver qué se hizo". Porque un polvaredón. Usted cree pa chocar con el poste. Ya cuando se quitó así poquito la polvareda **que lo vamos viendo**, dijo Alonso "No, pues está bien golpeado".* (Chih'97#22B)
'That day I was even screaming, "Oh, go and see what happened to him". Because there was so much dust. You can imagine, since he crashed into the post. Then when the dust lifted a little we suddenly saw him (literally: **we go seeing**), Alonso said, "Yes, he's badly hit".'

5.5.2 Experiential uses with statives

The examples of *estar*-plus-stative we find can be subsumed under the label of experiential. This includes expression of speaker attitude toward a new situation, as in the following example with *sintiendo* 'feeling'.

(39) *...ahí en Juárez pues ya **no se están sintiendo** — fíjate qué cosa tan curiosa — muy **muy mexicanos** [ ]. Porque ahí pos ya andan en dólares. [ ] Aquí no, ahí en Juárez no tienen el problema de las devaluaciones y todo...* (Chih'97#15A)
'...there is Juárez now **they are not feeling** — what a strange thing — **very Mexican**. Because, well, they already do everything in dollars. Here no. There in Juárez they don't have the problem of devaluations and all that...'

The speaker, who is from the state capital Chihuahua, is commenting on the border city Juárez. The contrast with Chihuahua is indicated by distal *ahí*. Cooccurring *ya* is consistent with change from the norm and subjective evaluation (Section 5.3.2 above). The speaker also interjects *fíjate qué cosa tan curiosa* 'what a strange thing'.

The following example, with *teniendo* 'having', from the New Mexico bilingual corpus is a good example of subjectivity. The strong disapproval of the quoted speaker is evident from *fregatal* 'a whole bunch' and *tanta* 'so much'.

(40) *...él quería quizas algo más de su hijo que se casara y tuviera un fregatal de familia. Siempre me decía "Yo no sé por qué **están***

> *teniendo tanta familia. Yo no sé como les van a dar de comer a todos."* (NMbil/Nin)
> '…perhaps he wanted something more of his son than marrying and having a bunch of kids. He always told me, "I don't know why **you are having such a big family**. I don't know how you're going to feed them all.'

Quesada (1995: 14) gives a nearly identical example from his San José, Costa Rica corpus, *la cosa no está para estar teniendo chiquitos* 'the situation is not one for having kids'. Other examples with *estar teniendo* include *problemas* 'having problems' (Butt and Benjamin 1994: 235), *fiebre* 'having fever' (Gómez Torrego 1998: 146), and *tiempo* 'having time' (Westfall 1995: 322–3). It is interesting that all of these may be troubling (negative) situations.

Another component of *estar*-plus-stative is active subject involvement, which with a mental or emotion verb means intensity of the cognitive process or feeling, as in *estoy deseando* 'I am desiring' (Zdenek 1972: 498) or *estoy queriendo* 'I am wanting' (Roca Pons 1958: 67). In the next example, involvement and intensity is corroborated by the tonic first person object pronoun *a mí* and the expression *ojalá* 'if only, I hope'. The speaker has attempted four times to see the piece of land that "is interesting him" but each time the owner cannot find the key.

> (41) *Y vamos a ir a ver un terreno, que a mí **me está interesando** para para la cuestión de mi mamá. Ojalá que tenga la idea, no más que como cuatro veces he ido y dice que "no encuentro la llave".* (Chih'97#5A)
> 'And we're going to go see a piece of land, that **is interesting me** for my mother. Hopefully he'll agree, except that I've gone about four times and he says "I can't find the key".'

Estar viviendo 'be living' makes up 2.8% (10/356) of all *estar* + *-ndo* tokens in the Chihuahua data and 2.6% (3/117) in the New Mexico bilingual data, not a negligible amount. Frequencies are comparable in other corpora: 1.8% (3/165) in Parisi's (1992) *habla culta* corpus and 2.3% (8/340) in MexPop. *Estar viviendo* has spawned quite a variety of opinions. Gili Gaya (1964: 59, 114) had suggested that *estar* retains its locative meaning in construction with another stative or locative, as in *Está viviendo con sus padres* 'he is living with his parents'. On the other hand, Rallides (1966: 108) starred *estoy viviendo as ungrammatical, precisely because *vivir* is inherently "continuous". Lope

Blanch (1962) ascribed a sense of transitoriness to Gili Gaya's example: "del sujeto sólo decimos que vive (temporalmente) con sus padres" 'of the subject we are only saying that he lives (temporarily) with his parents' (cf. Luna 1980: 202, note 433). More generally, Olbertz (1998: 330) holds that *estar*-plus-state expresses temporariness. In view of recalcitrant *está viviendo* examples, Squartini (1998: 110) adds that in Spanish (as opposed to Italian) a temporary situation may "characterize the life of the subject".

I claim that it is not no much transitoriness but a subjective meaning component that describes *estar viviendo* and other *estar*-plus-stative uses. In the first example below, *están viviendo* and *estamos viviendo* involve a contrast with the past and the place where the subject lived his childhood; in the second example, contrast blends with disapproval. The living arrangements may or may not be temporary.

(42) A: *No más que yo también trabajé de chico aquí pizcando algodón.*
...
M: *Cómo no. Sí le tocó, sí me acuerdo. Sí. ¿Y* **están viviendo** *en Chihuahua? ¿O en Juárez?*
A: *No, estamos viviendo en Albuquerque.* (Chih'97#21B)
'A: I also worked when I was growing up here picking cotton.
M: Of course. Yes, you did too, yes I remember. Yes. And **are you living** in Chihuahua? Or in Juárez?
A: No, we're living in Albuquerque.'

(43) **Está viviendo** *con él. Ahora agarran una idea, no sé. Se me hace a mí una idea muy cochina. Que se junten, juntos. Antes, si tú querías el muchacho, t- tenías que casarte.*(NMbil/Beatriz)
'**She is living** with him. Nowadays they grab onto an idea, I don't know. It seems to me a very dirty idea. That they get together, live together. Before, if you wanted the young man you had to get married.'

Additional support for the proposal that *estar*-plus-stative expresses speaker point of view is provided by the grammatical-person-index (Section 5.3.2). Of 26 tokens in the Chihuahua data, including *estar viviendo*, ten are first person (including one impersonal *se* and one infinitive with a first person matrix), another two are second person, and six more have first person object pronoun clitic *me* or *nos*, for a total of 18/26 = 69%. Another three have a cooccurring deictic locative or temporal, leaving only five cases, or about one-fifth, without an explicit linguistic indication of speaker involvement. A second fact from tense forms provides additional support: *estar*-plus-stative occurs overwhelmingly in the Present, with 24/26 tokens, or 92% (there was one Imperfect, *estaba sintiendo* 'I was feeling', and an Infinitive, *estar viviendo* 'be living'). Finally, *estar*-plus-stative probably occurs more in oral than in written language, with 5–7% in our oral (Chihuahua and New Mexico) data and 3% in journalism (Olbertz 1998: 330). Westfall (1995: 289, 297–8, 322–3) reports that she found no literary examples with statives but that these "abound" in the oral data she examined.

5.6 Subjective vs. transitory: Back to locative origins

Goldsmith and Woisetschlaeger (1982) distinguish between "phenomenal" and "structural" description in their discussion of what they call "metaphysical" use of the English Progressive. They illustrate this distinction with the following example:

(44) a. The engine isn't smoking anymore.
b. The engine doesn't smoke anymore.

According to these authors, (a) is an observation, you would have to start the engine first, while (b) is appropriate after repairing it by changing a defective part, whether or not you actually test the engine. The first is said to express knowledge about "what things happen in the world", the second about "how the world is made that such things may happen in it" (Goldsmith and Woisetschlaeger 1982: 80).

Langacker (1996: 293) instead describes the first example as either "actual" (phenomenal) or "temporarily structural", pointing out that (a) may indicate ongoingness at the moment of reference but also a transitory habitual situation. In his account, "the progressive is merely symptomatic of perfectivity (bounding)". Langacker (1991: 95) discusses the interaction between aspect and scope of predication in examples such as *Thelma is dyeing her hair (these days)*, where, although hair-dyeing is now a regular practice, it is viewed as only a "bounded episode" within a broader portion of Thelma's lifespan, hence temporary. Thus, transitoriness in *estar + -ndo* may be attributed to temporal bounding roughly as follows: dynamic > limited duration > temporal precision > temporariness (cf. Westfall 1995: 371).

An alternative account might emphasize the contribution of *estar* to the construction in accounting for transitory meaning. *Estar* is said to be a stage-level stative referring to transitory properties or contingent states (e.g. Squartini 1998: 22; Westfall 1995: 293–4). The origin of the construction as a locative supports a direct relation between location and contingency, as suggested by Fernández (1960) (Chapter 4, Section 4.3.1). Comrie (1976: 103–5) gives examples from several languages that use locative constructions or etymologically locative verbs to express a transitory state, including, of course, Spanish *estar*. This view of the transitory connotations of *estar + -ndo* is congruent with Gili Gaya's (1964: 62; cf. Bull 1965) analysis of *estar* as expressing the result of change, whether real or possible. As this eminent Hispanist explained, one can say *este jarro está intacto* 'this jar is intact' just as well as *este jarro está roto* 'this jar is broken' when "ha cruzado por nuestra mente la posibilidad de algún precance" 'the possibility of a mishap has crossed our mind'. Transitoriness may be subjective in that, as Goldsmith and Woisetschlaeger (1982: 83) observe, it is not just about time but involves an epistemic evaluation of the probability of a situation's continuing.

The most stative of the examples I have in the Chihuahua data is with *colindar* 'be adjacent'. The speaker is talking about an *ejido* or piece of common land. Transitoriness is precluded here.

(45) - *¿Cuántos ejidos son aquí en Asce- es un solo ejido para-?*
- *Bueno. Lo componen varios, verdad, pero en el caso, si hablamos del ejido de Ascención, es un ejido. Pero entonces ya, dentro del municipio existen varios ejidos. Me entiende.* **Está**, *por ejemplo, ee* **el ejido Colonia Díaz, que está colindando aquí, aquí está**, *hay el el ejido Seis de Enero, ee hay la colonia Victoria, que esa es de colonos...*(Chih'97#21A)
- How many *ejidos* are there here in Asce-, is it just one for-?
- Well. A number of them make it up, right, but in the case of, if we're talking about the *ejido* of Ascención, there is one. But then within the municipality there are various *ejidos*, right. There **is**, for example, **the *ejido* Colonia Díaz, which** adjoins (literally: **is adjoining**) **here, it is here**, there is the *ejido* Seis de Enero, there is the *colonia* Victoria, and that one is of settlers...

The use is experiential in the expression of proximity and overtness (evidentiality) from the point of view of the speaker: I have experienced the contiguousness of this *ejido*, it is part of my life. Support for this interpretation is the cooccurrence of *aquí* 'here' and its repetition in *aquí está* 'it is here'. Another contributing factor may be the use of *estar* as a presentational instead of *hay* 'there is' or *existen* 'there are', as for the other *ejidos* listed; prior use of *estar* may prime the *estar* + *-ndo* expression. An experiential analysis nicely suits examples like this that are recalcitrant to a transitoriness explanation.

Langacker (1991: 94–6) links construal with aspect in his discussion of examples such as:

(46) a. A statue of George Lakoff stands in the plaza
     b. A statue of George Lakoff is standing in the plaza

(a) indicates the statue's permanent location, while (b) either indicates temporary location or "reports on someone's immediate (hence temporary) perception of its location". In this analysis, it is temporal bounding that gives rise to the personal perception meaning component, via scope of predication. Langacker (1991: 96) illustrates this nicely with *This road winds/is winding through the mountains*, the simple Present used when looking at a map, the Progressive used when actually driving. The difference lies in the scope of predication with respect to *road*, a holistic construal in *winds* but a restricted one in *is winding*.

The problem is that a necessary link with temporal bounding and, more generally, the permanent versus transitory axis, excludes examples such as *está colindando* 'is being adjacent'. We find synchronically that real *estar*-plus-stative examples similar to Langacker's *a statue is standing* occur with deictic locatives, as in *está colindando aquí* 'is adjoining here' (example 45), or the following example with *ahí*, cited in Squartini (1998: 110) from the Lima *habla culta* corpus (Caravedo 1989: 209):

(47) *A mí me tocó la casona más vieja, o sea la questaba lado de la propia iglesia [ ] hacia donde**está mirando la estatua** del padre Jorge; **ahí***
    'I had the oldest house, namely the one which was close to the church [ ] towards where **the statue** of Father Jorge **is looking** (facing); **there**'

Rather than a temporary or even new location for the statue, *está mirando* conveys the speaker's particular perception of the location in relationship to his house. It would be important for empirical studies to show the frequency with which actual examples along the lines of *a statue is standing* cooccur with deictic locatives.

Thus, our data support a link between construal and aspect, but not as a consequence of temporal bounding per se. Rather, diachronic data provide evidence that this link arises from the locative origin of the progressive, and that it is temporal bounding linked to spatial bounding that gives rise to personal involvement and construal.

A diachronic view of the locative origins of the construction is important, because it allows us to tie together spatial circumscription with both temporal bounding, as per Langacker (1996), and active subject participation in an overt activity, as per Hatcher (1951). We argued in Chapter 4 that experiential uses of *estar* + *-ndo* derive from locative meaning by showing a relationship between being located and being engaged in a highly overt or perceptible activity. This relationship was manifested in the Old Spanish data in the relatively frequent occurrence of *estar* + *-ndo* in clauses subordinated to perception verb *ver* (Section 4.3). We can complete our diagram of the locative origins of speaker participation (Figure 8, Chapter 4) by adding in subject participation, as in Figure 13:

VIEWABLE (overtness, evidentiality, speaker participation)

CIRCUMSCRIBED IN SPACE (location) = CIRCUMSCRIBED IN TIME (temporal bounding)

INTENSE (subject participation)

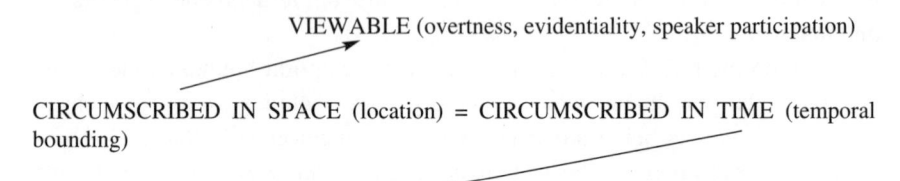

Figure 13. Locative — temporal bounding and speaker — subject participation (Locative origins, part II)

Speaker and/or subject participation in the situation is carried over into habitual uses of *estar* + *-ndo*, so that experiential habitual involves a subjective construal, specifically, the speaker's view that a situation is noteworthy. It is important that experiential meaning derives from the locative origins of *estar* + *-ndo*. The present data and analysis refute an understanding of *estar* + *-ndo* based on the presence versus absence of features in a system of contrasts and support a positive view of grammatical morphemes as having inherent semantic content (Bybee et al. 1994: 138).

A final note concerns the relationship of register to subjectivity. In sociolinguistic approaches, register or situational variation has been studied mostly in terms of objective or structural factors such as social role relations among participants, setting, and channel, for example, written versus spoken (cf. Biber and Finegan 1994). More recently, sociolinguists are exploring "the expressive use of variation" (Eckert 1996, 2000). In a study of 19th century letters by English writers, Arnaud (1998) found that women use progressive forms more frequently than men, and furthermore, that frequencies increase with more intimate correspondents. Similarly, we may think of variation in the frequency of *estar* + *-ndo* as not just conveying objective social and situational information but as a device that speakers can manipulate for interpersonal functions, for example, to express a greater degree of intimacy. Initial findings in this study suggest new avenues of research on Spanish *estar* + *-ndo* in relation to social, stylistic, and also expressive factors.

Having said all this, it is important to note that *estar* + *-ndo* does not always add an obvious connotation of transitoriness, newsworthiness, or speaker attitude to habitual aspect. Such nuances are not immediately apparent in the next example, as indicated by the appropriateness of the English Present Tense in the translation. The speaker works in a factory that makes parts shipped to an auto assembly plant in the United States.

(48) *Porque con un cable que vaya defectuoso, ellos pierden. Por ejemplo una hora de, de trabajo allá. Y hora- en una hora de trabajo salen, pues salen,* **un carro cada cinco minutos, está saliendo,** *completito ya con-* (Chih'97#VIII)
'Because with just one defective wire that gets by, they [the owners] lose. For example, one hour of work over there [in the assembly plant]. And in one hour of work they come out, well, they come out, **one car every five minutes,** comes out (literally: **is coming out**), all readied up, with…'

Still, one indication of experiential meaning in this example is the beginning of a description of the car as it gets off the assembly line, *completito ya con…* 'all readied up, with…'. The use of *estar* + *-ndo* to introduce a description indicates overtness, "as if [the situation] were actually taking place and being viewed by the speaker", in King and Suñer's (1980b: 226) words. The affective diminutive suffix on *completito* 'all readied up' adds further support to this interpretation. Nevertheless, I note this example as one which is not as obviously an experiential habitual as others we have seen, since it appears in the monolingual data and cannot be attributed to loss of pragmatic constraints in a language contact situation. Rather, as we have seen, increased frequency is driving *estar + -ndo* into habitual territory.

5.7 Summary

We may summarize our conclusions as follows. First, we found no evidence for an increase in the frequency of *estar + -ndo* in bilingual varieties with respect to comparable monolingual Spanish. To the contrary, frequency increases are a diachronic process, one effect of which is the growing restriction of the simple Present to non-progressive uses, especially in oral varieties. These findings cast doubt on the notion that increased frequencies of *estar + -ndo* among bilinguals are the result of convergence with English. Second, we saw that another frequency effect is continued semantic generalization. The next step in this evolution is extension to habitual contexts with an experiential meaning component, which derives from the locative origin of construction. Experiential meaning includes connotations of change, contrast, or transitoriness and the expression of speaker involvement, as measured by patterns of cooccurrence with grammatical person and time-place deictic elements.

We found no evidence of innovative futurate or present progressive uses of Present-tense *estar + yendo* 'going' among bilinguals. Nevertheless, *estar*-plus-motion verb combinations have a higher relative frequency in comparison with monolingual data. There are indications that increased frequency of *estar*-plus-motion verb may result in further semantic generalization in the extension of experiential habitual uses from general-motion verbs (*yendo*) to specific-motion verbs (*caminando* 'walking'). Finally, newer uses with statives accord with an analysis of present habitual uses of *estar + -ndo* as experiential rather than simply transitory, in both the Chihuahua and New Mexico data.

Notes

1. Figures from Nehls (1988) and Meir and Hundt (1995) are converted from a 100,000-word-based to a 10,000-word-based calculation.
2. On the obligatoriness of *estar + -ndo* to express present progressive with telic predicates ("verbos perfectivos" or Bello's "desinentes"), see Lenz (1925: 399 (§256), 417 (§270),

463 (§301)). On "terminative" verbs and "get" reflexives (e.g. *Me impaciento con los estudiantes haraganes* 'I get impatient with (the) lazy students'), see King and Suñer (1980b: 229–31).

3. Squartini (1998: 90–103) accounts for so-called innovative uses with achievements in Latin American Spanish, for example, *Te estás matando* 'You are killing yourself', as [-ASPECT], [-ACTIONALITY]. That is, unlike Standard (European) Spanish, Latin American varieties are said not to be restricted to a durative actional value.

4. There is a greater proportion of cooccurring *siempre* in the transitional bilingual group, at 25% (3/12), or 43% (3/7) if tokens without any temporal adverbial are subtracted. The sample is much too small, however, to draw any conclusions.

5. Parisi (1992: 98) lists *hacer* 'to do' as the most frequent *estar* + *-ndo* main verb, with 17% (28/165), but does not distinguish different predicates, for example *haciendo desastres* 'creating disasters' or *haciendo el test* 'taking the examination'. It would be interesting to see if "general activities" make up a bigger proportion of Present-tense versus Imperfect *estar* + *-ndo* as a possible measure of present — past asymmetries in the extension of the construction into habitual territory.

6. With respect to subject animacy, the Chih'97 figure for human subjects (86%, Table 47) is lower than the MexPop figure (91%, Table 35), at p = .0331.

7. It is possible that first person object pronouns *me/nos* cooccur more with *estar* than with the motion verb *-ndo* auxiliaries. In the Chihuahua data, *me/nos* occurred with third-person subjects, singular and plural, 13% of the time for *estar* + *-ndo* (26/200), 3.6% for *ir* + *-ndo* (2/55), and 8.5% for *andar* + *-ndo* (4/47).

8. I did not include NM monolingual data in Table 50 since there were only 19 Present-tense *estar* + *-ndo* tokens. The larger proportion of past tense forms in this corpus than in Chih'97 and NMbil is congruent with the type of discourse mostly obtained in the interviews, expositions of memories of the past.

9. To really evaluate the importance of cooccurring deictics such as *ahora* with *estar* + *-ndo* we would have to compare simple verb forms and other constructions. A preliminary comparison with *ir* + *-ndo*, however, indicates that *ahora* may cooccur with Present *estar* + *-ndo* in a higher proportion than with other constructions: there were no Present-tense *ir* + *-ndo* tokens with cooccurring *ahora/ita* in the Chihuahua data; on the other hand, there were three *ahorita* + Present *andar* + *-ndo* tokens, or 8% (3/37).

10. On future uses of Present-tense *estar* + *-ndo*, see Squartini (1998: 95ff.). Butt and Benjamin (1994: 235) mention immediate future uses of Present-tense *estar yendo* 'be going' in Chile and present progressive uses in the Andean region.

11. On the "redundant" possessive construction in example (26), see Company (1995). In this example, *su mamá de ella* 'her mother of her' refers to the mother of one of the participants in the conversation.

12. I did not include in the *ya* count one case of *ya no más* 'as soon as' (*ya no más van llegando a depositar [] entonces ya se lo dan a usted*- Chih'97#21A 'as soon as people arrive to deposit, then [the bank] gives you [the money]'.

13. On *estar siendo*, see Butt and Benjamin (1994: 235); De Bruyne (1995: 559, 574); Kany (1951: 237–8); Lorenzo (1971: 124, note 26); Ozete 1983: 76; Squartini (1998: 104–7).

Conclusion

We have traced the evolution of Spanish *-ndo* constructions through a study of distribution and cooccurrence patterns. Our primary goal has been to show how a diachronic approach provides insights on synchronic variation and language contact phenomena.

Diachronic changes in distribution and cooccurrence patterns reveal that change in the grammaticization of *-ndo* constructions is reductive. Reductive change is manifested in both form and meaning. Evidence of formal reduction is the fixing of the position of the auxiliary and the gerund, the decline in multiple-gerund sequences, the decrease in open class material intervening between the auxiliary and the gerund, and the increased positioning of object clitic pronouns preposed to the auxiliary. This series of changes contributes to the emergence of auxiliary-plus-gerund sequences as fused units. Indices of semantic reduction are the spread to more main verb classes, tense forms, and inanimate subjects. The decreased frequency of cooccurring locatives shows that these constructions originate as spatial expressions and that their grammaticization involves gradual loss of spatial features of meaning.

Reductive change is driven by frequency increases. There is a steady diachronic process of increases in construction frequency, a measure combining the absolute token frequency of auxiliary-plus-gerund sequences and the proportion of gerunds participating in such sequences. The role of frequency is shown by indices of formal and semantic reduction, which vary in tandem with construction frequency. We saw that spatial meaning is reduced in frequent collocations with main verbs not typically associated with physical location or motion, for example, *estar hablando* and *ir creciendo*. In present-day Spanish, high frequency collocations of *estar* with general activity main verbs, in particular, *estar trabajando*, contribute to the extension of *estar + -ndo* to habitual uses. The diachronic reversal in the relative frequency of auxiliaries *estar* and *ir* and concomitant generalization of *estar + -ndo* to erstwhile *ir + -ndo* contexts (for example, with motion and process verbs) provides additional evidence for the role of frequency in grammaticization.

Locutionary subjectivity — the expression of speaker point of view — is important throughout the development of *estar + -ndo*. Progressive meaning is conventionalized in the context of high frequency collocations with "talking" and "bodily activity" main verbs, such as *hablando* 'talking' and *llorando* 'crying', which entail active involvement by an agent — experiencer. Active involvement from the perspective of the subject is complemented by overtness or evidentiality from the perspective of the speaker. *Estar + -ndo* is thus an "experiential" (Lyons 1982) progressive. It is important that experiential progressive meaning involves neither metaphor nor pragmatic strengthening, but follows from the original locative meaning of the construction. Newer habitual uses, including combinations with motion verbs and stative predicates, are experiential rather than simply transitory.

Present-day variation in Spanish *-ndo* constructions reflects both reduction and retention in grammaticization. Semantic reduction or bleaching along parallel evolutionary paths results in layering in the domain of progressive — continuous aspect, so that different *-ndo* constructions compete as aspectual expressions. At the same time, retention of features of the original meaning of the source constructions results in the specification of additional features of meaning, such as gradual development for *ir + -ndo* and frequentative for *andar + -ndo*. Retention is shown in the distribution of auxiliaries with respect to locatives, temporals, and main verbs.

Given retention on the one hand, and semantic reduction on the other, variation in *-ndo* constructions is both meaningful and non-meaningful with respect to aspectual differences. Besides persisting meaning differences, an important factor in the choice of auxiliary is the routinization of frequent collocations that were once meaningful, such as *estar hablando, ir creciendo*, and *andar buscando*. Another set of factors is sociolinguistic, with register considerations paramount.

We have seen that the frequency of *-ndo* constructions and the relative frequency of *-ndo* auxiliaries is stratified by register. Overall token frequencies of the set of *-ndo* constructions as well as the relative frequency of *estar + -ndo* are higher in oral, popular, informal varieties than in written, formal varieties. The acceleration of frequency increases this century and the increasing restriction of the simple Present to non-progressive uses in the spoken language suggest a change in progress in the status of *estar + -ndo* toward becoming an obligatory expression of progressive aspect.

Register differences are important in evaluating the effects of language contact. In comparing New Mexico and Mexico data, we find no evidence for convergence with English. Overall token frequencies are not greater in bilingual speakers than in comparable oral monolingual data. Nor, crucially, do we find futurate uses or increased use of intervening material between the auxiliary and the gerund, neither of which would agree with internal diachronic trends. The hypothesis of acceleration of change in language contact is more difficult to evaluate. On most counts there are no differences between the bilingual New Mexican and monolingual Mexican data, for example, clitic climbing frequencies, the average number of cooccurring locatives and temporals, and the proportion of inanimate subjects.

The most important change with respect to monolingual varieties is the drop in the relative frequency of *ir* + *-ndo*. Diachronic changes in the relative frequency of *ir* + *-ndo* suggest that a process of specialization in favor of *estar* is more advanced in bilingual varieties. However, the evidence is against convergence and simplification as the mechanism of change, since the other motion verb auxiliary, *andar*, appears to be maintained. Rather, the decline of *ir* + *-ndo* seems to be associated with oral as opposed to written registers. The increased frequency of *estar*-plus-motion verb and possible extension of present habitual uses from general motion verbs (*estar yendo*) to more specific or lexically rich motion verbs (*estar caminando*) among bilinguals follows from the increased relative frequency of *estar* + *-ndo*. In other words, we see the same processes that have been operating in diachronic developments, frequency increases and semantic reduction.

The study leaves a number of important questions for further research. It is evident that there is dialectal, social, and stylistic variation in the frequency, distribution, and uses of *-ndo* constructions. Of broader interest to grammaticization studies is the changing relationship between simple and *estar* + *-ndo* forms and what this can tell us about the creation of obligatory progressives. Finally, *-ndo* constructions provide a promising area for further investigation into priming and repetition effects in language use and change.

References

Alarcos Llorach, E. 1980 [1970]. "Sobre la estructura del verbo español". In *Estudios de gramática funcional del español*, 50–89. Madrid: Gredos.
Alcina Franch, J. and Blecua, J. M. 1975. *Gramática española*. Barcelona: Ariel.
Alonso, A. 1954 [1939]. "Sobre métodos: construcciones con verbos de movimiento en español". In *Estudios lingüísticos: temas españoles*, 330–387. Madrid: Gredos.
Alonso, A and Henríquez Ureña, P. 1969. *Gramática castellana*. Buenos Aires: Losada.
Alonso, D. 1958. *De los siglos oscuros al de oro*. Madrid: Gredos.
Alonso Pedraz, M. 1964. *Evolución sintáctica del español. Sintaxis histórica del español desde el iberorromance hasta neustros días*. Madrid: Aguilar.
Amastae, J. and Elías Olivares, L. (eds). 1982. *Spanish in the United States: Sociolinguistic Aspects*. New York: Cambridge University Press.
Anderson, J. M. 1973. *An Essay Concerning Aspect: Some Considerations of a General Character Arising from Abbé Darrigol's Analysis of the Basque Verb*. The Hague: Mouton de Gruyter.
Arce-Arenales, M., Axelrod, M. and Fox, B.A. 1993. "Active voice and middle diathesis: A cross-linguistic perspective". In *Voice: Form and Function*, B. Fox and P. Hopper (eds), 1–21. Amsterdam: John Benjamins.
Arjona Iglesias, M. 1991. "El gerundio perifrástico". In *Estudios sintácticos sobre el habla popular mexicana*, 113–133. México: UNAM.
Arnaud, R. 1998. "The development of the progressive in 19th century English: A quantitative survey". *Language Variation and Change* 10: 123–152.
Baugh, J. and Sherzer, J. (eds). 1984. *Language in Use: Readings in Sociolinguistics*. Englewood, NJ: Prentice-Hall.
Bell, A. 1984. "Language style as audience design". *Language in Society* 13: 145–204.
Bello, A. 1978 [1847]. *Gramática de la lengua castellana*. Buenos Aires: Sopena.
Benveniste, E. 1968. "Mutations of linguistic categories". In *Directions for Historical Linguistics: A Symposium*, W. P. Lehmann and Y. Malkiel (eds), 85–94. Austin: University of Texas Press.
———. 1971. *Problemas de lingüística general, I*. Traducción de Juan Almela. México: Siglo Veintiuno.
Bernal Enríquez, Y. 1996. "Las relaciones entre el español nuevomexicano, el chicano, y el mexicano: Datos sobre cambio dialectal del NMCOSS". University of New Mexico, ms.
———. 1999. "La relación entre el uso y el dominio en el español chicano de la Nueva México y sus implicaciones para la revitalización". Paper presented at Dolores Gonzales Colloquy Series, University of New Mexico.

Bhat, D.N.S. 1999. *The Prominence of Tense, Aspect and Mood*. Amsterdam: John Benjamins.
Biber, D. 1986. "Spoken and written textual dimensions in English: Resolving the contradictory findings". *Language* 62: 384–414.
Biber, D. and Finegan, E. (eds). 1994. *Perspectives on Register: Situating Register Variation within Sociolinguistics*. Oxford: Oxford University Press.
Binnick, R. I. 1991. *Time and the Verb*. Oxford: Oxford University Press.
Blansitt, E. L., Jr. 1975. "Progressive aspect". *Stanford University Working Papers on Language Universals* 18: 1–34.
Bolinger, D. 1963. "Reference and inference: Inceptiveness in the Spanish preterite". *Hispania* 46: 128–135.
———. 1971. "The nominal in the progressive". *Linguistic Inquiry* 2: 246–250.
———. 1973. "Essence and accident: English analogs of Hispanic *ser–estar*". In *Issues in Linguistics: Papers in Honor of Henry and Renee Kahane*, B.B. Kachru et al. (eds), 58–69. Chicago: University of Illinois Press.
Bouzet, J. 1953. "Orígenes del empleo de *estar*". In *Estudios dedicados a Menéndez Pidal*, vol. IV, 37–58. Madrid: CSIC.
Brinton, L. J. 1988. *The Development of English Aspectual Systems: Aspectualizers and Post-Verbal Particles*. Cambridge: Cambridge University Press.
Bruyne, J. de. 1995. *A Comprehensive Spanish Grammar*. Oxford: Blackwell.
Bull, W. E. 1965. *Spanish for Teachers*. New York: Ronald Press.
Butt, J. and Benjamin, C. 1994. *A New Reference Grammar of Modern Spanish*, 2nd edition. Lincolnwood, IL: NTC.
Bybee, J. L. 1985. *Morphology: A Study of the Relation between Meaning and Form*. Amsterdam: John Benjamins.
———. 1994. "The grammaticization of zero: Asymmetries in tense and aspect systems". In Pagliuca (ed.), 235–254.
———. 1995. "Regular morphology and the lexicon". *Language and Cognitive Processes* 10: 425–455.
———. 1998. "The emergent lexicon". *Chicago Linguistic Society* 34.
———. (forthcoming) "Mechanisms of change in grammaticization: The role of frequency". In Handbook of Historical Linguistics, R. Janda and B. Joseph (eds). Oxford: Blackwell.
Bybee, J. and Dahl, O. 1989. "The creation of tense and aspect systems in the languages of the world". *Studies in Language* 13: 51–103.
Bybee, J. and Fleischman, S. (eds). 1995. *Modality in Grammar and Discourse*. Amsterdam: John Benjamins.
Bybee, J. and Pagliuca, W. 1985. "Cross-linguistic comparison and the development of grammatical meaning". In *Historical Semantics, Historical Word Formation*, J. Fisiak (ed.), 59–83. Berlin: Mouton de Gruyter.
———. 1987. "The evolution of future meaning". In *Papers from the 7th International Conference on Historical Linguistics*, A.G. Ramat, O. Carruba, and G. Bernini (eds), 109–122. Amsterdam: John Benjamins.
Bybee, J. and Thompson, S. 1997. "Three frequency effects in syntax". *Berkeley Linguistics Society* 23.

Bybee, J., Perkins, R. and Pagliuca W. 1994. *The Evolution of Grammar: Tense, Aspect, and Modality in the Languages of the World*. Chicago: University of Chicago Press.
Cameron, R. 1996. "A community-based test of a linguistic hypothesis". *Language in Society* 25: 61–111.
———. 1998. "A variable syntax of speech, gesture, and sound effect: Direct quotations in Spanish". *Language Variation and Change* 10: 43–83.
Caravedo, R. (ed.). 1989. *El español de Lima: Materiales para el estudio del habla culta*. Lima: Pontificia Universidad Católica del Perú, Fondo Editorial.
Chafe, W. L. 1970. *Meaning and the Structure of Language*. Chicago: University of Chicago Press.
Chaston, J. M. 1991. "Imperfect progressive usage patterns in the speech of Mexican American bilinguals from Texas". In *Sociolinguistics of the Spanish-Speaking World: Iberia, Latin America, United States*, C. A. Klee and L. A. Ramos-García (eds), 299–311. Tempe, AZ: Bilingual Press.
Claudi, U. and Heine, B. 1985. "From metaphor to grammar: some examples from Ewe". *Afrikanische Arbeitspapiere* (Köln) 1: 17–54.
Clegg, J. H. nd. "English syntactic interferences in Puerto Rican Spanish". Brigham Young University, ms.
———. and Rodríguez, J.D. 1993. "Progressive constructions in the speech of U.S. Hispanics". Paper presented at the XIV Spanish in the United States, San Antonio.
Coates, J. 1983. *The Semantics of Modal Auxiliaries*. London: Croom Helm.
———. 1995. "The expression of root and epistemic possibility in English". In Bybee and Fleischman (eds), 55–66.
Company, C. 1995. "Cantidad vs. cualidad en el contacto de lenguas: Una incursión metodológica en los posesivos redundantes del español americano". *Nueva Revista de Filología Hispánica* XLIII.2: 305–39.
Comrie, B. 1976. *Aspect*. Cambridge: Cambridge University Press.
Coseriu, E. 1977a. [1962]. "Sobre las llamadas "Construcciones con verbos de movimiento": Un problema hispánico". In *Estudios de lingüística románica*, 70–78. Madrid: Gredos.
———. 1977b. [1968]. "El aspecto verbal perifrástico en griego antiguo (y sus reflejos románicos)." In *Estudios de lingüística románica*, 231–263. Madrid: Gredos.
———. 1996 [1976]. "Tiempo y aspecto: El sistema románico de las categorías verbales". In *El sistema verbal románico*, compilación y redacción de Hansbert Bertsch, 95–125. México: Siglo XXI.
Criado de Val, M. 1966. *Gramática española*. Madrid: SAETA.
Cuervo, R. J. 1994 [1886, 1893]. *Diccionario de construcción y régimen de la lengua castellana*. Bogotá: Instituto Caro y Cuervo.
Dahl, O. 1985. *Tense and Aspect Systems*. Oxford: Blackwell.
Davies, M. 1998. Corpus of historical Spanish prose. http://138.87.135.33/~mdavies/espanol.htm
Dennis, L. 1940. "The progressive tense: Frequency of its use in English". *Publications of the Modern Language Association of America* 55: 855–865.
Deyermond, A. D. 1971. *A Literary History of Spain: The Middle Ages*. New York: Barnes & Noble.

Dietrich, W. 1983. *El aspecto verbal perifrástico en las lenguas románicas*. Trans. Marcos Martínez Hernández. Madrid: Gredos.
Dik, S. C. 1987. "Copula auxiliarization: how and why?" In Harris and Ramat (eds), 53–84.
———. 1989. *The Theory of Functional Grammar, Part 1: The Structure of the Clause*. Dordrecht: Foris.
Dorian, N. 1981. *Language Death: The Life Cycle of a Scottish Gaelic Dialect*. Philadelphia: University of Pennsylvania Press.
Douglass, T. R. 1967. "Gerundive and non-gerundive forms". *Hispania* 50: 99–103.
Dowty, D. 1979. *Word Meaning and Montague Grammar*. Dordrecht: Reidel.
Eckert, P. 1996. "(ay) goes to the city: Exploring the expressive use of variation". In: *Towards a Social Science of Language, Vol. 1, Variation and Change in Language and Society*, Gregory R. Guy et al. (eds), 47-68. Amsterdam: John Benjamins.
———. 2000. *Linguistic Variation as Social Practice*. Oxford: Blackwell.
Esgueva, M. and Cantarero, M. 1981. *El habla de la ciudad de Madrid*. Madrid: C.S.I.C.
Espinosa, A. M., Jr. 1975 (1957). "Problemas lexicográficos del español del sudoeste". In *El lenguaje de los chicanos: Regional and Social Characteristics of Language Used by Mexican-Americans*, E. Hernández-Chávez, A. D. Cohen, and A. F. Beltramo (eds), 13–18. Arlington, VA: Center for Applied Linguistics.
Espunya I Pratt, A. 1996. "The realization of the semantic operator progressive in English and Romance languages". *Language Sciences* 18: 295–303.
Fernández de Castro, F. 1990. *Las perífrasis verbales en español*. Oviedo: Publicaciones del Departameno de Filología Española.
Fernández Ramírez, S. 1960. "Algo sobre la fórmula *estar* + gerundio". In *Studia Philologica: Homenaje ofrecido a Dámaso Alonso por sus amigo y discípulos con ocasión de su 60o aniversario*, Vol. I, 509–516. Madrid: Gredos.
Finegan, E. 1995. "Subjectivity and subjectivisation: An introduction". In Stein and Wright (eds), 1–15.
Floyd, M. B. 1978. "Verb usage in Southwest Spanish: A review". The *Bilingual Review/La Revista Bilingüe* 5: 86–90.
Fontanella de Weinberg, B. 1970. "Los auxiliares españoles". *Anales del Instituto de Lingüística de la Universidad de Cuyo* X: 61–73.
Gerli, E. M. 1975. "Ars predicandi and the structure of Arcipreste de Talavera, Part I". *Hispania* 58: 430–441.
Gervasi, K. 1997. "Aspectos discursivos y sociolingüísticos de las cláusulas relativas en español". University of Southern California, ms.
Gili Gaya, S. 1964 [1943]. *Curso superior de sintaxis española*. Barcelona: Vox, 9th edn.
Givón, T. 1975. "Serial verbs and syntactic change: Niger — Congo". In *Word Order and Word Order Change*, C. N. Li (ed.), 47–112. Austin: University of Texas Press.
———. 1979. *On Understanding Grammar*. New York: Academic Press.
———. 1984/1990. *Syntax. A Functional-Typological Introduction*, Vol. I and Vol. II. Amsterdam: John Benjamins.
Goldberg, A. E. 1995. *Constructions: A Construction Grammar Approach to Argument Structure*. Chicago: The University of Chicago Press.
——— (ed.). 1996. *Conceptual Structure, Discourse and Language*. Stanford, CA: CSLI.
———. (2000). "Patient arguments of causative verbs can be omitted: The role of information structure in argument distribution." *Language Science*, N. Gisborne (ed.).

Goldsmith, J. and Woisetschlaeger, E. 1982. "The logic of the English progressive". *Linguistic Inquiry* 13: 79–89.
Gómez Torrego, L. 1988. *Perífrasis verbales*. Madrid: Arco Libros.
Gonzales, P. 1995. "Progressive and nonprogressive imperfects in Spanish discourse". *Hispanic Linguistics* 6/7: 61–92.
Green, J. N. 1987. "The evolution of Romance auxiliaries: Criteria and chronology". In Harris and Ramat (eds), 257–267.
———. 1988. "Spanish". In *The Romance Languages*, M. Harris and N. Vincent (eds), 79–130. Oxford: Oxford University Press.
Greenberg, J. H. 1966. *Language Universals*. The Hague: Mouton de Gruyter.
———. 1991. "The Semitic "intensive" as verbal plurality". In *Semitic Studies in Honor of Wolf Leslau, Vol. I*, A. S. Kaye (ed.), 577–587. Wiesbaden: Harrassowitz.
Gumperz, J. and Wilson, R. 1971. "Convergence and creoliation: A case from the Indo-Aryan/Dravidian border in India". In *Pidginization and Creolization of Languages*, D. Hymes (ed.), 151–167. Cambridge: Cambridge University Press.
Gutiérrez, M. J. 1992. "The extension of *estar*: A linguistic change in progress in the Spanish of Morelia, Mexico". *Hispanic Linguistics* 5: 109–141.
Haiman, J. 1994. "Ritualization and the development of language". In Pagliuca (ed.), 3–28.
Halliday, M. A. K. 1988. "On the language of physical science". In *Registers of Written English*, M. Ghadessy (ed.), 162–178. London: Pinter.
Hamplová, S. 1968. "Acerca de la manera de acción y el problema de su expresión mediante las perífrasis verbales en español". *Philologica Pragensia* 11: 209–231.
Harre, C. E. 1991. *Tener + Past Participle: A Case Study in Linguistic Description*. London: Routledge.
Harris, A. C. and Campbell, L. 1995. *Historical Syntax in Cross-Linguistic Perspective*. Cambridge: Cambridge University Press.
Harris, M. and Ramat, P. (eds). 1987. *Historical Development of Auxiliaries*. Berlin: Mouton de Gruyter.
Hatcher, A. G. 1951. "The use of the progressive form in English". *Language* 27: 254–280.
Heine, B. 1993. *Auxiliaries. Cognitive Forces and Grammaticalization*. Oxford: Oxford University Press.
———. 1994a. "Grammaticalization as an explanatory parameter". In Pagliuca (ed.), 255–287.
———.1994b. "On the genesis of aspect in African languages: The proximative". *Berkeley Linguistics Society* 20: 35–46.
———, Claudi, U. and Hünnemeyer, F. 1991. "From cognition to grammar: Evidence from African languages". In Traugott and Heine (eds), Vol I, 149–187.
Hernández-Chávez, E. 1992. "Language policy and language rights in the United States". Paper presented at 1st International Conference on Language Rights, Tallinn, Estonia.
———. 1993. "Native language loss and its implication for the revitalization of Spanish in Chicano communities". In *Language and Culture in Learning: Teaching Spanish to Native Speakers of Spanish*, B. Merino et al. (eds), 58–74. London: Falmer Press.
Hidalgo, M. 1987. "Español mexicano y español chicano: Problemas y propuestas fundamentales". *Language Problems and Language Planning* 11: 166–193.
Hook, P. 1992. "The emergence of perfective aspect in Indo-Aryan languages". In Traugott and Heine (eds), Vol II, 59–89.

Hopper, P. J. 1979. "Aspect and foregrounding in discourse". In *Discourse and Syntax* (Syntax and Semantics 12), T. Givón (ed.), 213–241. New York: Academic Press.
———. 1982a. "Aspect between discourse and grammar: An introductory essay for the volume". In Hopper (ed.), 3–18.
———, (ed.). 1982b. *Tense-Aspect: Between Semantics and Pragmatics*. Amsterdam: John Benjamins.
———. 1987. "Emergent grammar". *Berkeley Linguistics Society* 13: 139–157.
———. 1991. "On some principles of grammaticization". In Traugott and Heine (eds), Vol I, 17–35.
——— and Traugott, E.C. 1993. *Grammaticalization*. Cambridge: Cambridge University Press.
Hudson, A., Hernández Chávez, E. and Bills, G. 1995. "The many faces of language maintenance: Spanish language claiming in five southwestern states". In *Spanish in Four Continents*, C. Silva-Corvalán (ed.), 165–183. Washington, D.C.: Georgetown University Press.
Hudson-Edwards, A. and Bills, G. 1982. "Intergenerational language shift in an Albuquerque barrio". In Amastae and Olivares (eds), 135–153.
Israel, M. 1996. "The way constructions grow". In Goldberg (ed.), 217–230.
Jacobson, T. 1986. "¿Aspecto antes que tiempo? Una mirada a la adquisición temprana del español". In *Adquisición del lenguaje/Aquisição da linguagem*, J. M. Meisel (ed.), 97–114. Frankfurt/M: Vervuert.
Jakobson, R. 1938. "Sur la théorie des affinités phonologiques entre des langues". In *Actes du Quatrième Congrès International de Linguistes*, 48–59. Copenhagen: Munksgaard.
———. 1971. "Shifters, verbal categories, and the Russian verb". In *Selected Writings* II, 130–147. The Hague: Mouton de Gruyter.
Jesperson, O. 1931. *A Modern English Grammar on Historical Principles*, Part IV Syntax, Vol 3. London: George Allen and Unwin.
Jonge, B. de. 1993. "(Dis)continuity in language change: *Ser* and *estar* in Latin-American Spanish". In *Linguistics in the Netherlands*, F. Drijkoningen and K. Hengeveld (eds), 69–80. Amsterdam: John Benajmins.
Kany, C. E. 1951. *American-Spanish Syntax*, 2nd edition. Chicago: University of Chicago Press.
Kattán-Ibarra, J. and Pountain, C. J. 1997. *Modern Spanish Grammar: A Practical Guide*. New York: Routledge.
Kay, P. and Fillmore, C. J. 1999. "Grammatical constructions and linguistic generalizations: The *What's X doing Y?* construction". *Language* 75: 1–33.
Keniston, H. 1936. "Verbal aspect in Spanish". *Hispania* 19: 163–176.
———. 1937a. *The Syntax of Castilian Prose: The Sixteenth Century*. Chicago: University of Chicago Press.
———. 1937b. *Spanish Syntax List*. New York: Henry Holt and Company.
King, L. D. 1992. *The Semantic Structure of Spanish*. Amsterdam: John Benjamins.
King, L. D. and Suñer, M. 1980a. "On the notion of stativity in Spanish and Portuguese". In *Contemporary Studies in Romance Languages*, F. H. Nuessel (ed.), 183–201. Bloomington: Indiana University Linguistics Club.
———. 1980b. "The meaning of the progressive in Spanish and Portuguese". The *Bilingual Review/La Revista Bilingüe* 7: 222–238.

Klein, F. 1980. "A quantitative study of syntactic and pragmatic indicators of change in the Spanish of bilinguals in the United States". In *Locating Language in Time and Space*, W. Labov (ed.), 69–82. New York: Academic Press.

———. 1985. "La cuestión del anglicismo: Apriorismos y métodos". *Thesaurus* 40: 533–548.

Kock, J. de. 1975. "Pour une nouvelle définition de la notion d'auxiliarité". *Linguistique* 11.2: 81–92.

Koike, D. A. 1996. "Functions of the adverbial *ya* in Spanish narrative discourse". *Journal of Pragmatics* 25: 267–279.

Krug, M. 2000. *Emerging English Modals. A Corpus-Based Study of Grammaticalization*. Berlin: Mouton de Gruyter.

Labov, W. 1972a. *Sociolinguistic Patterns*. Philadelphia: University of Pennsylvania Press.

———. 1972b. "The transformation of experience in narrative syntax". In *Language in the Inner City: Studies in the Black English Vernacular*, 354–405. Philadelphia: University of Pennsylvania Press.

———. 1984. "Field methods of the project on linguistic change and variation". In Baugh and Sherzer (eds), 28–52.

———. 1994. *Principles of Linguistic Change: Internal Factors*. Oxford: Blackwell.

Labov, W. and Waletzky, J. 1967. "Narrative analysis: Oral versions of personal experience". In *Essays on the Verbal and Visual Arts*, J. Helm (ed.), 12–44. Seattle: University of Washington Press.

Lakoff, G. 1987. *Women, Fire, and Dangerous Things*. Chicago: University of Chicago Press.

Langacker, R. 1987. *Foundations of Cognitive Grammar*, Vol. 1. Stanford, CA: Stanford University Press.

———. 1991. *Concept, Image, and Symbol. The Cognitive Basis of Grammar*. Berlin: Mouton de Gruyter.

———. 1996. "A constraint on progressive generics". In Goldberg (ed.), 289–302.

Lavandera, B. 1981. "Lo quebramos, but only in performance". In *Latino Language and Communicative Behavior*, R. P. Duran (ed.), 49–67. Norwood: Ablex.

———. 1984. *Variación y significado*. Buenos Aires: Hachette.

Lawrence, Helen. 1999. "How's it going? The development of the progressive in British English". Paper presented at New Ways of Analyzing Variation (NWAVE)-28, Toronto.

Lehmann, C. 1985. "Grammaticalization: Synchronic variation and diachronic change". *Lingua e Stile* XX: 303–318.

———. 1995 (1982). *Thoughts on Grammaticalization*. München — Newcastle: LINCOLM EUROPA.

Lenz, R. 1925. *La oración y sus partes*, 2a ed. Madrid: Centro de Estudios Históricos.

Lightfoot, D. 1991. *How to Set Parameters: Arguments from Language Change*. Cambridge, MA: MIT Press.

Lipski, J. M. 1990. *The Language of the Isleños: Vestigial Spanish in Louisiana*. Baton Rouge: Louisiana State University Press.

1993a. "Creoloid phenomena in the Spanish of transitional bilinguals". In *Spanish in the United States: Linguistic Contact and Diversity*, A. Roca and J. M. Lipski (eds),155–182. Berlin: Mouton de Gruyter.

———. 1993b. "Origin and development of *ta* in Afro-Hispanic Creoles". In *Atlantic Meets Pacific: A global view of Pidginization and Creolization*, F. Byrne and J. Holm (eds), 217–231. Amsterdam: John Benjamins.
———. 1994. "A new perspective on Afro-Dominican Spanish: The Haitian contribution". *Latin American Institute Research Paper Series*, 26. Albuquerque: University of New Mexico.
———. 1996. Review of *Language Contact and Change*, by Carmen Silva-Corvalán. *Language* 72: 146–150.
Lloyd, P. M. 1993. *Del latín al español*. Madrid: Gredos.
Lope Blanch, J. M. 1953. *Observaciones sobre la sintaxis del español hablado en México*. México: Publicaciones del Instituto Mexicano de Investigaciones Científicas.
———. 1962. "Sobre la oración gramatical". *Nueva Revista de Filología Hispánica* XVI: 416–422.
———. 1971. *El habla de la ciudad de México. Materiales para su estudio*. México: Centro de Lingüística Hispánica (UNAM).
———. 1986. *El estudio del español hablado culto: Historia de un proyecto*. Mexico: UNAM.
———. 1990. *El español hablado en el suroeste de los Estados Unidos. Materiales para su estudio*. México: UNAM.
Lorenzo, E. 1971. *El español de hoy, lengua en ebullición*. Madrid: Gredos.
Luján, M. (1980). "Clitic promotion and mood in Spanish verbal complements". *Linguistics* 18: 381–484.
Luna Trail, E. 1980. *Sintaxis de los verboides en el habla culta de la ciudad de México*. México: UNAM.
Lunn, P. V. and DeCesaris, J. A. 1992. *Investigación de gramática*. Boston: Heinle and Heinle.
Lyons, J. 1977. *Semantics*, 2 vols. Cambridge: Cambridge University Press.
———. 1982. "Deixis and subjectivity: loquor, ergo sum?" In *Speech, Place, and Action: Studies in Deixis and Related Topics*, R. J. Jarvella and W. Klein (eds), 101–124. New York: John Wiley & Sons.
———. 1994. "Subjecthood and subjectivity". In *Subjecthood and Subjectivity: The Status of the Subject in Linguistic Theory*, M. Yaguello (ed.), 9–17. Paris: Ophrys.
———. 1995. *Linguistic Semantics*. Cambridge: Cambridge University Press.
Mair, C. and Hundt, M. 1995. "Why is the progressive becoming more frequent in English?" *ZAA: A Quarterly of Language, Literature and Culture (Zeitschrift für Anglistik und Amerikanistik)* 2: 112–122.
Maldonado, R. 1999. *A media voz: Problemas conceptuales del clítico "se"*. México: UNAM.
Marchand, H. 1955. "On a question of aspect: A comparison between the progressive form in English and that in Italian and Spanish". *Studia Linguistica* 9: 45–52.
Markič, J. 1990. "Sobre las perífrasis verbales en español". *Linguistica* 30: 169–206.
Medina-Rivera, A. 1996. "Discourse genre, type of situation, and topic of conversation in relation to phonological variables in Puerto Rican Spanish". In *Sociolinguistic Variation: Data, Theory, and Analysis*, J. Arnold et al. (eds), 209–222. Stanford, CA:CSLI.
Meillet, A. 1921 (1914). "Le problème de la parenté des langues". In *Linguistique historique et linguistique générale*, 76–101. Paris: Champion.

Menéndez Pidal, R. 1964. *Cantar de Mio Cid. Texto, gramática y vocabulario*. 4th ed., 3 vols. Madrid: Espasa-Calpe.

Moliner, M. 1966–7. *Diccionario de uso del español*. Madrid: Gredos.

Montes Giraldo, J. J. 1963. "Sobre las perífrasis con *ir* en el español de Colombia". *Thesaurus* (Boletín del Instituto Caro y Cuervo) 18: 384–403.

Moreno de Alba, J. G. 1978. *Valores de las formas verbales en el español de México*. México: UNAM.

Mougeon, R. and Beniak, E. 1991. *Linguistic Consequences of Language Contact and Restriction*. Oxford: Oxford University Press.

Mrak, N. A. 1998. "El discurso de pasado en el español de Houston: Imperfectividad y perfectividad verbal en una situación de contacto". *Southwest Journal of Linguistics* 17: 115–128.

Myhill, J.1988a. "Variation in Spanish clitic climbing". In *Synchronic and Diachronic Approaches to Linguistic Variation and Change* (GURT `88), T. J. Walsh (ed.), 227–250. Washington, D.C.: Georgetown University Press.

———. 1988b. "The grammaticalization of auxiliaries: Spanish clitic climbing". *Berkeley Linguistics Society* 14: 352–363.

Nehls, Dietrich. 1988. "On the development of the grammatical category of verbal aspect in English". In *Essays on the English Language and Applied Linguistics*, J. Klegraf and D. Nehls (eds), 173–198. Heidelberg: Groos.

Olbertz, H. 1998. *Verbal Periphrases in a Functional Grammar of Spanish*. Berlin: Mouton de Gruyter.

Ozete, O. 1983. "On the so-called Spanish gerund/participle". *Hispania* 66: 75–83.

Pagliuca, W. (ed.). 1994. *Perspectives on Grammaticalization*. Amsterdam: John Benjamins.

Parisi, C. 1992. Descriptive semantics and syntax of Modern Spanish 'estar' progressives. Ann Arbor, MI: University of Michigan dissertation.

Poplack, S. 1982. ""Sometimes I'll start a sentence in Spanish y termino en español": Toward a typology of code-switching". In: Amastae and Olivares (eds), 230–263.

———. 1989. "The care and handling of a megacorpus: the Ottawa-Hull French Project". In: *Language Change and Variation*, R. Fasold and D. Schiffrin (eds), 411–451. Amsterdam: John Benjamins.

———. 1992. "The inherent variability of the French subjunctive". In *Theoretical Analyses in Romance Linguistics*, C. Laefer and T. A. Morgan (eds), 235–263. Amsterdam: John Benjamins.

———. 1993. "Variation theory and language contact". In *American Dialect Research*, D. R. Preston (ed.), 251–286. Amsterdam: John Benjamins.

———. 1997. "The sociolinguistic dynamics of apparent convergence". In *Towards a Social Science of Language: Papers in Honor of William Labov, Vol 2: Social Interaction and Discourse Structures*, G. Guy et al. (eds), 285–309. Amsterdam: John Benjamins.

Pousada, A. and Poplack, S. 1982. "No case for convergence: The Puerto Rican Spanish verb system in a language-contact situation". In *Bilingual Education for Hispanic Students in the United States*, J. A. Fishman and G. D. Keller (eds), 207–237. New York: Teachers College Press.

Quesada, J. D. 1995. "*Estar* + *-ndo* y el aspecto progresivo en español". *Iberoromania* 42: 8–29.

Rallides, C. 1966. "Differences in aspect between the gerundive forms and the nongerundive forms of the Spanish verb". *Hispania* 19: 107–114.

———. 1971. *The Tense Aspect System of the Spanish Verb as Used in Cultivated Bogotá Spanish*. The Hague: Mouton de Gruyter.

Ramat, P. 1987. "Introductory paper". In Harris and Ramat (eds), 3–19.

Ramos, M. A. 1972. "El fenómeno de "estar siendo"". *Hispania* 55: 128–131.

Ramos-Pellicia, M. F. 1998. "Progressive constructions in the Spanish spoken in Puerto Rico". Paper presented at the XVI Spanish in the United States, Albuquerque.

Real Academia Española (RAE). 1990 [1732]. *Diccionario de autoridades, Edición facsímil, D-Ñ*. Madrid: Gredos.

———. 1931. *Gramática de la lengua española*. Madrid: Espasa-Calpe.

———.1973. *Esbozo de una nueva gramática de la lengua española*. Madrid: Espasa Calpe.

Rivero, M. L. 1970. "A surface structure constraint in negation". *Language* 46: 640–666.

———. 1986. "Parameters in the typology of clitics in Romance and Old Spanish". *Language* 62: 774–807.

Rizzi, L. 1982. "A restructuring rule in Italian syntax". In *Issues in Italian Syntax*, 1–48. Dordrecht: Foris.

Roca Pons, J. 1954. "Sobre el valor auxiliar y copulativo del verbo *andar*". *Archivum* 4: 166–182.

———. 1958. *Estudios sobre perífrasis verbales del español*. Revista de Filología Española, Anejo 67.

Saffran, J. R., Aslin, R. N and Newport, E. L. 1996. "Word segmentation: The role of distributional cues". *Journal of Memory and Language* 35: 606–621.

San Román, G. 1987. "Sentence and word-length as indicators of register in Arcipreste de Talavera, parts I and II: An exercise in quantitative stylistics". *La Corónica* 15: 213–224.

Sánchez, R. 1982. "Our linguistic and social context". In Amastae and Elías-Olivares (eds), 9–36.

Sankoff, D. 1988. "Sociolinguistics and syntactic variation". In *Linguistics: The Cambridge survey, IV*, F. Newmeyer (ed.), 140–161. Cambridge: Cambridge University Press.

Sankoff, D. and Laberge, S. 1978. "The linguistic market and the statistical explanation of variability". In *Linguistic Variation: Models and Methods*, D. Sankoff (ed.), 239–250. New York: Academic Press.

Sapir, E. 1921. *Language*. New York: Harcourt Brace & Company.

Scherre, M. M. Pereira and Naro, A. (1991). "Marking in discourse: "Birds of a feather."" *Language Variation and Change* 3: 23–32.

Schwenter, S. A. 1994. "The grammaticalization of an anterior in progress: Evidence from a peninsular Spanish dialect". *Studies in Language* 18: 71–111.

Seco, M. 1989. *Gramática esencial del español: Introdución al estudio de la lengua, 2a ed*. Madrid: Espasa-Calpe.

Seco, R. 1966. *Manual de gramática española, 8a ed*. Madrid: Aguilar.

Shirai, Y. 1994. "On the overgeneralization of progressive marking on stative verbs: Bioprogram or input?" *First Language* 14: 67–82.

Silva-Corvalán, C. 1991. "Invariant meanings and context-bound functions of tense in Spanish". In *The function of Tense in Texts*, J. Gvozdanovic and T. Janssen (eds), 255–270. Amsterdam: North-Holland.

———. 1992. "Estructura y lengua en el discurso hipotético". In *Homenaje a Humberto López Morales*, M. Vaquero and A. Morales (eds), 285–299. Madrid: Arco/Libros.

———. 1994. *Language Contact and Change: Spanish in Los Angeles*. Oxford: Clarendon Press.

———. 1995. "Contextual conditions for the interpretation of *poder* and *deber* in Spanish". In Bybee and Fleischman (eds), 67–105.

———. 1997a. "Variación sintáctica en el discurso oral: Problemas metodológicos". In *Trabajos de sociolingüística hispánica*, F. Moreno Fernández (ed.), 115–135. Alcalá, España: Universidad de Alcalá.

———. 1997b. "Gramática y pragmática discursiva". Plenary presentation at II Coloquio Latinoamericano de Analistas del Discurso, Argentina.

Silverstein, M. 1976. "Shifters, linguistic categories, and cultural description". In Meaning in Anthropology, K. H. Basso and H. A. Selby (eds), 11–55. Albuquerque: University of New Mexico Press.

Smith, C. S. 1991. *The Parameter of Aspect*. Dordrecht: Kluwer Academic Publishers.

Solé, Y. R. 1990. "Valores aspectuales en español". *Hispanic Linguistics* 4: 57–86.

Solé, Y. R. and Solé, C.A. 1977. *Modern Spanish Syntax: A Study in Contrast*. Lexington, MA: Heath.

Spaulding, R. K. 1926. "History and syntax of the progressive constructions in Spanish". *University of California Publications in Modern Philology* 13: 229–284.

Squartini, M. 1998. *Verbal Periphrases in Romance: Aspect, Actionality, and Grammaticalization*. Berlin: Mouton de Gruyter.

Stein, D. and Wright, S. (eds). 1995. *Subjectivity and Subjectivisation: Linguistic Perspectives*. Cambridge: Cambridge University Press.

Stockwell, R. P., Bowen, J. D, and Martin, J. W. 1965. *The Grammatical Structures of English and Spanish*. Chicago: University of Chicago Press.

Strang, B. M. H. 1982. "Some aspects of the history of the Be + ing construction". In *Language Form and Linguistic Variation: Papers Dedicated to Angus McIntosh*, J. Anderson (ed.), 427–474. Amsterdam: John Benjamins.

Sweetser, E. 1988. "Grammaticalization and semantic bleaching". *Berkeley Linguistics Society* 14: 389–405.

Talmy, L. 1991. "Path to realization: A typology of event conflation". *Berkeley Linguistics Society* 17: 480–519.

Taylor, J. R. 1995. *Linguistic Categorization: Prototypes in Linguistic Theory*, 2nd ed. London: Clarendon.

Thomason, S. G. and Kaufman, T. 1988. *Language Contact, Creolization, and Genetic Linguistics*. Berkeley: University of California Press.

Thompson, S. A. and Mulak, A. 1991. "A quantitative perspective on the grammaticization of epistemic parentheticals in English". In Traugott and Heine (eds), Vol II, 313–329. Amsterdam: John John Benjamins.

Timberlake, A. 1982. "Invariance and the syntax of Russian aspect". In Hopper (ed.), 305–347.

Torres Cacoullos, R. 1999a. "Variation and grammaticization in progressives: Spanish *-ndo* constructions". *Studies in Language* 23.1. 25–59.

———. 1999b. "Construction frequency and reductive change: Diachronic and register variation in Spanish clitic climbing". *Language Variation and Change* 11: 143–170.

——— and Hernández, J. E. 1999. "*A trabajarle*: La construcción intensiva en el español mexicano". *Southwest Journal of Linguistics* 18: 79–100.

Traugott, E. C. 1978. "On the expression of spatio-temporal relations in language". In *Universals of Human Language, Vol. 3*, J. Greenberg, C. Ferguson, and E. Moravcsik (eds), 369–400. Stanford, CA: Stanford University Press.

———. 1989. "On the rise of epistemic meanings in English: An example of subjectification in semantic change". *Language* 65: 31–55.

———. 1995. "Subjectification in grammaticalization". In Stein and Wright (eds), 31–54.

Traugott, E. and Heine, B. (eds). 1991. *Approaches to Grammaticalization*, 2 vols. Amsterdam: John Benjamins.

Traugott, E. and König, E. 1991. "The semantics-pragmatics of grammaticalization revisited". In Traugott and Heine (eds), Vol I, 189–218.

Universidad Nacional Autónoma de México (UNAM). 1976. *El habla popular de la Ciudad de México: Materiales para su estudio*. México: Publicaciones del Centro de Lingüística Hispánica.

Vásquez, I. 1989. "Construcciones de gerundio en el habla culta de San Juan". *Asomante* 3: 211–220.

Vendler, Z. 1967. "Verbs and times". In *Linguistics in Philosophy*, 97–121. Ithaca, NY: Cornell University Press.

Vigil, N. A. and Bills, G. D. 1993. "The New Mexico/Colorado Spanish Survey: Methodology and techonology". Paper presented at VIII International Conference on Methods in Dialectology, Vancouver, August 1993.

———. 1998. "El español de Nuevo México: Hablamos mexicano". Paper presented at V Encuentro Internacional de Lingüística en el Noroeste, Hermosillo, Mexico, November 1998.

Visser, F. Th. 1973. *An Historical Syntax of the English Language. Part Three, Second half, Syntactical Units with Two and with More Verbs*. Leiden: E.J. Brill.

Weiner, E. J. and Labov, W. 1983. "Constraints on the agentless passive". *Journal of Linguistics* 19: 29–58.

Weinreich, U. 1953. *Languages in Contact*. New York: Publications of the Linguistics Circle of New York.

Westfall, R. E. 1996. Simple and progressive forms of the Spanish past tense system: A semantic and pragmatic study in viewpoint contrast. Austin, TX: University of Texas dissertation.

Whitley, S. M. 1986. *Spanish/English Contrasts: A Course in Spanish Linguistics*. Washington, D.C.: Georgetown University Press.

Wright, S. 1995. "Subjectivity and experiential syntax". In Stein and Wright (eds), 151–172.

Yllera, A. 1980. *Sintaxis histórica del verbo español: Las perífrasis medievales*. Zaragoza: Universidad de Zaragoza.

Zdenek, J. W. 1972. "Another look at the progressive". *Hispania* 55: 498–499.

Appendices

Appendix I. Corpora, word counts, and *-ndo* construction totals

Corpus	Word count		Total *-ndo* constructions
Old Spanish (OldSp)	7 texts	579,800	616
Mexico City Popular (MexPop)	35 "muestras"	172,700	648
Essays	9 texts	376,300	278
Chihuahua (Chih'97)	37 speakers	150,000	587
New Mexico (NMmon/bil/tb)	35 speakers	101,100	260

Word counts were calculated as follows:

1. OldSp: The word counts for the *Cid*, *EE1*, *LBA*, and *Celestina* are the Microsoft Word "word count" of the electronic versions of these texts. The word counts for the *Lucanor* and *Corbacho* are from Davies (1998).
2. MexPop: Word count as reported in Clegg and Rodríguez (1993).
3. Essays: I estimated the word count by counting the number of words on pp.87–88 of Castellanos (1966), which was the book with the smallest page size and relatively large letter case. The count was 286 and 282, respectively. Then I multiplied the page total of 1344 (Appendix IIIB) by 280. The result most likely underestimates the word count.
4. Chih'97: Estimated by calculating that one hour of recording is about 10,000 words. MexPop's 172,700 words (Clegg and Rodríguez 1993) correspond to 17 hours of recordings (Arjona 1991:113).
5. NM corpus: Microsoft Word "word count" of transcribed portions of NMCSS tapes and a calculation of 10,000 words for every hour I recorded. Based on 15 NMmon speakers (34,900 words–76 *-ndo* constructions), 11 NMbil speakers (49,700–145) and 9 NMtb speakers (16,500–39).

Appendix II: Old Spanish corpus: Editions, concordances, translations

PMC
Electronic version of Menéndez Pidal paleographic edition.*
Bolaño e Isla, A. 1976. *Poema de Mio Cid*. Versión antigua con prólogo y versión moderna de Amancio Bolaño e Isla. México: Porrúa.
Hamilton, R. and Perry, J. 1975. *The Poem of the Cid*. With an introduction and notes by Ian Michael together with a new prose translation by Rita Hamilton and Janet Perry. Manchester: Manchester University Press.
Salinas, P. 1963. *Poema del Cid*. Texto antiguo y versión en romance moderno de Pedro Salinas. Introducción de Pedro Henríquez Ureña. Buenos Aries: Losada.
Such, P. and Hodgkinson, J. 1987. *The Poem of my Cid*. Translated with an introduction and commentary by Peter Such and John Hodgkinson. Warminster, England: Aris and Phillips Ltd.
Waltman, F. M. 1972. *Concordance to Poema de Mio Cid*. University Park, PA: The Pennsylvania State University Press.

Apol
Alvar, M. 1976. *Libro de Apolonio. Estudios, ediciones, concordancias*, 3 vols. Madrid: Castalia.

EE1
Kasten, L., Nitti, J. and Jonxis-Henkemans, W. 1997. *The Electronic Texts and Concordances of the Prose Works of Alfonso X, El Sabio*. Madison, WI: HSMS. (CD-ROM).
[EE1 1270–1284 Estoria de España: Escorial: Monasterio Y.I.2]

LBA
Electronic version of Salamanca ms.*
Joset, J. 1990. *Juan Ruiz, Arcipreste de Hita "Libro de buen amor"*. Madrid: Clásicos Taurus.
Jauralde, P. 1988. *Libro de buen amor/Arcipreste de Hita*. Edición, notas y versión moderna de Pablo Jauralde. Barcelona: PPU.
Mignani, R., Di Cesare, M.A. and Jones, G.F. 1977. *A Concordance to Juan Ruiz "Libro de Buen Amor"*. Albany, NY: State University of New York Press.
Singleton, M. 1975. *The Book of the Archpriest of Hita (Libro de Buen Amor)*, translated by Mack Singleton. Madison: Hispanic Seminary of Medieval Studies, 1975.
Willis, R. S. 1972. *Juan Ruiz, Libro de Buen Amor*. Princeton, NJ: Princeton University Press.

---

* I thank Anthony Cárdenas for copies of the electronic versions of the PMC and LBA, graciously provided by the Hispanic Seminary of Medieval Studies (University of Wisconsin).

Luc
Keller, J. E. and Keating, L. C. 1977. *The Book of Count Lucanor and Patronio. A translation of Don Juan Manuel's El Lucanor.* Lexington: The University Press of Kentucky.
Sotelo, A. I. 1976. *Don Juan Manuel "Libro de los enxiemplos del Conde Lucanor e de Patronio".* Madrid: Cátedra.

Corb
De Gorog, R. 1978. *Concordancias del "Arcipreste de Talavera".* Madrid: Gredos.
Gerli, M. 1987. *Alfonso Martínez de Toledo "Arcipreste de Talavera o Corbacho".* Madrid: Cátedra.
Simpson, L. B. 1959. *Little Sermons on Sin.* Berkeley: University of California Press.

C01
Corfis, I.A., O'Neill, J. and Beardsley, T.S., Jr. 1997. *Early Celestina Electronic Texts and Concordances.* Madison, WI: HSMS (CD-ROM)
Simpson, L. B. 1955. *The Celestina* (translated from the Spanish). Berkeley, CA: University of California Press.
Singleton, M. H. 1958. *Celestina* (translated from the Spanish). Madison, WI: The University of Wisconsin Press.

Appendix IIIA: Essays corpus (in alphabetical order, by author)*

Castellanos, R. 1966. *Juicios sumarios. Ensayos.* Xalapa: Cuadernos de Facultad de Filosofía, Letras y Ciencias (Universidad Veracruzana). [pp. 13–113]
García Canclini, N. 1990. *Culturas híbridas. Estrategias para entrar y salir de la Modernidad.* México: Grijalbo. [pp. 31–93]
García Canclini, N, coordinador. 1993. *El consumo cultural en México.* México: Consejo Nacional para la Cultura y las Artes. [pp. 86–196]
Lope Blanch, J. M. 1983. *Análisis gramatical del discurso.* México: UNAM. [pp.11–175 = all]
Martínez, J.L. (ed.). 1958. *El ensayo mexicano moderno.* México: Fondo de Cultura Económica. [pp. 9- 409 = all]
Monsiváis, C. 1995. *Los rituales del caos.* México: Era. [pp.15–113]
Montemayor, C. 1985. *El oficio literario.* Xalapa, México: Universidad Veracruzana. [pp. 9–111 = all.]
Paz, O. 1959. *El laberinto de la soledad.* México: Fondo de Cultura Económica. [pp. 9–105]
Reyes, A. (1927). *Cuestiones gongorinas.* Madrid: Espasa-Calpe. [pp. 5–268, except for IV (pp. 90–132)]

---

* I did not include footnotes or quoted material in the count of *-ndo* constructions.

Appendix IIIB: -*ndo* construction frequencies in Essays texts (listed in order of date of publication)

	ESTAR N	IR N	SEGUIR N	TOTAL* N	Aver**
Reyes (212 pp.)	0	10	8	20	9.4
Martínez (400 pp.)	30	36	34	111	27.7
Paz (96 pp.)	0	0	4	4	4.2
Castellanos (100 pp.)	10	14	4	38	38
Montemayor (102 pp.)	3	3	7	13	12.7
Canclini (62 pp.)	10	13	9	35	56.4
Monsivías (98 pp.)	8	8	5	22	22.4
Lope Blanch (164 pp.)	4	10	7	22	13.4
Canclini, ed. (110 pp.)	2	7	3	13	11.8

* Total includes cases of *continuar* + -*ndo*, *venir* + -*ndo*, *andar* + -*ndo*.
** Average number of occurrences per 100 printed pages.

Index

A
acceleration hypothesis 16, 17, 65, 68, 109, 196
acquisition 24, 214
agent 121, 130, 133, 140, 158, 163, 166, 175, 176, 195
aktionsart 10, 113, 182
Alarcos Llorach, E. 181
Alcina Franch, J. 178
Alonso, A. 157, 158, 162, 163
Alonso, D. 61
Alonso Pedraz, M. 204
ambiguity 9, 51, 66, 67, 70, 73
analogy 84–88
andar buscando 27, 168, 175, 228
Anderson, J. M. 71, 86
animacy 90, 95, 100, 133, 144, 154, 157, 165–166, 176, 195–198, 200, 225
Arce-Arenales, M. 94
Arjona Iglesias, M. 7, 22, 28, 110, 132, 150, 169, 189, 204
Arnaud, R. 62, 223
Aslin, R. N. 58
attrition 24, 208
autonomy 9, 32, 34, 35, 59
Axelrod, M. 94

B
Bell, A. 60
Bello, A. 178, 179, 224
Beniak, E. 24, 29
Benjamin, C. 6, 28, 166, 178, 184, 192, 204, 217, 225

Benveniste, E. 8, 195
Bernal Enríquez, Y. 23, 24, 28
Bhat, D.N.S. 113
Biber, D. 22, 60, 62, 187, 223
bilingualism 23–24, 68, 187
Bills, G. 23, 24, 25, 68
binary features 28, 119
Binnick, R. I. 103, 214
Blansitt, E. L. 183, 192, 204
bleaching 3, 9, 10, 12, 45, 46, 54, 60, 71, 83, 84, 119, 120, 129, 130, 140, 150, 151, 152–157, 168, 189
Blecua, J. M. 178
Bolinger, D. 86, 146, 161, 215
borrowing 25, 26
Bouzet, J. 84
Brinton, L. J. 192
Bruyne, J. de. 6, 158, 181, 225
Bull, W. E. 179, 181, 192, 204, 220
Butt, J. 6, 28, 166, 178, 184, 192, 204, 217, 225
Bybee, J. L. 1, 2, 4, 12, 13, 28, 31, 32, 34, 38, 41, 45, 54, 55, 59, 60, 69, 71, 72, 75, 91, 97, 112, 119, 121, 131, 136, 143, 144, 145, 151, 156, 157, 180, 184, 188, 189, 201, 206, 215, 222

C
Cameron, R. 68, 187
Campbell, L. 16
Cantarero, M. 62, 116
Caravedo, R. 221
categorization 9

Celestina 11, 21, 34, 52–54, 61–62, 91, 103, 134, 136, 139, 141–142, 152
Chafe, W.L. 192
change in progress 45, 185, 186
Chaston, J. M. 16, 44, 204, 207
Claudi, U. 12, 54, 71
Clegg, J. H. 7, 19, 20, 22, 29, 44, 58, 62, 155, 185
clitic climbing 9, 45–55, 63–65, 94, 117, 127
Coates, J. 9
code-switching 25, 26, 42, 208
comitative 77
Company, C. 225
Comrie, B. 6, 20, 86, 99, 146, 158, 180, 181, 182, 189, 192, 205, 214, 220
construction frequency 12, 18, 55–60, 115, 177
continuative 97, 98, 109, 111, 118, 119, 127, 151
conventionalization 13, 55, 109–111, 120, 127, 128, 177
convergence 15, 16, 17, 19, 20, 67, 68, 181, 195, 224
copula 133, 143, 161
Corbacho 21, 34, 61, 92, 98, 136, 139, 144, 152
Coseriu, E. 7, 28, 171
creoles 32
Criado de Val, M. 178
Cuervo, R. J. 166, 178

D
Dahl, O. 31, 32, 184, 186, 189
dative 29, 154, 176, 194, 195, 197
decategorialization 9
DeCesaris, J. A. 28
definite article 76, 215
deixis 82, 112, 200–203, 209, 221, 222, 224
demonstrative 76, 200, 209
Dennis, L. 185
desemanticization 8, 12
Deyermond, A. D. 21, 61, 92, 134
dialect 6, 19, 23, 29, 169, 174, 175, 202

Dietrich, W. 7, 28, 99, 171, 178, 187
Dik, S. C. 7
discourse function 133, 134, 138
distal 209, 216
Dorian, N. 18, 19, 24
Douglass, T. R. 179, 181
Dowty, D. 113
durativity 178, 179, 191, 192
dynamic verbs 179, 182, 183, 188, 189, 206

E
Eckert 223
enclitic 45, 73
English Progressive 17, 20, 62, 133, 134, 180, 185, 186, 192, 196, 219
entrenchment 128
epistemic 45, 201, 220
Esgueva, M. 62, 116
Espinosa, A. M., Jr. 67
Espunya I Pratt, A. 99
estar creciendo 150, 173–174, 207
estar hablando 13, 27, 77, 129, 132, 168, 175, 227, 228
estar trabajando 14, 132, 154, 194
estar yendo 105, 145, 204–208, 225
Estoria de España 4, 21, 36, 38, 61, 80, 85, 95, 113, 117, 124, 144, 152, 159, 161, 166, 176
evidential 14, 132, 136, 140, 141, 163, 175, 220, 222, 228
experiencer 121, 130, 140, 167, 175, 195
experiential 14, 132–133, 139, 140–142, 210, 216–224
experiential habitual 107, 177, 188–195, 204–210, 213

F
Fernández de Castro, F. 9
Fernández Ramírez, S. 6, 136, 180, 220
Fillmore, C. J. 6
Finegan, E. 14, 60, 132, 187, 223
Floyd, M. B. 16
Fontanella de Weinberg, B. 9

foreground 99, 103, 138
formality 61–64
Fox, B. A. 94
frequentative 81, 104, 111, 113, 119, 154, 158, 159, 160, 161, 162, 163, 165, 167, 175, 188, 193, 228
frequentative adverbials 90–91, 107, 193
fusion (in formal reduction) 32, 35, 36, 38–41, 45, 49, 54–55, 59, 60, 177
futurate uses 17, 205, 213, 224

G

general activity verbs 14, 131, 132, 158, 160–161, 172–173, 194–195
generic 180, 183, 192, 205
genre 18, 61, 63, 113, 187
Gerli, E. M. 61
Gervasi, K. 187
Gili Gaya, S. 6, 8, 28, 45, 157, 178, 217, 218, 220
Givón, T. 12, 18, 63, 197, 214
Goldberg, A. E. 6, 211
Goldsmith, J. 219, 220
Gómez Torrego, J. 9, 188, 217
Gonzales, P. 134, 180
gradual development 4, 79–80, 99–101, 108, 109, 111, 119, 142–144, 151
grammatical person 198–200, 224
Green, J. N. 6, 8, 9
Greenberg, J. H. 158, 159
Gumperz, J. 15
Gutiérrez, M. J. 157

H

habitual 3, 9, 18, 90–91, 107, 111, 119, 160, 180, 188–195, 201, 204–212
habitual, lexical 81
habitual, past 207, 209–210
habitual, simple Imperfect 179, 180
habitual, simple Present 180, 182–183, 204
Haiman, J. 13, 60, 130
Halliday, M. A. K. 60
Hamplová, S. 7, 28, 99, 100, 110, 132, 133, 157, 166, 179, 180, 204

harmony 120, 142, 143, 151
Harre, C. E. 9
Harris, A. C. 16
Hatcher, A. G. 132, 133, 222
Heine, B. 8, 9, 12, 28, 54, 71, 108, 110, 144, 189
Henríquez Ureña, P. 159
Hernández, J. E. 29
Hernández-Chávez, E. 19, 24
Hidalgo, M. 19
Hook, P. 173
Hopper, P. J. 1, 2, 4, 11, 13, 55, 60, 75, 99, 119, 157, 170
Hudson, A. 24, 29
Hundt, M. 28, 62, 186, 224
Hünnemeyer, F. 12, 54

I

Imperfect — Preterite ratio 153
impersonal *se* 194, 199, 218
inceptive 72, 93–99, 101, 102, 119, 146, 151, 215–216
informality 62
interference 43–44, 204, 208
interrogative 133, 183–184
intimacy 62, 223
ir creciendo 13, 27, 150–151, 168, 173, 207
ir viendo 110, 146, 215–216
Israel, M. 151
Italian 191, 218
iterative 91, 97, 137, 158, 159, 162, 179, 188, 191

J

Jacobson, T. 214
Jakobson, R. 16, 195
Jesperson, O. 92, 135
Jonge, B. de 202
journalistic data 186, 214, 219

K

Kany, C. E. 225
Kattán-Ibarra, J. 6, 183, 187, 192
Kaufman, T. 16, 23

Kay, P. 6
Keniston, H. 7, 8, 21, 28, 34, 45, 56, 69, 70, 99, 100, 115, 116, 118, 155, 158, 166, 181, 185
King, L. D. 28, 119, 132, 138, 179, 181, 188, 192, 213, 223, 225
Klein, F. 6, 15, 16, 20, 67, 181
Kock, J. de 8
Koike, D. A. 200, 202
König, E. 12, 96
Krug, M. 58

L
Laberge, S. 29
Labov, W. 51, 60, 63, 65, 67, 68, 180
Lakoff, G. 9
Langacker, R. 14, 128, 158, 219, 221, 222
language contact 15–20, 23–26, 43, 65–68, 109, 170–175, 177, 211–213, 224
Latin 21, 117, 124, 176
Latin American Spanish 225
Lavandera, B. 16, 18
Lawrence, H. 134
layering 1–2, 6, 118, 119, 151, 168, 171
Lehmann, C. 12, 28, 170
Lenz, R. 6, 8, 9, 45, 64, 95, 187, 214, 224
lexical permeability 174, 207
Libro de buen amor 22
Lightfoot, D. 9
Lipski, J. M. 18, 24, 29, 32
Lloyd, P. M. 117
locative adverbials 43, 53–54, 104–106, 127–129, 151, 165, 166, 203, 221, 222
locative origins of *estar* + *-ndo* 14, 76–78, 84, 124–129, 140–141, 219–222
Lope Blanch, J. M. 19, 22, 62, 110, 179, 182, 192, 218
Lorenzo, E. 99, 109, 178, 225
Lucanor 22, 61, 136, 137, 159
Luján, M. 54
Luna Trail, E. 6, 7, 28, 57, 99, 100, 110, 132, 133, 169, 189, 204, 214, 218

Lunn, P. V. 28
Lyons, J. 14, 77, 132, 143, 204, 228

M
main clause 99, 134, 139, 182
Mair, C. 28, 62, 186
manner expressions 35, 38, 43, 57, 101, 135, 142, 147–149
Marchand, H. 181
markedness 159
Medina-Rivera, A. 68, 187
Meillet, A. 16
Menéndez Pidal, R. 85, 151
metaphor 12, 71, 72, 84–86, 111–112
Moliner, M. 180
Montes Giraldo, J. J. 110
Moreno de Alba, J. G. 182, 183, 188, 189
morphologization 60
Mougeon, R. 24, 29
Mrak, N. A. 16
Mulak, A. 182
Myhill, J. 9, 45, 46, 60

N
Naro, A. 65
negative attitude 92, 103, 166–168, 209, 217
negative polarity 133, 167
Nehls, D. 186, 224
network model 128, 157
Newport, E. L. 58

O
obligatorification 170, 171
obligatoriness 20, 142, 180–187
Olbertz, H. 7, 13, 28, 62, 116, 124, 142, 155, 169, 174, 186, 214, 218, 219
overtness 132, 133, 137–141, 175, 179, 195, 210, 220, 222, 223
Ozete, O. 132, 225

P
Pagliuca, W. 1, 4, 12, 32, 75
parallel reduction hypothesis 32, 69

Index

Parisi, C. 132, 179, 191, 192, 195, 200, 214, 217, 225
Peninsular Spanish 174, 184, 186
Pereira Scherre, M. M. 65
performative 182
Perkins, R. 1, 32
plural objects 148, 158, 159
Poema de mio Cid 11, 21, 33, 38, 93, 110, 117, 124, 144, 152, 153, 171
Poplack, S. 15, 17, 18, 23, 24, 26, 68, 169, 181
possessive 76, 139, 142, 225
postural meaning, source 117, 124, 125, 128
Pountain, C. J. 6, 183, 187, 192
Pousada, A. 15
pragmatic constraints 16, 195, 207, 224
pragmatic strengthening 12, 140–142
priming 64, 157
process verbs 131, 145, 152, 173, 174
prospective 8, 10, 11
proximative 108, 110

Q

quedar(se) + *-ndo* 7, 8, 118, 125–127, 171
Quesada, J. D. 10, 13, 179, 180, 183, 188, 217

R

Rallides, C. 179, 217
Ramat, P. 9
Ramos, M. A. 214
Ramos-Pellicia, M. F. 204
Real Academia Española (RAE) 8, 178
reduplication 150
reflexive 50, 51, 66, 67, 70, 94, 96, 101, 197, 225
register 18, 19, 23, 57, 60–65, 68, 70, 169, 175, 186, 213, 223
relative clause 135–137, 141
relative frequency (of *-ndo* auxiliaries) 11, 115–118, 156, 161, 169, 170, 177, 213
retention 4–6, 73–75, 111, 118, 151, 166, 168

retrospective 8, 10, 11, 171–172
Rivero, M. L. 46, 47, 54
Rizzi, L. 54
Roca Pons, J. 6, 8, 28, 97, 99, 109, 146, 158, 166, 184, 217
Rodríguez, J. D. 7, 19, 20, 22, 29, 58, 62, 155, 185
Romance 7, 8, 28, 45, 191
routinization 6, 119, 168, 169, 175

S

Saffran, J. R. 58
San Román, G. 61
Sánchez, R. 19
Sankoff, D. 1, 29
Sapir, E. 31
schema 13, 87, 112, 125, 128, 130, 144, 151, 157
Schwenter, S. A. 110
Seco, M. 178, 187
Seco, R. 178
seguir + *-ndo* 7, 8, 9, 98, 109, 118, 119, 127, 151, 169, 171, 214
semantic generalization 12, 71, 83, 91, 120, 156, 213, 224
Shirai, Y. 214
Silva-Corvalán, C. 15, 16, 20, 24, 45, 64, 65, 67, 109, 169, 170, 174, 175, 180, 186, 187, 195, 197, 201, 206, 207, 208, 212, 214
Silverstein, M. 14
simplification 17, 20, 170, 175, 213
Smith, C. S. 89, 90, 103, 180, 191
social effects 17, 18, 61, 62, 169, 170, 213
Solé, C. A. 6, 178, 181, 184, 204
Solé, Y. R. 6, 8, 28, 100, 110, 171, 178, 181, 183, 184, 204
spatial meaning 13, 112, 227
Spaulding, R. K. 6, 8, 13, 21, 28, 63, 69, 98, 109, 118, 126, 168, 169, 187
speaker involvement 14, 132–142, 178, 195, 197–218, 224
specialization 11, 20, 120, 170–175, 177, 213

Squartini, M. 9, 13, 99, 100, 103, 110, 147, 158, 165, 168, 171, 180, 191, 192, 218, 220, 221, 225
stative 14, 18, 63, 90, 94, 101, 109, 146, 182, 189, 201, 204, 210, 211, 212, 213–221
Stockwell, R. P. 178, 179, 181
Strang, B. M. H. 62, 134, 137, 180, 186
structuralism 1, 119, 179, 181
style. See register
subject involvement 14, 129–132, 139, 140, 217
subjectification 14, 140
subjectivity 14, 121, 132, 139, 142, 178, 184, 194–204, 216, 223
subordinate clause 134–136, 148
Suñer, M. 132, 138, 179, 188, 213, 223, 225
Sweetser, E. 71

T
Talmy, L. 100, 149
Taylor, J. R. 9
teleology 181
telicity 145, 146, 187, 224
temporal adverbials 44, 84, 88–104, 107, 108, 109–111, 179, 193, 200–202, 205
temporal bounding. See transitoriness
Thomason, S. G. 16, 23
Thompson, S. A. 13, 54, 112, 157, 182
Timberlake, A. 2
token frequency 13, 19, 23, 32, 55–57, 59, 61, 63, 64, 65, 67, 115, 120, 128, 129, 130, 154–156, 165, 173, 185–187
Torres Cacoullos, R. 22, 29, 65, 110, 144

transfer 24, 44, 174, 207, 212
transitional bilingual 24, 26, 207, 208
transitoriness 14, 133, 178, 190, 192, 204, 206, 218–222
Traugott, E. C. 1, 12, 14, 55, 60, 71, 96, 140, 157
type frequency 13, 55, 120, 130

V
variation 1, 2, 169, 170, 189
Vásquez, I. 43, 44
Vendler, Z. 146, 191, 211
venir + *-ndo* 6, 7, 8, 10, 11, 171, 172
Vigil, N. A. 23, 25, 68
Visser, F. Th. 185

W
Waletzky, J. 180
Weiner, E. J. 65
Weinreich, U. 16, 23
Westfall, R. E. 132, 180, 187, 209, 210, 217, 219, 220
Whitley, S. M. 6, 28
Wilson, R. 15
Woisetschlaeger, E. 219, 220
Wright, S. 14, 132, 133, 134
written varieties 18, 19, 155, 169, 186, 214, 219

Y
Yllera, A. 13, 21, 85, 94, 98, 113, 117, 118, 123, 143, 146, 151, 166, 176, 192

Z
Zdenek, J. W. 132, 192, 217

In the STUDIES IN LANGUAGE COMPANION SERIES (SLCS) the following volumes have been published thus far or are scheduled for publication:

1. ABRAHAM, Werner (ed.): *Valence, Semantic Case, and Grammatical Relations. Workshop studies prepared for the 12th Conference of Linguistics, Vienna, August 29th to September 3rd, 1977.* Amsterdam, 1978.
2. ANWAR, Mohamed Sami: *BE and Equational Sentences in Egyptian Colloquial Arabic.* Amsterdam, 1979.
3. MALKIEL, Yakov: *From Particular to General Linguistics. Selected Essays 1965-1978.* With an introd. by the author + indices. Amsterdam, 1983.
4. LLOYD, Albert L.: *Anatomy of the Verb: The Gothic Verb as a Model for a Unified Theory of Aspect, Actional Types, and Verbal Velocity.* Amsterdam, 1979.
5. HAIMAN, John: *Hua: A Papuan Language of the Eastern Highlands of New Guinea.* Amsterdam, 1980.
6. VAGO, Robert (ed.): *Issues in Vowel Harmony. Proceedings of the CUNY Linguistics Conference on Vowel Harmony (May 14, 1977).* Amsterdam, 1980.
7. PARRET, H., J. VERSCHUEREN, M. SBISÀ (eds): *Possibilities and Limitations of Pragmatics. Proceedings of the Conference on Pragmatics, Urbino, July 8-14, 1979.* Amsterdam, 1981.
8. BARTH, E.M. & J.L. MARTENS (eds): *Argumentation: Approaches to Theory Formation. Containing the Contributions to the Groningen Conference on the Theory of Argumentation,* Groningen, October 1978. Amsterdam, 1982.
9. LANG, Ewald: *The Semantics of Coordination.* Amsterdam, 1984.(English transl. by John Pheby from the German orig. edition *"Semantik der koordinativen Verknüpfung",* Berlin, 1977.)
10. DRESSLER, Wolfgang U., Willi MAYERTHALER, Oswald PANAGL & Wolfgang U. WURZEL: *Leitmotifs in Natural Morphology.* Amsterdam, 1987.
11. PANHUIS, Dirk G.J.: *The Communicative Perspective in the Sentence: A Study of Latin Word Order.* Amsterdam, 1982.
12. PINKSTER, Harm (ed.): *Latin Linguistics and Linguistic Theory. Proceedings of the 1st Intern. Coll. on Latin Linguistics, Amsterdam, April 1981.* Amsterdam, 1983.
13. REESINK, G.: *Structures and their Functions in Usan.* Amsterdam, 1987.
14. BENSON, Morton, Evelyn BENSON & Robert ILSON: *Lexicographic Description of English.* Amsterdam, 1986.
15. JUSTICE, David: *The Semantics of Form in Arabic, in the mirror of European languages.* Amsterdam, 1987.
16. CONTE, M.E., J.S. PETÖFI, and E. SÖZER (eds): *Text and Discourse Connectedness.* Amsterdam/Philadelphia, 1989.
17. CALBOLI, Gualtiero (ed.): *Subordination and other Topics in Latin. Proceedings of the Third Colloquium on Latin Linguistics, Bologna, 1-5 April 1985.* Amsterdam/Philadelphia, 1989.
18. WIERZBICKA, Anna: *The Semantics of Grammar.* Amsterdam/Philadelphia, 1988.
19. BLUST, Robert A.: *Austronesian Root Theory. An Essay on the Limits of Morphology.* Amsterdam/Philadelphia, 1988.
20. VERHAAR, John W.M. (ed.): *Melanesian Pidgin and Tok Pisin. Proceedings of the First International Conference on Pidgins and Creoles on Melanesia.* Amsterdam/Philadelphia, 1990.

21. COLEMAN, Robert (ed.): *New Studies in Latin Linguistics. Proceedings of the 4th International Colloquium on Latin Linguistics*, Cambridge, April 1987. Amsterdam/Philadelphia, 1991.
22. McGREGOR, William: *A Functional Grammar of Gooniyandi*. Amsterdam/Philadelphia, 1990.
23. COMRIE, Bernard and Maria POLINSKY (eds): *Causatives and Transitivity*. Amsterdam/Philadelphia, 1993.
24. BHAT, D.N.S. *The Adjectival Category. Criteria for differentiation and identification*. Amsterdam/Philadelphia, 1994.
25. GODDARD, Cliff and Anna WIERZBICKA (eds): *Semantics and Lexical Universals. Theory and empirical findings*. Amsterdam/Philadelphia, 1994.
26. LIMA, Susan D., Roberta L. CORRIGAN and Gregory K. IVERSON (eds): *The Reality of Linguistic Rules*. Amsterdam/Philadelphia, 1994.
27. ABRAHAM, Werner, T. GIVÓN and Sandra A. THOMPSON (eds): *Discourse Grammar and Typology*. Amsterdam/Philadelphia, 1995.
28. HERMAN, József: *Linguistic Studies on Latin: Selected papers from the 6th international colloquium on Latin linguistics, Budapest, 2-27 March, 1991*. Amsterdam/Philadelphia, 1994.
29. ENGBERG-PEDERSEN, Elisabeth et al. (eds): *Content, Expression and Structure. Studies in Danish functional grammar*. Amsterdam/Philadelphia, 1996.
30. HUFFMAN, Alan: *The Categories of Grammar. French lui and le*. Amsterdam/Philadelphia, 1997.
31. WANNER, Leo (ed.): *Lexical Functions in Lexicography and Natural Language Processing*. Amsterdam/Philadelphia, 1996.
32. FRAJZYNGIER, Zygmunt: *Grammaticalization of the Complex Sentence. A case study in Chadic*. Amsterdam/Philadelphia, 1996.
33. VELAZQUEZ-CASTILLO, Maura: *The Grammar of Possession. Inalienability, incorporation and possessor ascension in Guaraní*. Amsterdam/Philadelphia, 1996.
34. HATAV, Galia: *The Semantics of Aspect and Modality. Evidence from English and Biblical Hebrew*. Amsterdam/Philadelphia, 1997.
35. MATSUMOTO, Yoshiko: *Noun-Modifying Constructions in Japanese. A frame semantic approach*. Amsterdam/Philadelphia, 1997.
36. KAMIO, Akio (ed.): *Directions in Functional Linguistics*. Amsterdam/Philadelphia, 1997.
37. HARVEY, Mark and Nicholas REID (eds): *Nominal Classification in Aboriginal Australia*. Amsterdam/Philadelphia, 1997.
38. HACKING, Jane F.: *Coding the Hypothetical. A Comparative Typology of Conditionals in Russian and Macedonian*. Amsterdam/Philadelphia, 1998.
39. WANNER, Leo (ed.): *Recent Trends in Meaning-Text Theory*. Amsterdam/Philadelphia, 1997.
40. BIRNER, Betty and Gregory WARD: *Information Status and Noncanonical Word Order in English*. Amsterdam/Philadelphia, 1998.
41. DARNELL, Michael, Edith MORAVSCIK, Michael NOONAN, Frederick NEWMEYER and Kathleen WHEATLY (eds): *Functionalism and Formalism in Linguistics. Volume I: General papers*. Amsterdam/Philadelphia, 1999.

42. DARNELL, Michael, Edith MORAVSCIK, Michael NOONAN, Frederick NEWMEYER and Kathleen WHEATLY (eds): *Functionalism and Formalism in Linguistics. Volume II: Case studies.* Amsterdam/Philadelphia, 1999.
43. OLBERTZ, Hella, Kees HENGEVELD and Jesús Sánchez GARCÍA (eds): *The Structure of the Lexicon in Functional Grammar.* Amsterdam/Philadelphia, 1998.
44. HANNAY, Mike and A. Machtelt BOLKESTEIN (eds): *Functional Grammar and Verbal Interaction.* 1998.
45. COLLINS, Peter and David LEE (eds): *The Clause in English. In honour of Rodney Huddleston.* 1999.
46. YAMAMOTO, Mutsumi: *Animacy and Reference. A cognitive approach to corpus linguistics.* 1999.
47. BRINTON, Laurel J. and Minoji AKIMOTO (eds): *ollocational and Idiomatic Aspects of Composite Predicates in the History of English.* 1999.
48. MANNEY, Linda Joyce: *Middle Voice in Modern Greek. Meaning and function of an inflectional category.* 2000.
49. BHAT, D.N.S.: *The Prominence of Tense, Aspect and Mood.* 1999.
50. ABRAHAM, Werner and Leonid KULIKOV (eds): *Transitivity, Causativity, and TAM. In honour of Vladimir Nedjalkov.* 1999.
51. ZIEGELER, Debra: *Hypothetical Modality. Grammaticalisation in an L2 dialect.* 2000.
52. TORRES CACOULLOS, Rena: *Grammaticization, Synchronic Variation, and Language Contact.A study of Spanish progressive -ndo constructions.* 2000.
53. FISCHER, Olga, Anette ROSENBACH and Dieter STEIN (eds.): *Pathways of Change. Grammaticalization in English.* n.y.p.